THE 1960s

OPPOSING VIEWPOINTS®

Other Books of Related Interest:

THE 1960s

OPPOSING VIEWPOINTS®

David L. Bender, *Publisher*
Bruno Leone, *Executive Editor*

William Dudley, *Series Editor*
John C. Chalberg, Ph.D., professor of history,
　Normandale Community College, *Consulting
　Editor*

William Dudley, *Book Editor*

AMERICAN HISTORY SERIES

Greenhaven Press, Inc.
San Diego, California

Cover photographs, clockwise from top: 1) American soldier in Vietnam (AP/Wide World Photos); 2) Televised debate between John F. Kennedy and Richard M. Nixon, 1960 (UPI/Bettmann); 3) Black Power protest at the 1968 Olympics in Mexico City (UPI/Bettmann); 4) People at Woodstock, 1969 (AP/Wide World Photos)

Library of Congress Cataloging-in-Publication Data

The 1960s : opposing viewpoints / William Dudley, book editor
    p. cm. — (American history series)
  Includes bibliographical references and index.
  ISBN 1-56510-526-5 (lib. : alk. paper). — ISBN 1-56510-525-7 (pbk. : alk. paper)
    1. United States—History—1961–1969—Sources. 2. United States—Politics and government—1961–1963—Sources. 3. United States—Politics and government—1963–1969—Sources. 4. United States—Social conditions—1960–1980—Sources. I. Dudley, William, 1964– . II. Series: American history series (San Diego, Calif.)
E838.3.A16 1997   96-49282
973.923—dc21   CIP

"America was born of revolt, flourished in dissent, became great through experimentation."

Henry Steele Commager, American Historian

Contents

Foreword

Aboard the *Arbella* as it lurched across the cold, gray Atlantic, John Winthrop was as calm as the waters surrounding him were wild. With the confidence of a leader, Winthrop gathered his Puritan companions around him. It was time to offer a sermon. England lay behind them, and years of strife and persecution for their religious beliefs were over, he said. But the Puritan abandonment of England, he reminded his followers, did not mean that England was beyond redemption. Winthrop wanted his followers to remember England even as they were leaving it behind. Their goal should be to create a new England, one far removed from the authority of the Anglican church and King Charles I. In Winthrop's words, their settlement in the New World ought to be "a city upon a hill," a just society for corrupt England to emulate.

A Chance to Start Over

One June 8, 1630, John Winthrop and his company of refugees had their first glimpse of what they came to call New England. High on the surrounding hills stood a welcoming band of fir trees whose fragrance drifted to the *Arbella* on a morning breeze. To Winthrop, the "smell off the shore [was] like the smell of a garden." This new world would, in fact, often be compared to the Garden of Eden. Here, John Winthrop would have his opportunity to start life over again. So would his family and his shipmates. So would all those who came after them. These victims of conflict in old England hoped to find peace in New England.

Winthrop, for one, had experienced much conflict in his life. As a Puritan, he was opposed to Catholicism and Anglicanism, both of which, he believed, were burdened by distracting rituals and distant hierarchies. A parliamentarian by conviction, he despised Charles I, who had spurned Parliament and created a private army to do his bidding. Winthrop believed in individual responsibility and fought against the loss of religious and political freedom. A gentleman landowner, he feared the rising economic power of a merchant class that seemed to value only money. Once Winthrop stepped aboard the *Arbella*, he hoped, these conflicts would not be a part of his American future.

Yet his Puritan religion told Winthrop that human beings are fallen creatures and that perfection, whether communal or individual, is unachievable on this earth. Therefore, he faced a paradox: On the one hand, his religion demanded that he attempt to live a perfect life in an imperfect world. On the other hand, it told him that he was destined to fail.

Soon after Winthrop disembarked from the *Arbella*, he came face-to-face with this maddening dilemma. He found himself presiding not over a utopia but over a colony caught up in disputes as troubling as any he had confronted in his English past. John Winthrop, it seems, was not the only Puritan with a dream of a heaven on earth. But others in the community saw the dream differently. They wanted greater political and religious freedom than their leader was prepared to grant. Often, Winthrop was able to handle this conflict diplomatically. For example, he expanded, participation in elections and allowed the voters of Massachusetts Bay greater power.

But religious conflict was another matter because it was grounded in competing visions of the Puritan utopia. In Roger Williams and Anne Hutchinson, two of his fellow colonists, John Winthrop faced rivals unprepared to accept his definition of the perfect community. To Williams, perfection demanded that he separate himself from the Puritan institutions in his community and create an even "purer" church. Winthrop, however, disagreed and exiled Williams to Rhode Island. Hutchinson presumed that she could interpret God's will without a minister. Again, Winthrop did not agree. Hutchinson was tried on charges of heresy, convicted, and banished from Massachusetts.

John Winthrop's Massachusetts colony was the first but far from the last American attempt to build a unified, peaceful community that, in the end, only provoked a discord. This glimpse at its history reveals what Winthrop confronted: the unavoidable presence of conflict in American life.

American Assumptions

From America's origins in the early seventeenth century, Americans have often held several interrelated assumptions about their country. First, people believe that to be American is to be free. Second, because Americans did not have to free themselves from feudal lords or an entrenched aristocracy, America has been seen as a perpetual haven from the troubles and disputes that are found in the Old World.

John Winthrop lived his life as though these assumptions were true. But the opposing viewpoints presented in the American History Series should reveal that for many Americans, these assumptions were and are myths. Indeed, for numerous Americans, liberty has not always been guaranteed, and disputes have been an integral, sometimes welcome part of their life.

The American landscape has been torn apart again and again by a great variety of clashes—theological, ideological, political, economic, geographical, and social. But such a landscape is not necessarily a hopelessly divided country. If the editors hope to prove anything during the course of this series, it is not that the United States has been destroyed by conflict but rather that it has been enlivened, enriched, and even strengthened by Americans who have disagreed with one another.

Thomas Jefferson was one of the least confrontational of Americans, but he boldly and irrevocably enriched American life with his individualistic views. Like John Winthrop before him, he had a notion of an American Eden. Like Winthrop, he offered a vision of a harmonious society. And like Winthrop, he not only became enmeshed in conflict but eventually presided over a people beset by it. But unlike Winthrop, Jefferson believed this Eden was not located in a specific community but in each individual American. His Declaration of Independence from Great Britain could also be read as a declaration of independence for each individual in American society.

Jefferson's Ideal

Jefferson's ideal world was composed of "yeoman farmers," each of whom was roughly equal to the others in society's eyes, each of whom was free from the restrictions of both government and fellow citizens. Throughout his life, Jefferson offered a continuing challenge to Americans: Advance individualism and equality or see the death of the American experiment. Jefferson believed that the strength of this experiment depended upon a society of autonomous individuals and a society without great gaps between rich and poor. His challenge to his fellow Americans to create—and sustain—such a society has itself produced both economic and political conflict.

A society whose guiding document is the Declaration of Independence is a society assured of the freedom to dream—and to disagree. We know that Jefferson hated conflict, both personal and political. His tendency was to avoid confrontations of any sort, to squirrel himself away and write rather than to stand up and speak his mind. It is only through his written words that we can grasp Jefferson's utopian dream of a society of independent farmers, all pursuing their private dreams and all leading lives of middling prosperity.

Jefferson, this man of wealth and intellect, lived an essentially happy private life. But his public life was much more troublesome. From the first rumblings of the American Revolution in the 1760s to the North-South skirmishes of the 1820s that ultimately produced the Civil War, Jefferson was at or near the center of American political history. The issues were almost too many—and too crucial—for one lifetime: Jefferson had to choose between supporting or rejecting the path of revolution. During and after the ensuing war, he was at the forefront of the battle for religious liberty. After endorsing the Constitution, he opposed the economic plans of Alexander Hamilton. At the end of the century, he fought the infamous Alien and Sedition Acts, which limited civil liberties. As president, he opposed the Federalist court, conspiracies to divide the union, and calls for a new war against England. Throughout his life, Thomas Jefferson, slaveholder, pondered the conflict between American freedom and American slavery. And from retirement at his Monticello retreat, he frowned at the rising spirit of commercialism he feared was dividing Americans and destroying his dream of American harmony.

No matter the issue, however, Thomas Jefferson invariably supported the rights of the individual. Worried as he was about the excesses of commercialism, he accepted them because his main concern was to live in a society where liberty and individualism could flourish. To Jefferson, Americans had to be free to worship as they desired. They also deserved to be free from an over-reaching government. To Jefferson, Americans should also be free to possess slaves.

Harmony, an Elusive Goal

Before reading the articles in this anthology, the editors ask readers to ponder the lives of John Winthrop and Thomas Jefferson. Each held a utopian vision, one based upon the demands of community and the other on the autonomy of the individual. Each dreamed of a country of perpetual new beginnings. Each found himself thrust into a position of leadership and found that conflict could not be avoided. Harmony, whether communal or individual, was a forever elusive goal.

The opposing visions of Winthrop and Jefferson have been at the heart of many differences among Americans from many backgrounds through the whole of American history. Moreover, their visions have provoked important responses that have helped shape American society, the American character, and many an American battle.

The editors of the American History Series have done extensive research to find representative opinions on the issues included in these volumes. They have found numerous outstanding opposing viewpoints from people of all times, classes, and genders in American history. From those, they have selected commentaries that best fit the nature and flavor of the period and topic under consideration. Every attempt was made to include the most important and relevant viewpoints in each chapter. Obviously, not every notable viewpoint could be included. Therefore, a selective, annotated bibliography has been provided at the end of each book to aid readers in seeking additional information.

The editors are confident that as this series reveals past conflicts, it will help revitalize the reader's views of the American present. In that spirit, the American History Series is dedicated to the proposition that American history is more complicated, more fascinating, and more troubling than John Winthrop or Thomas Jefferson ever dared to imagine.

John C. Chalberg
Consulting Editor

Introduction

*"What makes the 1960s distinctive . . . is that
protest of America's status quo moved from the
margins of American society to center stage."*

One day in August 1965, the midpoint of a turbulent decade,
civil rights leader Martin Luther King Jr. was walking in the black
community of Watts, Los Angeles. What he saw resembled a war
zone. A dispute between white police officers and the black
driver and passenger of a car pulled over for a traffic violation
had erupted into six days of rioting that left 34 people dead, 864
hospitalized, and whole city blocks torched to the chanting of
"Burn, baby, burn!" Four thousand people were arrested, and
about two hundred businesses were destroyed.

The race riot in Watts was shocking not only for its scope and
violence but also for its timing. It began just five days after President
Lyndon B. Johnson signed the Voting Rights Act, a historic
law mandating federal government intervention to ensure that
blacks were not denied the right to vote because of their race. The
law was hailed as a turning point for African Americans and a triumph
for the black civil rights movement.

As King and civil rights colleague Bayard Rustin were walking
through the streets of Watts, some black teenagers approached
King, shouting, "We won!" King angrily asked how they could
consider the riots, which not only resulted in numerous deaths
and widespread destruction but also turned many whites against
the civil rights cause, to be a victory. "We won," replied one
youth, "because we made them pay attention to us."

Although King and the youth disagreed on whether violence
was justified in order to effect social change, their beliefs and actions
were similar in many respects. Both King and the people who
rioted in Watts were—in very different ways—challenging the status
quo. Both were doing so in ways that broke the law. And both,
arguably, were attempting to raise the consciousness of Americans.
They shared all these characteristics with people involved in many
of the important political and social movements of the decade, including
the protest against the war in Vietnam and the widespread
cultural ferment that came to be called the counterculture.

15

Challenging the Status Quo

Both King and the rioters in Watts were challenging an American status quo that restricted the freedoms and opportunities of its black minority. As the 1960s began, African Americans continued to be held back from full participation in the "American Dream" by racial prejudice and discrimination. In the South, where discrimination was most blatant, blacks were expected to defer to whites, and those who attempted to vote, assert their rights, or improve their economic condition were often intimidated or even killed by whites—with the complicity of local authorities. Racism and its effects were also evident, however, in black inner-city communities outside the South. Discrimination in housing kept blacks away from white neighborhoods and contributed to overcrowding. Public schools in black communities such as Watts were often substandard. Discrimination by banks and other lenders stunted the economy of black communities. This situation, combined with racial barriers in the job market, helped contribute to a high unemployment rate among blacks. For example, the unemployment rate in 1965 in Los Angeles was three times as high for blacks as for whites. Police officers in many cities were overwhelmingly white (200 out of 205 officers in Watts in 1965); many of them were admitted racists who were quick to use violence to maintain order in the "jungle."

By 1960, however, blacks had already had some victories in their struggle for equal rights, and many were hopeful about the intentions and abilities of John F. Kennedy, elected president that year. Because of these and other developments, including the civil rights movement itself and the widespread media coverage it attracted, many blacks had greater hopes for change in the 1960s than in previous decades. The "revolution of rising expectations" caused some blacks to explode when conditions seemed to be improving too slowly for them.

A combination of dissatisfaction with the present and hope for the future also spurred other challenges to the American status quo during the 1960s. College students on many campuses rebelled against restrictions on political activity, against university ties with the American military, and against restrictive social rules; in many cases their attempts at change were successful. Members of the counterculture decried the materialism and conformity of American society. Peace activists attempted to change America's policy in Vietnam; their numbers would swell as the war continued to escalate during the decade. Feminists worked to change customs and laws that discriminated against women.

Challenges to the American status quo were not unique to the 1960s; people in the United States have been challenging political, cultural, religious, and social authority for most, if not all, of the nation's history. What makes the 1960s distinctive, however, is that protest of America's status quo moved from the margins of American society to center stage. Barbara L. Tischler writes in her introduction to *Sights on the Sixties* that

> the dynamism of the 1960s and the conviction that the nation was ready for rapid and unconventional reform renders the decade almost unique in twentieth-century history. Not since the Depression had the nation experienced such dramatic tension and conflict over the legitimacy of institutions and individuals in positions of power to make policy.

Similarly, in his book *And the Crooked Places Made Straight*, historian David Chalmers argues that never before had so many fundamental questions been raised so openly by so many people:

> In a massing unique to the American experience, practically every classic social conflict or question erupted into the streets of the nation as a challenge to social stasis and stability; the individual vs. society, self-expression vs. authority, social justice vs. order, integration vs. separation, change vs. stability, reform vs. revolution, nonviolence vs. violence, spiritual values vs. materialism, and rationality vs. the irrational; war, peace, and the obligation to one's country; poverty, generational conflict, fathers and sons, black and white, empowerment, Chicanos, Native-Americans, male and female, lesbian and gay rights, sexual liberation, and the sensory exploration of the world of drugs. Never before had so many simultaneous challenges been loaded onto the circuits of American life.

A striking aspect of many sixties movements and developments, including the civil rights movement led by King and the riots in Watts and other cities, was that they went beyond political lobbying, campaigning for candidates for public office, legal appeals, and other conventional means of working "within the system" to effect social change. King and his followers used boycotts, mass protests, sit-ins, and other forms of nonviolent direct action, in many cases defying local law. The rioters in Watts and those who defended their actions argued that such unlawful behavior was necessary because only violence could force America to change. Both the civil disobedience of the civil rights movement and the violence of Watts and other sites of social unrest drew attention to the plight of African Americans, but both also created a backlash against the protesters and their cause.

Civil Disobedience

Civil disobedience, with its direct defiance of law and authority, was perhaps the most controversial aspect of the civil rights movement. King and others considered it a necessary step to confront America with what they believed to be unjust laws and customs. Others decried civil disobedience as a cause of social disorder. The black college students who created the sit-in movement by asking to be served at lunch counters in defiance of "whites only" signs were in many respects models of politeness and civility. Yet the *Nashville Banner* in 1960 called their actions an "incitation to anarchy" and many activists were arrested for creating a public disturbance. Several Alabama clergymen, responding to massive civil rights demonstrations in 1963 in Birmingham, addressed King in an open letter in which they argued that "when rights are consistently denied, a cause should be pressed in the courts and in negotiations with local leaders, and not in the streets."

Some observers maintained that King's civil disobedience doctrines were directly responsible for the riots in Watts and elsewhere that became common in the mid- and late 1960s. Richard Nixon, who was elected president in 1968 on a platform that included a call for "law and order," wrote in 1966:

> I think it is time the doctrine of civil disobedience was analyzed and rejected as not only wrong but potentially disastrous.

> If all have a right to engage in public disobedience to protest real or imagined wrongs, then the example set by the minority today will be followed by the majority tomorrow.

> Issues then will no longer be decided upon merit by an impartial judge. Victory will go to the side which can muster the greater number of demonstrations in the streets. The rule of law will be replaced by the rule of the mob.

King, on the other hand, defended civil disobedience by arguing that there are unjust laws. "I submit," he asserted in a famous letter written while in jail in Birmingham, Alabama, "that an individual who breaks a law that conscience tells him is unjust and willingly accepts the penalty by staying in jail to arouse the conscience of the community of its injustice, is in reality expressing the very highest respect for law."

Civil disobedience was also a hallmark of other noted movements of the 1960s. College students and antiwar protesters borrowed tactics from the civil rights movement, including sit-ins and mass marches. Thousands of young men openly defied the law by burning their draft cards and in other ways refusing to cooperate with military conscription as a protest against the war in Vietnam. Other peace activists broke into offices of draft boards to destroy files and thus disrupt the draft process.

Violence and Disorder

Violence was even more threatening to defenders of "law and order" than was civil disobedience. For many, the sixties are still remembered as a time of destructiveness and disorder. Many of the most memorable moments and developments of the 1960s were acts of violence, including the assassinations of John F. Kennedy in 1963 and Martin Luther King Jr. and Robert F. Kennedy in 1968; the clash between police and protesters at the Democratic Convention in Chicago in 1968; the continuing stories of violence and brutality in Vietnam; and the race riots in Watts and other places during the decade.

The violent riots in Watts, like later ones in Detroit, Newark, and other cities, were much analyzed during the 1960s; the nature and causes of the riots continue to be debated. A government commission appointed to study the Watts riots, chaired by former CIA director John McCone, argued that the riots were a "senseless" explosion created by a handful of marginal and alienated blacks. Historian Allen Matusow, in his book *The Unraveling of America*, argues that this conclusion was based on a misreading of the events. He contends that rather than a handful of people, at least thirty thousand blacks participated in the rioting, while twice that number were supportive spectators. "Moreover," he writes, "the typical rioter was not socially on the margin, but a young man somewhat better educated than the typical nonrioter and holding a job." In addition, rather than indulging in random or senseless violence, Matusow maintains that many riot participants intended to send the message that blacks

> would not passively submit to a life of discrimination and poverty. . . . The most arresting fact about Watts—and most of the other riots—was this: Looters and arsonists moved along the streets destroying white-owned stores, but ordinarily sparing stores with signs reading "Negro-owned" or "Blood.". . . Rioters were less hostile to the National Guard than to the local police and downright friendly to federal troops.

The question of whether violence had any legitimate place in a social protest movement was debated extensively. Until the end of his life, Martin Luther King Jr. consistently maintained his belief in nonviolent protest. But some black leaders embraced riots and violence as a means for black Americans to assert themselves and improve their lives. For example, H. Rap Brown, leader of the Student National Coordinating Committee (previously the Student Nonviolent Coordinating Committee), at one point urged blacks to "wage guerrilla war on the honkie white man." Such statements, and the continuing wave of violence, contributed to a political backlash against all radical movements. The election of Ronald Reagan to the California governorship in 1966—in retrospect a significant turning point for American conservatism—was based largely on appeals to restore the social "order" that many people believed was threatened by black and student militants.

Toward the end of the decade, activists in causes other than the civil rights movement began to advocate violence. The members of Students for a Democratic Society (SDS) originally sought to emulate the nonviolent activities of the civil rights movement; however, by the end of the decade, SDS had split into several short-lived factions, most of which were officially committed to violent revolution. The antiwar movement also became divided over whether to utilize violent tactics. Demonstrations were increasingly marked by violent clashes with the police. In 1969 and 1970 small groups of white revolutionaries attempted to set off bombs in war-related government buildings; a bombing at the University of Wisconsin at Madison killed a graduate student. Many observers and historians have argued that the growing extremism among sixties protest groups (including increasingly frequent calls for violence) was a product of a growing sense of urgency that resulted from the failure of efforts both to attain equality for blacks and to stop the war in Vietnam.

Changing People's Consciousness

In commenting privately that the 1954 Supreme Court decision *Brown v. Board of Education* (which outlawed racially segregated schools) was a mistake, President Dwight D. Eisenhower asserted, "I don't believe you can change the hearts of men with laws or decisions." In many respects, the activities of King, of the people in Watts, and of other sixties activists were based on the opposite presumption—that the hearts (and minds) of people can and should be changed through social activism.

King's words and actions were officially aimed at racial laws and customs, but they were also directed at raising America's consciousness. King wrote that racial segregation "distorts the soul and damages the personality. It gives the segregator a false sense of superiority and the segregated a false sense of inferiority." Chalmers writes:

> Particularly for King, . . . the attack on American racism sought to change people's ways of thinking and feeling. . . . The willingness to accept punishment for refusing to obey unjust laws was a psychological weapon to bolster the self-image of blacks and to put pressure on whites to face the evils of a system of racial dominance and subordination. Out of an awakened sense of injustice would come the institutional changes that would sweep away segregation and open up equal opportunity for all. That restructuring of society would in turn change behavior.

"The 1960s," Chalmers continues, "was particularly marked by the extent to which this strategy [of raising people's consciousness to effect social change] emerged as the chosen path." Many of the movements of the 1960s employed this strategy. Group consciousness emerged among the poor, the young, Native Americans, Hispanics, and gays. Activists against the Vietnam War sought to change public perceptions of the conflict and America's role in it. Student activist Gregory Calvert, in an influential 1967 paper, wrote that "the problem in white America is the failure to admit or recognize unfreedom. It is the problem of false consciousness." He went on to argue that the task of student radicals was "the encouragement or building of revolutionary consciousness, of consciousness of the conditions of unfreedom." Counterculture figures such as Timothy Leary advocated the use of drugs such as LSD, rather than political activism, to expand people's consciousness of the universe around them. Feminists endeavored to expose the extent to which traditional gender roles and stereotypes circumscribed women's lives and sought to transform society's beliefs concerning women's rights and abilities. Hippies created a counterculture in an effort to celebrate individual authenticity and expression rather than social conformity. "At its most heady," writes historian Kenneth Cmiel, "the counterculture thought of itself as a revolution in consciousness, something that could reshape the world."

The idea of changing consciousness also was used to defend and explain the riots in Watts and other American cities. The Watts youth's declaration that "We won because we made them pay attention to us" reveals the extent to which the riots were seen as a means to raise the consciousness of whites. Moreover, they were also thought to change the consciousness of blacks. Following riots in Detroit in 1967, an activist argued that "after the rebellion was over, there was a strong sense of brotherhood and sisterhood. We saw a very strong sense of camaraderie in the community." British journalist Geoffrey Hodgson wrote that black anger was directed at whites:

> It was no longer a matter of what whites could be persuaded to concede . . . it was a question of what degree of attention angry young blacks would demand. . . . It was a question of how much they could make white people respect them and therefore also a question of self-respect. It was a question of "consciousness."

Two Views of the 1960s

The civil rights movement and the riots in Watts are two of the various aspects of the 1960s that are covered in this volume. In addition to the war in Vietnam and the counterculture, the viewpoints in this book discuss the space race, President Lyndon B. Johnson's Great Society, the feminist movement, and other important issues and developments of the decade.

Americans remain divided about the 1960s. Some argue that the decade was a time in which the injustices of America were challenged—with some success. Others consider the decade a time when people engaged in pointless and irresponsible violence as well as drug use, promiscuous sexual activity, and other behaviors inconsistent with social norms. These critics believe the negative effects of these actions remain in America today. The divergent views of the 1960s help explain why Americans, in the words of historian David Farber, "cannot seem to let the sixties go gently into the night." The viewpoints in this book provide a small sampling of the debates, controversies, and passions of this decade and of the various movements to change America's society and America's consciousness.

CHAPTER 1

The New Frontier and the Great Society

Chapter Preface

From January 1961 to January 1969, the presidency of the United States was held successively by John F. Kennedy and Lyndon B. Johnson. These two disparate individuals did much to shape America in the 1960s.

The personalities of these two presidents (both Democrats) and the circumstances by which each gained power could scarcely have been more different. The Harvard-educated Kennedy, a member of a wealthy and politically ambitious family, was a U.S. senator with a relatively undistinguished record. Kennedy overcame questions concerning his youth and Roman Catholic background to win a very narrow victory over Richard Nixon in the 1960 presidential election. Energetic and witty, he promised a dynamic administration that would "get the country moving again" after what was widely perceived as the passive leadership style of President Dwight D. Eisenhower. Kennedy's "New Frontier" (the term used to describe the domestic agenda of his administration) included programs to fight poverty, stimulate the economy, and strengthen American defense. He sparked a rise of youthful idealism with the creation of the Peace Corps and captured the imagination of many Americans with his goal of sending a man to the moon before the end of the decade. However, his record of achievement as president was limited by a recalcitrant Congress, which failed to pass many of his proposals. It was his shocking assassination on November 22, 1963 (an event that some people say marks the true beginning of the 1960s), that lifted Kennedy to near-mythological status as one of America's most beloved presidents.

Kennedy's vice president and successor, Lyndon B. Johnson, in contrast, had risen from modest circumstances to achieve a formidable reputation as an accomplished senator. Physically imposing, he was considered by some to be crude and overbearing compared to his more polished predecessor. Nevertheless, he was able to achieve several things Kennedy could not, such as the passage of much of Kennedy's economic and social agenda—including civil rights legislation—that had been bottled up in Congress. Johnson went beyond Kennedy's New Frontier to enunciate his own vision of America as a nation using its wealth to create a "Great Society" of "success without squalor, beauty without barrenness." Such a society, Johnson argued, could be achieved through government measures and programs designed to fight and win a "War on Poverty," improve America's schools and universities, provide health care for the elderly, and protect consumers and the environment.

Unlike Kennedy, Johnson won an overwhelming electoral victory in 1964, taking 61.3 percent of the vote and all but six states from his Republican opponent, Barry Goldwater. Bolstered by his victory, Johnson successfully urged Congress to pass hundreds of pieces of legislation—ranging from the Medicare and Medicaid programs to federal subsidies for the arts—to put his Great Society into place. Between 1964 and 1972, social welfare expenditures grew from 25.4 percent to 41.3 percent of the federal budget and from 4.3 percent to 8.8 percent of America's gross national product.

Many Americans were inspired by and supportive of Johnson's vision. However, the Great Society also received criticism from different quarters. Conservatives decried it for what they viewed as harmful government intervention in the economy and the creation of wasteful government bureaucracies. It was also looked on with disfavor by many on the political left, who argued that the changes and programs it proposed amounted to woefully inadequate window dressing on a fundamentally undemocratic and unjust society.

The leadership and ideas of Presidents Kennedy and Johnson set the tone for much of the 1960s. The selections in this chapter analyze various aspects of Kennedy's New Frontier and Johnson's Great Society.

"I believe that this Nation should commit itself to achieving the goal, before this decade is out, of landing a man on the moon and returning him safely to earth."

America Should Send a Man to the Moon

John F. Kennedy (1917–1963)

John F. Kennedy was elected president of the United States in 1960, becoming, at forty-three, the youngest person to win election to that office. The telegenic Democratic senator from Massachusetts appealed to many Americans with his pledge to "get the country moving again" after eight years under Republican president Dwight D. Eisenhower.

In his acceptance speech for the Democratic nomination for president, Kennedy spoke of a "New Frontier" of American challenges for the upcoming decade. The phrase was later used to refer to his domestic agenda as president. However, Kennedy's New Frontier proved to be somewhat limited. He sent numerous legislative proposals to Congress, including bills for medical aid to the elderly, for federal spending for education, and for programs to rebuild America's inner cities, but these and other measures were rejected or stalled in Congress. Some of his actions, including his appointment of segregationist judges to the federal bench, his perceived failure to fully support or promote the civil rights movement, and his 20 percent increase in the defense budget, were disappointing to some of his liberal supporters.

One part of Kennedy's New Frontier that did receive congressional and public support was his call for a national effort to put a person on the moon before the end of the decade. By undertaking this venture, the United States escalated its "space race" with the Soviet Union, which began on October 4, 1957, when the So-

From John F. Kennedy's speech to the 87th Congress, May 25, 1961.

viet Union shocked many Americans by launching *Sputnik I*, the world's first artificial space satellite. On April 12, 1961, shortly after Kennedy took office as president, Soviet Yuri A. Gagarin became the first man in space. Alan B. Shepard became the first American in space a few weeks later on May 5.

On May 25, Kennedy made a special address to a joint session of Congress in which he proposed that America commit to a manned lunar expedition. Kennedy placed the idea in the context of a deadly serious Cold War competition with the "adversaries of freedom" (i.e., the Soviet Union and other communist nations) for world power and influence. Kennedy succeeded in rallying Congress and the nation to this effort. On July 20, 1969, after the United States had spent more than $24 billion, American astronaut Neil Armstrong became the first man to set foot on the moon.

Mr. Speaker, Mr. Vice President, my copartners in Government, and ladies and gentlemen: The Constitution imposes upon me the obligation to from time to time give to the Congress information on the state of the Union. While this has traditionally been interpreted as an annual affair, this tradition has been broken in extraordinary times.

These are extraordinary times. We face an extraordinary challenge. But our strength as well as our convictions have imposed upon this Nation the role of leader in freedom's cause. We face opportunities and adversaries that do not wait for annual addresses or fiscal years. This Nation is engaged in a long and exacting test for the future of freedom—a test which may well continue for decades to come. Our strength as well as our convictions have imposed upon this Nation the role of leader in freedom's cause.

No role in history could be more difficult or more important. It is not a negative or defensive role—it is a great positive adventure. We stand for freedom. That is our conviction for ourselves, that is our only commitment to others. No friend, no neutral, and no adversary should think otherwise. We are not against any man, or any nation, or any system, except as it is hostile to freedom. Nor am I here to present a new military doctrine bearing any one name or aimed at any one area. I am here to promote the freedom doctrine.

The great battleground for the defense and expansion of freedom today is the whole southern half of the globe—Asia, Latin

President Kennedy's vision of sending a person to the moon became a reality on July 20, 1969, when Neil Armstrong and Edwin "Buzz" Aldrin Jr. (pictured) became the first people to walk on the moon's surface.

America, Africa, and the Middle East—the lands of rising peoples. Their revolution, the greatest in human history, is one of peace and hope for freedom and equality, for order and independence. They seek an end, they seek a beginning. And theirs is a revolution which we would support regardless of the cold war, and regardless of which political or economic route they choose to freedom.

Adversaries of Freedom

For the adversaries of freedom did not create this revolution; nor did they create the conditions which compel it. But they are seeking to ride the crest of its wave, to capture it for themselves.

Yet their aggression is more often concealed than open. They have fired no missiles; and their troops are seldom seen. They send arms, agitators, aid, technicians and propaganda to every troubled area. But where the fighting is required, it is usually done by others, by guerrillas striking at night, by assassins striking alone, assassins who have taken the lives of 4,000 civil officers in the last 12 months in Vietnam, by subversives and saboteurs and insurrectionists, who in some cases control whole areas inside of independent nations.

They possess a powerful intercontinental striking force, large forces for conventional war, a well-trained underground in nearly every country, the power to conscript talent and manpower for any purpose, the capacity for quick decisions, a closed society without dissent or free information, and long experience in the techniques of violence and subversion. They make the most of their scientific successes, their economic progress and their pose as a foe of colonialism and friend of popular revolution. They prey on unstable or unpopular governments, unsealed or unknown boundaries, unfilled hopes, convulsive change, massive poverty, illiteracy, unrest and frustration.

With these formidable weapons, the adversaries of freedom plan to consolidate their territory, to exploit, to control, and finally to destroy the hopes of the world's newest nations, and they have ambition to do it before the end of this decade. It is a contest of will and purpose as well as force and violence, a battle for minds and souls as well as lives and territory. In that contest we cannot stand aside. . . .

There is no single simple policy with which to meet this challenge. Experience has taught us that no one nation has the power or the wisdom to solve all the problems of the world or manage all its revolutionary tides; that extending our commitments does not always increase our security; that any initiative carries with it the risk of temporary defeat; that nuclear weapons cannot prevent subversion; that no free peoples can be kept free without will and energy of their own; and that no two nations or situations are exactly alike.

Yet there is much we can do and must do. The proposals I bring before you today are numerous and varied. They arise from the host of special opportunities and dangers which have become increasingly clear in recent months. Taken together, I believe that they mark another step forward in our effort as a people. Taken together they will help advance our own progress, encourage our friends, and strengthen the opportunities for freedom and peace. I am here to ask the help of this Congress for freedom and peace. I am here to ask the help of this Congress and the Nation in approving these necessary measures. . . .

The Importance of Space

If we are to win the battle that is going on around the world between freedom and tyranny, if we are to win the battle for men's minds, the dramatic achievements in space which occurred in recent weeks should have made clear to us all, as did the sputnik in 1957, the impact of this adventure on the minds of men everywhere who are attempting to make a determination of which road they should take. Since early in my term our efforts in space have been under review. With the advice of the Vice President, who is Chairman of the National Space Council, we have examined where we are strong and where we are not, where we may succeed and where we may not. Now it is time to take longer strides—time for a great new American enterprise—time for this Nation to take a clearly leading role in space achievement which in many ways may hold the key to our future on earth.

I believe we possess all the resources and all the talents necessary. But the facts of the matter are that we have never made the national decisions or marshaled the national resources required for such leadership. We have never specified long-range goals on an urgent time schedule, or managed our resources and our time so as to insure their fulfillment.

Recognizing the head start obtained by the Soviets with their large rocket engines, which gives them many months of leadtime, and recognizing the likelihood that they will exploit this lead for some time to come in still more impressive successes, we nevertheless are required to make new efforts on our own. For while we cannot guarantee that we shall one day be first, we can guarantee that any failure to make this effort will find us last. We take an additional risk by making it in full view of the world—but as shown by the feat of Astronaut [Alan B.] Shepard, this very risk enhances our stature when we are successful. But this is not merely a race. Space is open to us now; and our eagerness to share its meaning is not governed by the efforts of others. We go into space because whatever mankind must undertake, freemen must fully share.

National Goals

I therefore ask the Congress, above and beyond the increases I have earlier requested for space activities, to provide the funds which are needed to meet the following national goals:

First, I believe that this Nation should commit itself to achieving the goal, before this decade is out, of landing a man on the moon and returning him safely to earth. No single space project in this period will be more exciting, or more impressive to mankind, or more important for the long-range exploration of space; and none will be so difficult or expensive to accomplish. Including necessary supporting research, this objective will require an additional $531 million this year and still higher sums in the future. We propose to accelerate development of the appropriate lunar spacecraft. We propose to develop alternate liquid and solid fuel boosters much larger than any now being developed, until certain which is superior. We propose additional funds for other engine development and for unmanned explorations—explorations which are particularly important for one purpose which this Nation will never overlook; the survival of the man who first makes this daring flight. But in a very real sense, it will not be one man going to the moon—we make this judgment affirmatively—it will be an entire nation. For all of us must work to put him there.

Second, an additional $23 million, together with $7 million already available, will accelerate development of the ROVER nuclear rocket. This is a technological enterprise in which we are well on the way to striking progress, and which gives promise of some day providing a means for even more exciting and ambitious exploration of space, perhaps beyond the moon, perhaps to the very ends of the solar system itself.

Third, an additional $50 million will make the most of our present leadership by accelerating the use of space satellites for worldwide communications. When we have put into space a system that will enable people in remote areas of the earth to exchange messages, hold conversations, and eventually see television programs, we will have achieved a success as beneficial as it will be striking.

Fourth, an additional $75 million—of which $53 million is for the Weather Bureau—will help give us at the earliest possible time a satellite system for worldwide weather observation. Such a system will be of inestimable commercial and scientific value; and the information it provides will be made freely available to all the nations of the world.

Let it be clear—and this is a judgment which the Members of the Congress must finally make—let it be clear that I am asking the Congress and the country to accept a firm commitment to a new course of action—a course which will last for many years and carry very heavy costs, $531 million in the fiscal year 1962 and an estimated $7–9 billion additional over the next five years. If we are to go only halfway, or reduce our sights in the face of difficulty, in my judgment it would be better not to go at all. This is a choice which this country must make, and I am confident that under the leadership of the Space committees of the Congress and the appropriations committees you will consider the matter carefully. It is a most important decision that we make as a nation; but all of you have lived though the last 4 years and have seen the significance of space and the adventures in space, and no one can predict with certainty what the ultimate meaning will be of the mastery of space. I believe we should go to the moon. But I think every citizen of this country as well as the Members of the Congress should consider the matter carefully in their judgment, to which we have given attention over many weeks and months, as it is a heavy burden; and there is no sense in agreeing, or desiring, that the United States take an affirmative position in outer space unless we are prepared to do the work and bear the burdens to make it successful. If we are not, we should decide today.

A National Commitment

Let me stress also that more money alone will not do the job. This decision demands a major national commitment of scientific and technical manpower, material and facilities, and the possibility of their diversion from other important activities where they are already thinly spread. It means a degree of dedication, organization, and discipline which have not always characterized our research and development efforts. It means we cannot afford undue work stoppages, inflated costs of material or talent, wasteful interagency rivalries, or a high turnover of key personnel.

New objectives and new money cannot solve these problems. They could, in fact, aggravate them further—unless every scientist, every engineer, every serviceman, every technician, contractor, and civil servant involved gives his personal pledge that this Nation will move forward, with the full speed of freedom, in the exciting adventure of space.

"If our national self-respect is on such a shaky basis that it cannot survive one more Russian triumph in space, we are in a bad way indeed."

America's Race to the Moon Is Misguided

Carl Dreher (1896–1976)

In May 1961 President John F. Kennedy captivated much of the nation with his call for a national effort to send a man to the moon within the decade. The National Aeronautics and Space Administration (NASA) began plans for a manned lunar expedition, and annual government appropriations for space exploration rose to $5 billion during the Kennedy administration. Many scientists and others questioned the wisdom of devoting so many national resources to the "space race" with the Soviet Union to land a man on the moon. Some people argued that the money spent on space exploration could be better used to fight poverty or other social problems. Several other concerns are expressed in the following viewpoint, taken from an article by Carl Dreher, science editor of the *Nation* magazine from 1961 to 1975. In the article, written for the *Nation* in 1962, Dreher notes such objections to a manned lunar expedition as excessive costs, the risks to astronauts, and the disadvantages of pursuing Cold War competition instead of international cooperation in the exploration of space. The American effort to send a person to the moon continued for most of the 1960s, culminating in the successful *Apollo 11* expedition in July 1969.

Before the [Soviet] Vostok III and IV flights, some prominent scientists and politicians were expressing misgivings about the

From Carl Dreher, "Wrong Way to the Moon," *Nation*, September 15, 1962. Reprinted with permission from the *Nation* magazine; © The Nation Company, L.P.

cost of American participation in the race to the moon. The rising volume of protest was drowned out by the cries of anguish over the manifest Soviet lead. Most of this clamor was quite baldly inspired by partisan and commercial considerations, and since the earlier criticism had and still has a solid technological basis, no doubt it will be voiced anew. Those who say what they think, rather than what the Pentagon and the aerospace industry would like them to say, will be helping to safeguard the lives of our astronauts, which are endangered by energetic space promoters like Vice President Lyndon Johnson, who incessantly warns us that "our future as a nation is at stake," and that "we dare not lose."

In the first place, we may lose even if we commit everything we have: neither men nor money will necessarily overcome a late start. In the second place, why don't we dare? The moon race has little to do with military power at the present time and, the Air Force and its Congressional reserve generals to the contrary, may never assume decisive military importance. A space war is much more likely to be fought in earth orbit. We cannot, then, be overwhelmed by a Soviet victory in the lunar sweepstakes. Nor has the breakneck effort now in the whooping-up stage anything to do with our industrial and agricultural capacity and our ability to aid other nations; rather, it detracts from these assets. And they are assets in that older race against hunger and disease; the sick and hungry are not interested in the moon, but in food and medicine. As for the things of the spirit, if our national self-respect is on such a shaky basis that it cannot survive one more Russian triumph in space, we are in a bad way indeed. The Russians launched the first satellite and we felt somewhat humiliated, yet here we are, five years later, still grappling with them and causing them as many worries as they cause us.

Aside from the extravagant and juvenile character of these alarms, their authors ignore the fact that a premature moon landing, followed by the death of the astronauts on the moon or subsequently in space, would not enhance national prestige. This is a risk for the Soviets as well as for us. The more sanguine contestant may fail; the more wary one may wait, learn from the other's disasters and succeed. That is, indeed, a likely denouement, for the lunar problem is one of enormous difficulty. Hans Thirring, the noted Austrian physicist, has likened it to the leveling of the Rocky Mountains. If the first attempts succeed, it will be little short of a miracle.

On the side of moderation there are some impressive names and arguments. Already in December, 1960, when plans and budgets were still relatively modest (and they will seem minuscule in another year), Dr. James R. Killian, chairman of the M.I.T. Corporation and President Eisenhower's first scientific adviser in the post-sputnik era, said, "Will several billion dollars a year additional for enhancing the quality of education not do more for the future of the United States and its position in the world than several billions a year additional for man in space?" More recently, General Eisenhower has inveighed against what he called "a mad effort to win a stunt race," which it is, and "a great boondoggle," which is rather an oversimplification. More conversant with the technological realities, Dr. Lee DuBridge, whose California Institute of Technology manages the Jet Propulsion Laboratory for the National Aeronautics and Space Administration [NASA], has referred to "space idiots" and shown that the arguments for a military crash program in space are fallacious. Dr. George B. Kistiakowsky, another scientific adviser to President Eisenhower, Dr. James Van Allen, Dr. Edward U. Condon and Senator William Proxmire have reasoned to much the same effect.

A Question of Priorities

Senator Paul Douglas of Illinois was among those who believed that too much money was being spent on the space program that could be better used on poverty and other social welfare concerns. The following passage is taken from his concluding remarks after questioning Charles L. Schultze, director of the Bureau of the Budget, in hearings on February 2, 1966.

I remember when this man-to-the-moon business first came up I asked Mr. [David] Bell, who was your predecessor, how much it would cost. He said a minimum of $20 billion. And I questioned whether it was worthwhile. One of my colleagues said: "Well, people questioned the expenditure to finance the experiments by Alexander Graham Bell and the telegraph." I replied: "That cost $40,000, and there is quite a difference between $40,000 and $20 billion."

My time is up. Now I simply want to say that a little critical judgment is needed on these measures. The public, the business community, the political world, is just carried away with the fascination of these subjects, and yet we ignore the human beings who live here in the United States of America, 20 million of whom live in abject poverty and 35 to 40 million living in poverty.

You can easily shift your sense of values from the human value to the spectacular mechanical value.

What profits a civilization if it has 20 million people in abject poverty and sends one man to the moon?

None of these critics can be brushed off, but perhaps the most cogent evaluation has been provided by Dr. Warren Weaver, former president of the American Association for the Advancement of Science and one of the most highly respected of scientists, in the *Saturday Review* of August 4 [1962]. Assuming that it would cost the United States $30 billion to put a man on the moon, Dr. Weaver pointed out that this would give a 10 per cent raise in salary to every teacher in the country over a ten-year period, give $10 million each to 200 of the best small colleges, finance seven-year scholarships (freshman through Ph.D.) for 50,000 new scientists and engineers, contribute $200 million each toward the creation of ten new medical schools, build and largely endow complete universities for all fifty-three of the nations added to the United Nations since its founding, create three more Rockefeller Foundations and still have $100 million left over to popularize science, which bestrides us like a colossus and of whose spirit, principles and procedures probably not one American in a hundred has the faintest conception.

Costs of the Space Race

We have got so used to throwing around billions that we no longer comprehend what a billion means in human terms, but even these comparisons fall far short of the actuality. There is no assurance that the moon operation will come in at $30 billion; all such forecasts have turned out to be low, and this one is little more than a guess. Before the House Appropriations Subcommittee, NASA Deputy Administrator Robert C. Seamans, Jr., estimated the agency would require $50–60 billion over the next ten years. The June [1962] *Fortune* put the cost of the space effort at about $20 billion *annually* by 1970 and calculated that by that time the United States will have spent $75–100 billion on space activities, while missiles will have accounted for another $50 billion. No downtrend in NASA's spending is expected after the moon has been conquered; races to Mars and Venus are planned next. And of course any slackening in the missile and nuclear bomb races would be over the dead bodies of thousands of admirals, generals, veterans, munition manufacturers, labor leaders and other dedicated patriots, aided by [Soviet] Marshal Rodion Y. Malinovsky who, after Major [Andrian G.] Nikolayev and Lieut. Col. [Pavel P.] Popovich landed [on earth following successful orbital flights], rubbed it in with the admonition: "Let our enemies know what techniques and what soldiers our Soviet power disposes of."

The monetary argument does carry some weight and should continue to be pressed, but it does not follow that because the money could be put to good use here below there will be a popular revulsion against shooting it off into space. The moon race, as Dr. Condon has pointed out, is a kind of lunar Olympic game, exciting to both Russians and Americans and providing a much-needed effervescence for millions of drab lives. The astronauts have largely supplanted movie stars and ordinary athletes as popular heroes.

Endangering Lives

Instead of talking only about money, therefore, we should be talking of ways to spare as many of these attractive young men as possible, rather than offering them as a human sacrifice on the altar of nationalistic passions. There will be fatalities in any event, but we cannot condemn the moon project on that account. There is nothing particularly admirable about dying in bed. The appeal, if it is to be effective, must be based on the fact that astronauts will die unnecessarily and, by accelerating the moon race, we shall be accessories to a crime.

Of this there can be no doubt in the mind of anyone who is willing to make an honest appraisal. The moon program is in a state of flux bordering on confusion. Up to a few months ago NASA seemed committed to the method of direct ascent. A single heavy vehicle would be put into a moon trajectory by an enormous rocket, on arrival would decelerate itself by proportionately powerful retro-rocket action, land, stay a while, then take off with another massive spurt of rocket power for the trip home. When it was realized that a booster large enough for this brute-force method could not be built until the 1970s, if then, the planners turned to earth orbit rendezvous and coupling—sending the astronauts and the moon vehicle, or the fuel, into earth orbit in separate packages and connecting them at an absolute speed of some 18,000 miles per hour and a differential speed of about a foot per second.

Although rendezvous and coupling is an untried procedure, a mishap in earth orbit would not necessarily be fatal. The man-carrying vehicle might be able to re-enter, or other vehicles might be orbited rapidly for rescue operations. But then, from earth-orbit planning, NASA switched to lunar rendezvous and coupling. This involves sending a duplex vehicle from the earth into moon orbit and dropping a part of the assembly with two men to the moon, while one man stays with the main vehicle. The ferry, or "bug," returns to lunar orbit for rendezvous with the mother ship, couples to it, the two lunar explorers go back into the main cabin, the bug is jettisoned, and the three astronauts return to earth in the remaining unit.

All the modes of getting to the moon (and getting back) must give the experienced engineer the shivers, but the lunar rendezvous technique seems the most perilous of all. The juncture must be accomplished hundreds of thousands of miles from earth, with very little chance of survival if something should go wrong. The rapid transition from direct ascent to earth orbit to lunar orbit also raises a question. Does it represent technological progress, or are the planners merely jumping from one tour de force to another?

Some of the NASA engineers contend that lunar rendezvous and coupling is not only the fastest and cheapest method, but the one most likely to succeed. It is true that takeoff from the moon will be in a relatively light vehicle, in an environment where gravity is only one-sixth that of the earth, and the "bug" may approach the mother ship at a relatively low speed—only about one mile per second. But there will still be the risk of takeoff from a probably unfavorable surface and topography and the subsequent problems of coupling will be extremely critical.

Just when these matters are being debated in NASA's conference rooms, the Department of Defense has adopted a policy of restrictions on information based on the "need to know" principle. Tight secrecy is likely to spread to NASA, if it has not already done so. This would be a disservice to all concerned. Scientists and engineers inside and outside the government should be able to obtain the facts on which to base an opinion, and to criticize the conclusions reached by the insiders if they wish. Above all, safety, not speed, should be the overriding consideration. James E. Webb, Lyndon Johnson's choice as NASA administrator, may deny that there is a lunar race, but of course there is one and this fact alone may influence the judgment of the teams inside the agency whose members are making crucial decisions that will affect not only their own careers, but decide the fate of the astronauts. The more publicity there is, the better the latter's chances. The scientists who have spoken out against the general aspects of the project as it is being conducted might well have something to say on the technical decisions as well.

Cooperation Can Reduce Risks

Another direction in which the risks of the lunar venture can be reduced is through cooperation between the contestants. Since, no matter what experiments precede the initial attempts to land on and escape from the moon, the odds will be against the early explorers, one would think that the two sides would at least exchange views on rescue techniques and perhaps work out a plan for common utilization of rescue facilities. They could still compete, but must it be a competition to the death? After the Nikolayev-Popovich flights the director of Britain's radio-astronomy and satellite-tracking station at Jodrell Bank, Sir Bernard Lovell, remarked, "More than ever one is appalled by the foolishness of these two countries attempting the moon problem in competition. After all, the common problem is the exploration of space and the manned conquest of the solar system." The common problem, unhappily, is subordinate to the separate problem of the superpowers, which is to do each other in by whatever means come to hand. Space may be infinite, but in the minds of the diplomats and militarists it is compressed into just one more counter in the war game. They brush off advice of the sort offered by Sir Bernard, just as they frustrate the attempts of the neutrals to get them to stop nuclear testing. They are perfectly ready to sacrifice the astronauts, their own lionized fellow countrymen, to national ambition, and in the fullness of their masculinity and patriotism the astronauts are willing and eager to take their chances.

VIEWPOINT 3

"This nation, this people, this generation, has man's first chance to create a Great Society: a society of success without squalor, beauty without barrenness."

The American People and Government Should Strive to Create a "Great Society"

Lyndon B. Johnson (1908–1973)

Lyndon B. Johnson became president of the United States following the assassination of John F. Kennedy on November 22, 1963. Johnson had been the Senate majority leader prior to his election as vice president in 1960, and he was able to use his experience and skills to shepherd much of Kennedy's stalled legislative proposals through Congress. He helped pass the landmark Civil Rights Act of 1964, declared a domestic "War on Poverty," and was rewarded with the Democratic Party's 1964 nomination for president.

Johnson first used the phrase "Great Society" in a May 1964 speech before graduates of the University of Michigan, in which he argued that the United States had an unprecedented opportunity to use its wealth and power to end social problems such as poverty and urban decay. In subsequent months he built on and expressed his vision of the Great Society while campaigning for the 1964 election. The following viewpoint is taken from remarks given at a Democratic Party fund-raising dinner in Detroit on June 26, 1964. Johnson handily defeated his opponent, Barry Goldwater, in the November 1964 election and made the Great

From Lyndon B. Johnson's remarks at a Democratic Party fund-raiser, in *Public Papers of the Presidents: Lyndon B. Johnson, 1963–64,* vol. 1 (Washington, DC: Government Printing Office, 1965).

Society a prominent theme of his presidency over the next few years. The term "Great Society" has subsequently been used to refer to Johnson's attempts to improve America's quality of life through government programs and legislation.

In 1960, in this city, John Fitzgerald Kennedy began his campaign for President. He asked you then to make a choice for progress. You made that choice. The result has been four years of unmatched progress in this nation.

This year you and all the American People are going to choose four more years of progress. . . .

With the help of all of you, all good Americans, doing what we conceive to be best for our country, we will continue to work together for the people of Michigan and the people of America. . . .

If we stand together, if we are united, if we join hands, there are some things that no party, no group, or no person is going to stop. No one will stop America from moving toward a world where every child will grow up free from the threat of nuclear war.

Do we stand together on that?

No one will stop America from wiping out racial injustice and liberating every citizen, of every race and color, to share in all the blessings of our freedom. No one will stop America from feeding the hungry, and caring for the helpless, and giving dignity and self-respect to the old.

Do we stand together on that?

No one is going to stop the great forward march that we began four years ago. Because you are not going to let them. The American people are not going to let them. And as long as I am President of the United States, so help me God, I am not going to let them. . . .

I am proud to say tonight that we are, tonight, entering our fortieth straight month without any indication of a recession. And we shall never again permit this country to retreat toward the ravages of economic decline.

We can all, each of us, take great pride in our own tax paying, profit-sharing, private-enterprise system of government where incentive has its reward, and all the nations of the world look to us with envy.

In every area of activity that we chose to be part of, we have moved farther and faster than at any time in our history. These have been exciting and these have been rewarding years. But the job is not yet done. We have barely begun our drive toward prosperity. Men of little vision and men of small vitality have always underestimated the American potential for progress. If we work together in a policy of prosperity, we can build an America where every man can meet his desires for a decent life, where no man lacks the dignity of labor.

A Policy for Prosperity

This is the kind of America that we are going to build. This is the policy we have. This is our policy for prosperity.

First, we will continue to direct the enormous impact of the federal budget toward stimulating growth and toward controlling inflation.

Second, we will work with industry and labor to discourage destructive inflation. The responsibility for prices and wage decision belongs to private enterprise. But we have a common interest in controlling inflation. For inflation undermines alike the profits of business, the wages of workers, and the savings and the profits of all of our people.

Third, we will encourage and expand investment in material and human resources. We will stimulate them. We will take great pride in aiding them and supporting them. This is the core of the poverty program. Our war against poverty seeks to give the desperate and the downtrodden the skills and the experience that they need to lift themselves from poverty. We are going to pass this program, and in our lifetime we, God willing and with your help, we are going to wipe out poverty in America.

Fourth, with the help of people of all faiths, doing it in the American way, we will bring resources together with needs, matching skills to jobs, incentives to lags, and focusing our help where help is most needed.

Fifth, we will encourage technology and modernization, through research and tax incentives. At the same time we will not forget our responsibility to find jobs for those thrown out of work by machines.

These policies offer us the prospect of an abundance beyond the furthest aims of an earlier generation. . . .

Quality of Life

But abundance is not an end in itself. Our concern is with the quality of the life of our people, not with just massive statistics, not with just mounting bank balances. The purpose and the values of our party and our nation can never be listed in the ledgers of accountants. They are inscribed in the hearts of our people, in the history of our nation, and the heritage of our civilization.

So the ultimate test of our beloved America is the larger purpose to which we turn our prosperity.

We must first turn it toward relief of the oppressed, the under-privileged, and the helpless. We must, in the words of the Bible, "Learn to do well, seek judgment, relieve the oppressed, judge the fatherless, plead for the widow."

The Great Society

President Lyndon B. Johnson first used the term "Great Society" in a commencement address at the University of Michigan at Ann Arbor on May 22, 1964. His speech included the following passages.

The purpose of protecting the life of our nation and preserving the liberty of our citizens is to pursue the happiness of our people. Our success in that pursuit is the test of our success as a nation.

For a century we labored to settle and to subdue a continent. For half a century we called upon unbounded invention and untiring industry to create an order of plenty for all of our people.

The challenge of the next half century is whether we have the wisdom to use that wealth to enrich and elevate our national life, and to advance the quality of our American civilization.

Your imagination, your initiative, and your indignation will determine whether we build a society where progress is the servant of our needs, or a society where old values and new visions are buried under unbridled growth. For in your time we have the opportunity to move not only toward the rich society and the powerful society, but upward to the Great Society.

The Great Society rests on abundance and liberty for all. It demands an end to poverty and racial injustice, to which we are totally committed in our time. But that is just the beginning.

The Great Society is a place where every child can find knowledge to enrich his mind and to enlarge his talents. It is a place where leisure is a welcome chance to build and reflect, not a feared cause of boredom and restlessness. It is a place where the city of man serves not only the needs of the body and the demands of commerce but the desire for beauty and the hunger for community.

It is a place where man can renew contact with nature. It is a place which honors creation for its own sake and for what it adds to the understanding of the race. It is a place where men are more concerned with the quality of their goals than the quantity of their goods.

But most of all, the Great Society is not a safe harbor, a resting place, a final objective, a finished work. It is a challenge constantly renewed, beckoning us toward a destiny where the meaning of our lives matches the marvelous products of our labor.

In this pursuit we will turn special attention to the problems of older Americans. Retirement should be a time of serenity and fulfillment, not deprivation and fear.

We are going to provide hospital care through Social Security to older Americans under a Democratic Administration, and that Administration will never permit a lifetime of savings to be wiped out by the ravages of illness.

And we will go on from this to increase benefits and build better housing, and expand employment opportunities, and do all in the power of a nation grateful for a lifetime of service and labor.

A New Era

But this is only part of our service.

We stand at the edge of the greatest era in the life of any nation. For the first time in world history we have the abundance and the ability to free every man from hopeless want, and to free every person to find fulfillment in the works of his mind or the labor of his hands.

Even the greatest of all past civilizations existed on the exploitation of the misery of the many.

This nation, this people, this generation, has man's first chance to create a Great Society: a society of success without squalor, beauty without barrenness, works of genius without the wretchedness of poverty. We can open the doors of learning. We can open the doors of fruitful labor and rewarding leisure, of open opportunity and close community—not just to the privileged few, but, thank God, we can open those doors to everyone.

For we will not allow the ancient values of the human spirit and the visions of the human heart to be submerged in unbridled change.

This is a vision and a task that is worthy of the highest labors of any generation. This is the vision and this is the task that the American people are asking of us tonight. And I pledge to you in your name and in mine, and in the name of our party and our country, we will be ready. . . .

In this land in which we live we have much to be proud of, much to protect and a great deal more to preserve. It is the kind of people like you who have made the sacrifice to come out here and spend this evening listening to speeches and to reach down in your pocket and pay the fare that supports one of the two great parties in America that are responsible for this great system that we have. . . .

And the almost 3 billion people in the rest of the world who have never known the pleasure and prosperity that is ours, who have never shared the freedom that belongs to us—they watch our every move to see which direction our life will take in the hope that they, too, some day, may enjoy the blessings that are ours.

VIEWPOINT 4

"Private property, free competition, hard work—these have been our greatest tools. Let us not discard them now!"

America's Greatness Demands a Reduction in Government

Barry Goldwater (b. 1909)

An Arizona senator and businessman, Barry Goldwater was a leader of the conservative wing of the Republican Party. His 1960 book *The Conscience of a Conservative*, in which he outlined his ideas, brought him national exposure, and in 1964 he was selected by the Republicans to run for president against Lyndon B. Johnson, the incumbent. In his campaign, Goldwater attacked Johnson's proposed Great Society and argued for both a limited national government in domestic life and a strong national defense against the Soviet Union. His views are given in the following viewpoint, excerpted from a campaign speech delivered in Prescott, Arizona, on September 3, 1964. Goldwater argues that the election of Johnson would result in a regimented society dominated by the federal government. He contends that a stronger national defense would preserve world peace and that morally lax government officials have contributed to a growing lack of respect for law and order in America. Goldwater carried only six states in the 1964 election, but his candidacy and its themes are credited by some with sparking a later conservative political revival in the United States.

From Barry Goldwater's campaign speech delivered at Prescott, Arizona, September 3, 1964.

This is truly the home of the free and of the brave. Our forefathers came here seeking a new life; a life that they could lead for themselves, with honor, with faith, and with a friendliness that need never be forced.

They hewed and fashioned that new life through hard work and sacrifice and they passed on to us our most cherished heritage—a free and orderly community of men.

Today that free and orderly community faces the grave danger of becoming merely another possession of the White House, and we who live here face the grave danger of becoming the servants of some Big Brother who lives there.

We all sense this danger, not only those of us gathered in this square, but all of us across this land. There is a stir in the land. There is a mood of uneasiness. We feel adrift in an uncharted and stormy sea. We feel that we have lost our way.

We must and we can find our way to the greatness and a purpose worthy of this nation and its people.

Today, with your help and with God's blessing, we go forward to greatness in this nation.

Greatness of purpose—to keep the peace and extend freedom.

Greatness of action—to speak clearly and to be heard respectively once again in the councils of the world.

Greatness of heart and self-restraint at home—to restore law and order, to make our streets safe, without losing liberty.

Greatness of vision—to see beyond the comforts and pleasures of the day toward the towering goals of tomorrow.

Greatness of soul—to restore inner meaning to every man's life in a time too often rushed, too often obsessed by petty needs and material greeds, and too often controlled by the pressure of groups rather than the conscience of the individual.

The individual, the private man, the whole man—you!—today stands in danger of becoming the forgotten man of our collectivized, complex times.

The private man, the whole man—you!—must and can be restored as the sovereign citizen, as the center of the family, the state, and as the prime mover and molder of the future.

Today, therefore, and again with your help, we also begin a great campaign to return the Government of this nation to the people of this nation.

Today we take a first step toward ending in our time the erosion of individual worth by a growing Federal bureaucracy.

This time, in this election, we have a choice. It is between far more than political personalities, far more than political promises, far more than political programs. It is a choice of what sort of people we want to be. It is the choice of what sort of world we want to live [in] and want to pass on to our children.

Choose the way of this present Administration and you will have chosen the way of the regimented society, with a number for every man, woman, and child; a pigeonhole for every problem, and a bureaucrat for every decision.

Choose the way of this present Administration and you have the way of mobs in the street, restrained only by the plea that they wait until after election time to ignite violence once again.

Choose the way of this present Administration and you choose the way of unilateral disarmament and appeasement in foreign affairs.

Choose the way of this present Administration and you make real the prospect of an America unarmed and aimless in the face of militant Communism around the world.

Instead, I ask that you join me in proving that every American can stand on his own, make up his own mind, chart his own future, keep and control his own family, asking for help and getting help only when truly overwhelming problems, beyond his control, beset him.

I ask you to join with me in finding 20th-century answers for 20th-century problems rather than relying on the old, disproved doctrine of turning our problems, our lives, and our liberties over to a supposed élite in an all-powerful central government.

The campaign we launch today is dedicated to that.

The campaign we launch today is dedicated to peace, to progress, and to purpose.

You have heard those words and phrases time after time. You know how empty they have become. Our task is to look beyond the words, to understand what the politicians really mean when they say them, to what they do with them when they get in office.

When we speak of these things we mean something far different from the opposition party. We mean:

Peace through preparedness;

Peace through freedom;

Purpose through constitutional order.

These are the themes that we shall make resound across this great land of ours, and across an anxious, troubled and listening world.

The Question of Peace

The question of peace, for instance, is basic to the differences between the two major parties today.

The present Administration does not understand the nature of the threats to the peace, the nature of the enemy who threatens the peace, or the nature of the conflict which, whether we like it or not, has been imposed upon the entire world.

47

What more flat evidence of this could there be than the fact that, in his acceptance speech, the leader of the present Administration did not even mention Communism?

Johnson's Patchwork Utopia

M. Stanton Evans, then associate editor of the National Review, *reacted unfavorably to President Johnson's January 1965 address to Congress, in which he described his Great Society proposals. Some of Evans's criticisms of Johnson, which were published in the February 2, 1965, issue of that conservative magazine, are excerpted here.*

Lyndon Johnson's outline of "the Great Society" in his first 1965 address to Congress puts this department in mind of the old saying: If we had some ham, we could have ham and eggs—if we had some eggs.

It begins to appear that in Johnson's patchwork Utopia, the same thought will apply: If we had some free enterprise, we could have free enterprise and economy in government—if we had some economy in government. For despite his obeisances to liberty and to reduction of "waste," it becomes clear that Johnson means to conduct us with all deliberate speed into a society which is at once compulsory and insolvent.

The President's "State of the Union" address [of January 1965] made it clear that, whatever the legislative specifics, he intends to thrust the authority of the Federal Government into every conceivable sector of national life. To elevate "the quality of our people," a dubious task for government, Johnson proposed new or enlarged federal intrusion into health, education, job training, unemployment compensation, area redevelopment, transportation, housing, dentistry, mental illness, municipal life, landscaping, training of law enforcement officers, air pollution, "natural beauty," and, of course, poverty. . . .

Should all the things Johnson mentioned be realized in legislation, America will have virtually completed its transition from free enterprise to the planned economy. This new overlay of paternalism would create a web of federal authority so far-reaching and powerful that it is doubtful the United States could recover the vigor of its once-free institutions. Even without Johnson's proposals, the reach of federal power is immense, much more so than is generally realized. What Johnson is proposing is to fill in the lacunae, to complete the edifice of power which has been a-building for 30 years.

The fact is that Communism is the only great threat to the peace! The fact is that Communism is a threat to every free man. It can't be ignored!

Republicans have proved that they understand these things. The Republican platform this year shows this understanding. Re-

48

publican performances in the White House and in the Congress have demonstrated this understanding.

A major concern of ours has been the military security of this nation. Some distort this proper concern to make it appear that we are preoccupied with war.

There is no greater political lie.

We are preoccupied with peace!

And we are fearful that this Administration is letting the peace slip away, as it has slipped three times since 1914, by pretending that there are no threats to it.

I am trying to carry to the American people this plain message: This entire nation and the entire world risks war in our time unless free men remain strong enough to keep the peace.

This Administration, which inherited the mightiest arsenal for the defense of freedom ever created on earth, is so dismantling it that we face the prospect of going into the decade of the nineteen-seventies with only a fraction of the flexible, balanced weapon systems which give us the vital options of controlled, graduated deterrence—rather than only a capacity for all-out nuclear confrontation. . . .

I promise an administration that will keep the peace—and keep faith with freedom at the same time.

The Republican party, this party of peace through strength, has no clearer message. Peace has no greater hope.

We cannot support this cause, however, on a base of sand at home. Our economy must underpin the strength with which peace can be kept as well as fill our needs at home. And the key to progress there, as it is to eventual peace in the world, is purely and simply—freedom.

A Free Economy

This country has grown great and strong and prosperous by placing major reliance on a free economy. What we have we owe to the ceaseless strivings of tens of millions of free men to better their own conditions and to provide better futures for their children and their children's children.

Private property, free competition, hard work—these have been our greatest tools. Let us not discard them now!

This system has preserved and protected our freedom, our right to disagree, our diversity, our independence from arbitrary interference in our affairs.

This system is the mighty engine of progress which enabled this country to develop from a small independent citizenry to become a multitude spanning the continent and living on a level that is the envy of the world.

Government-to-government aid from other countries did not do it for us. Hard work and freedom did it! Progress through freedom has been our heritage and must continue to be our goal.

Increasingly, however, government has been absorbing or controlling more and more of our resources, our energy, and our ambition.

Today you work from January through April just to provide government with the money it spends.

Until early February you are working to pay the expenses of local and state government. For twice as long thereafter you are working to pay the expenses of the Federal Government. Only then do you work for money that you yourself can use for what you yourself choose.

This cancerous growth of the Federal Government must and shall be stopped. A Republican Administration will let you use more of your money for yourself. . . .

The Purpose of Government

Perhaps even closer to our hearts, is the matter of purpose and order in our lives and our society.

Most of us have conceived of the purpose of our national Government as being service to the people, bringing them fair laws and fair administration, and doing those absolutely needed things which individuals, communities, or states cannot do by themselves.

But leaders of the present Administration conceive of government as master, not servant.

Responsibility has shifted from the family to the bureaucrat, from the neighborhood to the arbitrary and distant agency. Goals are set, roles are assigned, promises are made—all by the remote control of central government.

The leadership of this present Administration, which seeks this concentration of power as an announced article of its political faith, becomes the natural ally of all in our society who would monopolize power, centralize power, manipulate power, and grow rich from power.

This applies across the board, from the advocates of big government, to the bosses of big labor, to the bosses of big-city politics, as well as to those who would abuse great economic power in business.

Facing the power seekers is the lone man, the citizen, the forgotten man whose rights our Government was designed to make secure.

What have we been given by the politicians who want to tell you how to behave, how to think, how to live, what to study, and even where or if to pray?

What examples have been set, what lessons learned from this sort of leadership?

The shadow of scandal falls, unlighted yet by full answers, across the White House itself.

Public service, once selfless, has become for too many at its highest levels, selfish in motive and manner. Men who preach publicly of sacrifice, practice private indulgence.

The example this sets can be traced, tragically, through the easy morals and uneasy ethics which in private life disturb so many parents and lure so many young people.

If the tone of America is not set by men in public service it will be set, as unfortunately it is being set too often today, by the standards of the sick joke, the slick slogan, the off-color drama, and the pornographic book.

It is on our streets that we see the final, terrible proof of a sickness which not all the social theories of a thousand social experiments has even begun to touch.

Crime grows faster than population, while those who break the law are accorded more consideration than those who try to enforce the law. Law-enforcement agencies—the police, the sheriffs, the F.B.I.—are attacked for doing their jobs. Law breakers are defended.

Our wives, all women, feel unsafe on our streets.

Respect for the Law

And in encouragement of even more abuse of the law, we have the appalling spectacle of this country's Ambassador to the United Nations [Adlai E. Stevenson] actually telling an audience—this year, at Colby College—that "in the great struggle to advance civil human rights, even a jail sentence is no longer a dishonor but a proud achievement." Perhaps we are destined to see in this law-loving land people running for office not on their stainless records but on their prison records.

There are peaceful means of expressing a dissatisfaction. There are lawful ways. But no one can in deep conscience advocate lawlessness in seeking redress of a grievance!

When men will seek political advantage by turning their eyes away from riots and violence, we can well understand why lawlessness grows even while we pass more laws.

And when men use political advantage for personal gain we can understand the decline of moral strength generally.

It is a responsibility of the national leadership, regardless of political gain, political faction, or political popularity to encourage every community in this nation to enforce the law, not let it be abused and ignored.

It is not the responsibility nor is it the proper function of our national leadership to enforce local laws. But it is a responsibility of the national leadership to make sure that it, and its spokesmen and its supporters, do not discourage the enforcement or incite the breaching of these laws. And it is their responsibility to keep standards of common honesty high, turning on lights of integrity, not turning them off.

The leadership of this nation has a clear and immediate challenge to go to work effectively and go to work immediately to restore proper respect for law and order in this land—and not just prior to Election Day either!

This is not a challenge just for a few days or weeks, a problem to be put off until the voters are in.

This is a challenge to the overwhelming majority of Americans who share these basic beliefs with us:

That each man is responsible for his own actions.

That each man is the best judge of his own well-being.

That each man has an individual conscience to serve and a moral code to uphold.

That each man is a brother to every other man.

America's greatness is the greatness of her people. Let this generation, then, make a new mark for that greatness. Let this generation light a lamp of liberty that will illuminate the world. Let this generation of Americans set a standard of responsibility that will inspire the world.

We can do it! And God willing, together, we will do it.

VIEWPOINT 5

*"Many Great Society programs are marked by an
emphasis . . . on 'cost effectiveness.'"*

President Johnson's Great Society Is Providing Creative Solutions for America's Problems

Max Ways (1905–1985)

In the November 1964 elections, Lyndon B. Johnson defeated Barry Goldwater and Democrats took unprecedented majorities in both houses of Congress. Johnson's supporters in the election included corporate leaders, labor officials, liberals, and minorities. Backed by such a broad consensus, Congress and Johnson passed and signed into law numerous pieces of legislation between 1965 and 1968 meant to bring the president's promised "Great Society" to reality. Federal aid for education, urban renewal, and housing subsidies was greatly increased. The Medicare and Medicaid programs were established to provide health care to America's elderly and poor, respectively. The "War on Poverty," launched by Johnson in 1964, was expanded, and new "wars" on crime and disease were declared. Programs ranging from the National Endowment for the Arts and Humanities to the Job Corps were created—all in the context of a rapidly expanding economy.

Many Americans responded to this series of domestic reforms with hope and optimism. The following viewpoint is taken from a January 1966 article in *Fortune*, a business affairs magazine. Its author, Max Ways, served on the magazine's board of editors.

Ways contends that the initiatives and programs of "L.B.J.'s" Great Society are proving to be an effective means of dealing with problems such as poverty. He refutes conservative arguments that the federal government is growing too large or stultifying, arguing instead that Johnson is helping create new relationships between the federal government, state governments, businesses, and other institutions, bringing them together in practical ways to solve America's social problems.

There's much more to L.B.J.'s domestic policies than meets the eye. Government is learning from modern business that, when it comes to problem solving, power belongs out where the know-how is.

As the huge program enacted by Congress in 1965 moves into action, U.S. history is making a major turn from the politics of issues to the politics of problems, from an emphasis on need to an emphasis on opportunity, from struggle over the redistribution of what we have to the less crude and more intricate decisions about what we might become.

Salient features of the new package include aid to education, medicare and expanded federal activities in the health field, urban renewal and scores of other efforts to improve the physical environment. Since many of these topics have a long and embattled past in public discussion, some observers try to force the present programs into the mold of yesterday's debates. They see the new programs simply as another surge in the drive begun thirty years ago to expand the federal government's share of total power in order to right social wrongs. When the Johnson program is put into that context, liberals automatically applaud it and conservatives automatically denounce it. Both are missing the point.

A New Confidence

They fail to recognize that a fundamental break with the welfare-state trend occurred when this society made a different assessment of its own vigor. A new confidence in opportunity began to be reflected in politics fifteen years ago and was a factor in both of the Eisenhower elections. Although John F. Kennedy's 1960 campaign included appeals to the older kind of politics, his statements and policies as President seldom moved back toward the assumptions about U.S. society that characterized his party's dominance between 1933 and 1952. Lyndon Johnson even more explicitly has founded his Administration on the premise that U.S. society in general is exceedingly lively, increasing its rate of innovation and expanding its range of opportunity.

Two events early in Johnson's Administration indicated his commitment to this premise. One was the way he argued the case for the income-tax cut that Kennedy had proposed. Both Presidents, and especially Johnson, made it clear in the tax debate that they regarded the private economy, and not the pump of federal spending, as the main engine of economic growth. The second event was Johnson's Great Society speech at Ann Arbor in May, 1964. In some quarters this address has been misread as a threat to impose upon the U.S. future a federal-government blueprint of what the Great Society ought to be. But this interpretation is contradicted by the speech itself and Johnson's subsequent policies and words, including his 1964 campaign speeches. At Ann Arbor he was expressing, in his capacity of national leader, a bolder view of the prospect before the nation, the widening range of choice presented to all its people and all its institutions, public and private. Toward the end of the speech, he suggested that the federal government would have an important part to play in the quest for a better future. Neither then nor later, however, did he intimate that the federal role in the decisions ahead would be dominant or that Washington could supply the superior wisdom.

Creative Federalism

Along with the new assumptions of vigor in U.S. society came a new way of organizing federal programs. At Ann Arbor and on five public occasions since then, Johnson has used a phrase, "creative federalism," that has not received the attention it deserves. Federalism means a relation, cooperative and competitive, between a limited central power and other powers that are essentially independent of it. In the long American dialogue over states' rights, it has been tacitly assumed that the total amount of power was constant and, therefore, any increase in federal power diminished the power of the states and or "the people." Creative federalism starts from the contrary belief that total power—private and public, individual and organizational—is expanding very rapidly. As the range of conscious choice widens, it is possible to think of vast increases of federal government power that do not encroach upon or diminish any other power. Simultaneously, the power of states and local governments will increase; the power of private organizations, including businesses, will increase; and the power of individuals will increase.

Creative federalism as it is now developing emphasizes relationships between Washington and many other independent centers of decision in state and local government, in new public bodies, in universities, in professional organizations, and in business. This characteristic of the new programs is part of a rather belated application to government of the organizational habits developed by modern business. While everyone has been watching the influence of government policies on the economy, the impact of the economy's strength and its mode of organization have been quietly altering the way the government works. Tens of thousands of professional and managerial types, in and out of government service, are shaping and executing Great Society programs. This is as it should be, for professional and managerial men are preeminently oriented toward direction choosing and problem solving within a complex framework of many centers of decision.

This new outlook in Washington is the deepest reason for the rapprochement, during the Johnson Administration, between government and business. The two still have and will always have different responsibilities and aims. But they are beginning to use the same working language, depend on the same kinds of people, and get at tasks and decisions in the same way. More than administrative style is involved in this Washington shift. The whole framework of U.S. politics is changing.

The Old Politics and the New

Many observers have noted disparagingly that the Johnson program—with the significant exception of civil rights—does not generate much public "excitement." Those observers are conditioned to expect a certain kind of political excitement that arises when classes or other broad groups in a society—each armed with principles of ethics, justice, constitutional law, or ideology—clash over whether government power should be used to achieve or retain a group advantage. The twentieth century, at home and abroad, has produced so many exciting political conflicts of this sort that they have come to be considered as the whole of politics and even, perversely, as desirable.

The Johnson program's relative lack of this sort of exciting conflict should be read as a clue to its fundamental novelty. Civil rights, the single domestic issue that today creates the familiar kind of popular excitement, points up the contrast between the old politics and the new. The drive for Negro equality invokes principles of justice and ethics in demanding that the weight of government be employed to do for one large group what society itself has conspicuously failed to do. Government can do little for Negroes as a group without hurting (psychologically, if not materially) many whites most directly affected by such measures as school desegregation. When government must decide how far it will go in taking cherished advantages from one group in the course of helping another group, an exciting political issue arises.

Most issues of the 1930's had this same characteristic of taking from group A to give to group B. Indeed, a class redistribution of income and power was one of the stated aims of the New Deal. Thirty years ago belief was widespread that the U.S. economy was "mature," that a large and increasing proportion of all social initiative would have to be exercised through the federal government, that the hope of progress lay in the enlarged federal power to take from the "economic royalists" and give to the underprivileged. In the struggle arising from such beliefs the political positions called "radical," "liberal," and "conservative" jelled into their present meanings.

The Johnson program does not fit any of these molds. Except for the special case of the Negro, every group is now believed capable of advancing under its own steam. Consequently, the old welfarist arguments for government intervention lose some of their force and urgency while the newer problem-solving approach comes to the fore.

Medicare, when it was first seriously debated in the 1940's, was presented with an emphasis on what the young owed to the old and, especially, on what the fortunate owed to the unfortunate. Today the viewpoint has shifted. It is now recognized that this society as a whole has a problem of paying for the greatly enlarged medical services now available to the aged; medicare is put forward as a device to deal with the problem. Similarly, the programs to improve education, clean up rivers, beautify highways, and reduce air pollution are not struggles between broad social groups. And they are not ideological *issues*. They are efforts to deal with *problems* by a society that is becoming increasingly confident of its problem-solving ability.

Specific federal programs derived from this new approach may be good or bad, valuable or wasteful, disruptive or constructive. Each will certainly require close public scrutiny of its conception and execution. There will be plenty of chance for criticism and opposition when we learn to look at these programs in the context of the new politics. But effective criticism and opposition will not develop from the old yammer for or against any extension of the federal government's scope.

The Government as Junior Partner

Those Washington officials now busily setting up the programs like to describe the new roles for the federal government with the phrase "junior partner." An easy cynicism, bred of past conditions, is quick to suspect that this junior partner means to enlarge his scope until he takes over the shop. But an examination of the new programs in detail shows this cynicism is misplaced. These programs are so designed that they will work only if the "senior partners"—i.e., elements of the society other than the federal government—continue to grow and innovate vigorously. If that hope is disappointed, the federal "junior partner," instead of increasing his power, will be in trouble with the electorate.

President Lyndon B. Johnson, seen here visiting a farm family in 1964, helped create many government programs meant to aid farmers and the poor.

Because the Washington junior partners are aware of this danger, "creative federalism" includes a deliberate policy of encouraging the growth of institutions that will be independent of and, in part, antagonistic to the federal government power. Almost every part of every new program transfers federal funds to some outside agency. Nothing will be achieved if the recipients—universities, state and local educational authorities, hospitals, medical schools, and poverty-program councils—merely become subservient arms directed by the central federal power. Tension between Washington and other independent centers is required by the whole body of experience out of which the notion of "creative federalism" comes.

This way of doing things entered the government by osmosis from corporate management. Big corporations have been getting bigger, but executives are increasingly and justifiably impatient of outside criticism that, using the language of fifty years ago, attacks corporations as "monolithic" concentrations of power in a few hands. From the inside of any great corporation it is obvious that top management spends a great deal of its time trying to enlarge the responsibilities and strengthen the initiative of other power centers within the corporation. Such policies are pursued in the face of certain knowledge that the multiplied and strengthened power centers will develop troublesome tensions with top management and with one another. Top management does not pursue this "polycentric" policy out of altruism or masochism. It does so because the complexity of modern knowledge, reflected in the complexity of organized action, demands that much of the decision making be decentralized. Not only is a high degree of local autonomy required but, even more significantly, a high degree of professional autonomy. Engineering decisions have to be made by engineers. Accountants, architects, artists, and xerographers acquire similar "states' rights."

Yet it is not correct to assume that the over-all trend in modern organization is toward decentralization. Complexity has two sides: while specialization decentralizes, interdependence centralizes. The art of modern management consists largely in discovering what to centralize and what to decentralize, and in constructing the channels through which information and decision, generated at many levels, flow. An old-fashioned "captain of industry," an industrial absolutist of the Henry Ford type, would be driven screaming into the night by the restraints and complexities of modern corporate "federalism." But it works.

Those business executives who still see in recent Washington trends only a further expansion toward "absolute government" are as blind as those critics of Big Business who go on mouthing warnings against "monolithic" corporations. These business executives are doubly blind, because in the new federal patterns they do not recognize their own children.

The new patterns first entered Washington at the point where the connection between government, advanced business, and science is most intense—the Defense Department. During World War II, teams of analysts began to apply techniques of "operations research" to military decisions. In the postwar period this approach spread to analytical comparisons of "weapons systems" by methods that worked back from battlefield value to factory cost. Secretary of Defense [Robert S.] McNamara made the Pentagon a link in an informational and decision-making process stretching from White House policy decisions through prime contractors to thousands of subcontractors. No one can calculate whether the vast activity we call "defense" is more or less centralized than it was in 1960; and the answer, if we had it, would not be very important. What matters is that the total system has a more rational and a more effective way of relating the parts to the whole. There is a conscious, unceasing effort to ensure that any given decision will be made at the most appropriate place—high or low, in Washington or out—and on the basis of the best information.

Programs in Appalachia

Many Great Society programs are marked by an emphasis, similar to that of the Defense Department, on "cost effectiveness."

Take, for a sample, Appalachia. The casual reader of the news may assume that the program for stimulating this backward region is just another dribble of welfarist pap from the Washington udder. The casual reader will be wrong. And he will be missing one of the most interesting of recent political innovations.

The act of Congress creating the program contains a remarkable clause: within Appalachia federal funds are to be "concentrated in areas where there is a significant potential for future growth, and where the expected return on public dollars invested will be the greatest." This method of allocation runs counter both to the old congressional pork-barrel system and to the welfarist system that allocated funds on the basis of "need." Appalachia's "need" is such that the $1.1 billion authorized by Congress would be frittered away if it were concentrated on the neediest hollows, the deadest hamlets, and the most eroded hillsides.

By making the greatest investment potential its basic criterion, the Appalachian Act directs the program to concentrate in another way. Within Appalachia there are, right now, a number of economically vigorous towns that may be stimulated to greater growth. There are other areas where local initiative and private enterprise can make a case for a high potential return on investment. The new criterion of public spending leads the men in the Appalachian program to talk in businesslike terms about market analysis and plant-location strategy rather than in terms of social work. John L. Sweeney, federal cochairman of the Appalachian Regional Commission, does not try to wring the reporter's heart with statistics of beriberi and illiteracy in Appalachia. Instead, he makes his pitch like a chamber-of-commerce secretary, about how Appalachia, lying between the two great markets of the U.S.—the eastern seaboard and the Great Lakes complex—may have a glittering economic future.

But how will concentration on the growth counties of Appalachia help the people of the back hollows? How can it relieve them of the grim choice between continued poverty and psychologically disruptive migration to Chicago, Detroit, and other great industrial centers? In answer, Sweeney turns to a map. A large proportion of federal funds for Appalachia will be spent to aid the construction of a road network that would allow the hill dwellers to live in the land they love and commute by bus or car to jobs in the growing centers of the region. Motorized transit offers the possibility of large labor pools without a megalopolis.

One danger of all this is that the federal government, in moving away from welfarist standards, will find it has let in the seven worse devils of rigid central planning. But the Appalachian program is set up in a way that minimizes this danger. The key power center is not Sweeney's office but a commission made up of the governors of the twelve Appalachian states. States, counties, towns, colleges, and private businesses have already been stimulated to compete in presenting to the commission proposals based upon the test of "greatest potential." If this local initiative continues to wax, federal coordinating functions will be a small part of the total activity. If the local initiative subsides there won't be anything worth coordinating and the Appalachian program will be a clear-cut failure. In neither case will Washington have increased its "control" of Appalachia.

Higher Education

The same organizational principles can be seen at work in the government's relations with one of the most advanced sectors of U.S. life, higher education. John W. Gardner, the recently appointed Secretary of Health, Education, and Welfare, did much shrewd and unconventional thinking about this subject when he was head of the Carnegie Corporation of New York. Over a year ago in a speech to university people he took aim at the familiar charge that the flow of federal money to universities represents a dangerous increase in federal power and a threat to academic independence. He pointed out that there was another side to the story. "To the old-line federal official, used to a world in which government funds were spent for purposes defined by government and administered by hierarchically organized departments under complete government control, the new trend looks like a grievous *loss* of government power," he said. "Wherever he looks, he sees lay advisory bodies recommending how government money shall be spent, and he sees nongovernmental organizations spending it."

A government agency, because it is accountable to Congress and the taxpayer, wants to define quite precisely what is to be done with public money that it hands over to a university research project. The university, accustomed to the notion that science works best when it is free of externally imposed conditions, resists the definitions, restrictions, and reviews insisted upon by the agency.

Gardner has urged university people to give more sympathetic understanding to the government view, and he has urged government officials to see the university view. But he does not believe—and this is the important point—that the tension between them will or should disappear. "Actually, there is some advantage to the public interest in keeping a certain adversary quality in the relationship."

This thought gets close to the heart of "creative federalism." In the context of modern knowledge and work, whether we are talking about business or government, the over-all degree of centralization or decentralization is seldom an interesting or useful question. What matters is the quality of an ever evolving process of deciding which functions to centralize and which to decentralize. . . .

Research and Development

Research and its more costly brother, development, turn up at point after point in the wide spectrum of enlarged federal activities enacted by the 1965 Congress. A small but interesting example is the Solid Waste Disposal Act. Hah, cry the alarmists, now the federal government is going into garbage collection; the last rampart of local autonomy has been stormed. But maybe not.

The technology of a nation that can put men in space may discover a more efficient manner of garbage and trash disposal than burning it, or dumping it, or hauling it by scow to the open sea—which will wash it up on the beach of some other municipality. Cities struggle along with one method or another, and few of them can afford a thoroughgoing R. and D. project to find better ways of coping with the garbage and trash explosion. New ideas for solid-waste disposal will have to be tried out in practice, and in the trying it may be desirable for Washington to make a grant to some city willing to be, if one may put it so, the guinea pig.

Similarly, we have federal programs for research into the causes of crime and delinquency and into better methods of transmitting information on suspected criminals. These do not necessarily imply that Washington is about to take over all the police work of the nation. We will not necessarily be forced to choose between the Keystone cops and the police state.

Health, including medicare, is the largest single category of increased federal spending projected by the 1965 legislative program. The fact that there is now a huge and increasing population over sixty-five years old represents medical triumphs in saving lives at all age levels. The public has shown its appreciation of the improved quality of medical care by increasing its payments for such services from a level of 4 percent of disposable income to 6 percent. Part of this increase represents the fact that "unit costs" of medical care have been rising somewhat faster than other costs. But in the main, the increase to the present level of nearly

$30 billion a year indicates that the public has decided that medical care is worth more than it used to be.

For the aged, especially, there are now many opportunities for treatment (e.g., the removal of eye pupils in cataract cases) that did not exist a generation ago. Once such treatment becomes medically feasible, this society raises its standards of what it considers essential. Lack of money, it says, must not be allowed to stand between an aged person and a chance to preserve his eyesight. Even though private health insurance, pension plans, and individual savings have expanded rapidly, they lagged behind the new standards of minimum medical service to the aged. In a problem-solving society medicare was seen as a way of closing a gap that medical progress had opened up.

Unquestionably, medicare will throw a new burden of demand on medical services that are already overloaded. Recent federal legislation provides funds to encourage the expansion of medical and nursing schools. . . .

Urban Renewal

In 1965 the federal government acquired a new Cabinet-level department—Housing and Urban Development. Over the last twenty years, as the problems of the cities have become more formidable, there has been a change in how we think about these problems. This new way of seeing the urban challenge works *against* the danger that the federal government will "take over" the cities.

A generation ago, "slum" had a simple, physical meaning. It signified a group of buildings that were overage, overpopulated, and underequipped. That simple meaning implied a remedy, which is now understood to be inadequate; "slum clearance" and "public housing" would replace bad buildings with better buildings. All that required was money and the federal government had it. In a program so conceived there would be some—but not much—inherent need for local decision making and local initiative. Federal housing on this model made some—but not much—improvement.

"Slum" today signifies a complex in which such elements as the quality of education and the morale of inhabitants are more important than the buildings themselves. Moreover, a slum is not thought of as an isolated "blighted area" that can be quarantined and dealt with independently of the rest of the city. We are now aware of "gray areas," which may be degenerating into slums faster than bulldozers can level old slums. From this and similar observations we have come to look upon the city as a process to be improved rather than as a product to be altered.

As any manager knows, improvement of a process requires

analysis of how its parts affect one another and how they can be better coordinated to obtain the chosen objectives. It is simply unimaginable that in any given city the federal government can play a major role in such coordination. The problems are, city by city, so unique that local coordination and local initiative must be the determining elements. Experience bears this out. Philadelphia, New Haven, Boston, are cities where urban renewal is making huge strides because bubbling local initiative and increasing professional competence make effective the spending of federal and other urban renewal money. By contrast, New York lags, not because it has been out of favor with Washington fund dispensers, but because it has lacked the local political and business leadership, which is more important than money from Washington. Members of Congress—relics of the old politics—who promise to "do more" in the way of increasing the flow of federal money to such laggard cities as New York will continue to be helpless until local initiative develops.

Urban renewal, far from being an extension of the "monolithic" federal power, has created or revived a host of local organizations, which have become centers of influence on reconstructing the process of living in cities. A Philadelphian involved in the revival of that city said: "Citizen organization is the principal phenomenon of this town." In other words, federal housing money in Philadelphia helped to create and strengthen decision-making centers that lie outside of federal control.

The New Limits of Government

It is as true today as it ever was that a free society must be vigilant against concentration of power in a few hands. It is also true that in the twentieth century many national governments, using humanitarian slogans, have tended to squash the sphere of local government and constrict the scope of private organizations and individuals. The U.S. has not been immune to this trend. Twenty-five years ago state and local government in the U.S. *was* anemic, and predictions—some approving, some despairing—were widely made that the federal political system must be transformed into a unitary national system on the British or French model. Twenty-five years ago the dispersed and competing power centers of private enterprise *were* being cramped by the encroaching power of Washington.

As resistance to this trend developed, the U.S. seemed to be in a struggle between what was politically practical and what was, by traditional interpretation, constitutional. The traditionalists lost ground steadily until it became much harder to see the tidy pigeonholes into which Americans used to separate what was private, what was governmental, what was state, what was federal.

Today the scope of federal action cannot be specifically defined by categories (e.g., defense and foreign affairs). The federal government may have a proper function in almost any field of action. This change raises a question: can a central government that has massive roles in business agriculture, schools, health, and even, perhaps, garbage collection truly be described as a "limited" federal government?

The answer, oddly, is yes. The new limits on federal power have been imposed by political practicality. Ironically, the popular hunger for progress that seemed to generate a threat to limited government has come to the rescue of limited government. An electorate that began to expect real results—and would not be fobbed off by such psychological titillations as "soaking the rich"—pressed political leaders toward more effective modes of action. These modes turned out to put a heavy *practical* emphasis on state and local government, on business freedom, on the market as a way of making economic decisions.

If in January, 1956, anybody had forecast a federal government budget of $175 billion by 1976, his prediction would have been taken to mean that more and more power would be concentrating in Washington. Today we can view the same prediction against a projected background of a 1976 gross national product of over a trillion dollars and understand that federal spending at $175 billion would take a smaller share of total national activity than the present budget does. Today we are less interested in the size of the total federal budget than in the relative "cost effectiveness" of the programs that make up the budget. The old public sector versus private sector argument is giving ground before a rising interest in good management, both government and private.

Outdated Oratory

Lyndon Johnson as Senate Majority Leader in the Eisenhower years showed that he sensed the new political framework. He muted the strident ideological slogans that had dominated his party in the years 1933–52 because these class struggle slogans in a rapidly progressing country were losing their appeal. As President, his much-derided insistence on "consensus politics" is in part a shrewd recognition that "issues" are no longer central. Knowing that his new programs will be judged more by what they accomplish than by the good intentions of their authors, he has warned administrators to build these programs soundly rather than quickly. Even so, several of the new programs— notably the "war on poverty"—have run into serious organizational difficulties. Johnson's fundamental difficulty is that many leaders of his party are still stuck in the old framework where ideology counted more than good management.

Many Republican leaders are also stuck there, still firing irrelevant ideological guns at a target area from which the enemy is decamping. The great Republican political asset for the future is its hold on a high proportion of the managers and professional men whose skills are especially needed in the conception, execution, and criticism of the new type of governmental program. Use of this asset requires close engagement with the new programs at local, state, and national levels. Beneath the surface of the last congressional session some exceedingly important work was done in improving Great Society measures proposed by the executive branch—and Republicans made a contribution to this improvement that has been somewhat masked by the party's own outdated oratory.

All through the postwar period, partisan political debate has lagged behind the radical change, generated outside politics, that has been sweeping through U.S. society. This accelerating rate of change, which appears to be a permanent condition, posed a challenge to the fundamental American political institutions. We are now emerging—successfully—from this period of challenge. In a way that was hardly conceivable twenty-five years ago, U.S. democratic institutions have proved flexible and adaptable and are becoming, once again, the objects of envy and admiration by discerning men in other countries. The American political genius is moving through creative federalism toward new ways of expanding individual choice while maintaining social cohesion.

VIEWPOINT 6

"Every element of the Great Society . . . is contaminated by . . . power lust, greed, and fear of change."

President Johnson's Great Society Is Not Solving America's Problems

Paul Goodman (1911–1972) and
Richard Flacks (b. 1938)

Critics of President Lyndon B. Johnson's "Great Society," the term used to describe Johnson's domestic agenda and, more specifically, the many programs passed by Congress in 1965, came from both the political right and left. Conservatives, such as Arizona senator Barry Goldwater, maintained that Great Society programs resulted in wasteful government spending and meddlesome government interference with business. But opposition to the Great Society was perhaps more intense from the left than from the right. Many people argued that the money committed to Great Society programs never lived up to the rhetoric—especially as the Vietnam War consumed more and more of the president's attention and the nation's resources. Other critics focused on the ideology and motives underlying the Great Society itself.

The following viewpoint consists of excerpts from two essays attacking the Great Society from radical perspectives. The first is by Paul Goodman, a writer of many novels and books of social criticism who influenced many college students to become politically active in the 1960s. In a 1965 article excerpted here, Goodman argues that most Great Society programs have failed to im-

Part I: Paul Goodman, "The Great Society," *New York Review of Books*, October 14, 1965. Copyright 1965 by Paul Goodman. Reprinted by permission of Sally Goodman. Part II: Richard Flacks, "Is the Great Society Just a Barbecue?" *New Republic*, 1966. Reprinted by permission of the *New Republic*, © 1966, The New Republic, Inc.

prove the lives of Americans and that the Great Society itself is a failed attempt by elite Americans of the "American Establishment" to justify and maintain their privileged places in American society. Part II of the viewpoint is taken from a 1965 article by Richard Flacks, one of the founding members of Students for a Democratic Society (SDS) who was then a professor of sociology at the University of Chicago. (He went on to become a professor at the University of California at Santa Barbara and to write several books on the 1960s and the student movement.) Flacks asserts that President Johnson has allied himself with American businesses to create a new politics of "liberal corporatism," and he contends that this new politics will fail to provide social justice for most Americans. He calls for greater grass-roots movements to "restore democracy" in America.

I

A reasonable function of government is to see to it that the conditions of life are tolerable. In modern societies this might involve considerable government intervention, to prevent or remedy social and physical evils, like urban poverty, exploitation of labor, traffic congestion, air pollution. But such a safeguarding function is entirely different from government's trying to make life excellent, to make society moral, civilized, or magnificent. Intellectual or moral excellence is not a likely province for rulers of any breed, and certainly not for American politicians who have risen to power by speaking banalities, making deals, and pandering, and who stay in power by avoiding the risks of sharp definition, imagination, scrupulous integrity, or even too much wit. Political arts have their use, but they are not the way to spiritual excellence.

Yet the last three Administrations have kept dabbling in this direction. President Eisenhower, who was hardly literate, ordered a commission to map our National Goals, and under him government agencies began to improve the school curricula and speed up intervention in scientific research. John Kennedy, who was stylish and had academic connections, called us to service and he wanted us to be respected for our civilization as well as our military and economic power. He was a champion of art centers, neoclassic architecture, and concerts at the White House; above all, he speeded up the harnessing of academic social sciences to government policy. And now Lyndon Johnson, who is culturally noted for monograms and driving fast, is going to inaugurate for us the Great Society.

I do not think this was only a campaign slogan. Even if it were, we must note the change in slogans. "Fair Deal" and "New Deal" used to refer to political economy and were a legitimate bid for votes; "New Frontier" and "Great Society" are more spiritual. (Barry Goldwater, correspondingly, threatened to restore us to Moral Order.) In any case, the President has carried his slogan over into 1965, and when his oblique eyes become dreamy and his voice avuncular on the theme of our future greatness, I am insulted by his pretension.

Do not misunderstand me. When the President speaks of trying to dissolve hard core poverty, assuring equal rights, opening to every child the opportunity for an education, or coping with the blight of cities, I assent. (It is said that this populist strain in LBJ is authentic, and I hope so.) But that is not the program of a great society but of any decent society. It should be urged modestly and executed resolutely. There is no cause for fanfare in doing justice where we have been unjust, conserving where we have been vandals, and spending for neglected public goods what a small country like Denmark or Holland provides as a matter of course.

Contamination of the Great Society

But the fact is that every element of the Great Society, including its war on poverty and its conservation, is contaminated by, compromised by, and finally determined by power lust, greed, and fear of change. No good thing is done for its own sake. Let me give half a dozen examples—I could give a hundred. The drive to schooling, even in its propaganda, is not to liberate the children and to insure that we will have independent and intelligent citizens (this was the educational aim of Jefferson); it is apprentice-training of the middle class for the corporations and military, and a desperate attempt to make slum children employable and ruly. Beautification and area development are treated as adjuncts of the automobile business. We will curb the billboards but multiply and landscape the highways that destroy country and city both. Eighty per cent of the billion for Appalachia is going for highways. Yet almost acute emergencies, like air and water pollution and the insecticides, are bogged in "research" because of hostile lobbies and because there is no money to be made of them. The cities are overcrowded, yet farm policy persistently favors food chains and big plantations and drives small farmers out, so beautiful, vast areas are depopulating and returning to swamp. In the cities, housing, renewal, and community development are tied to real-estate bonanzas, the alliance of national and municipal political machines, and even the aggrandizement of the welfare bureaucracy. In the crucial test case of Mobilization for Youth in New York, the move toward grass-roots democracy was swiftly crushed and brought under professional control, staffed by City Hall, Washington consenting. . . . In communications, there has ceased to be any attempt to decentralize television and get some variety, if not foliage, into the wasteland. Indeed, by temperament President Johnson hankers for consensus and managed news; he says he welcomes responsible criticism, but it's an angry welcome; and the projection of his personality and icons is beginning to resemble the style of Russia or Cuba. In forwarding the fine arts, the government neglects the traditional, useful, and safe method of underwriting standard repertory and editions of the American classics, but it toys with the obnoxious official art of Arts Councils, glamorous culture centers, and suppers for the famous. Meantime, free lances are bulldozed from their lofts and it is harder for creative people to be decently poor in their own way. The Department of Justice keeps whittling away at civil liberties, and the emasculation of Congress proceeds. The arms budget continues to increase. Now a spaceship will explicitly become a new grotesque weapon, and we explicitly use the adventure of exploration for propaganda. And it is hard to believe the President's moral commitment to civil rights at home when he dispatches marines and bombers to subjugate foreign peoples whose civil rights threaten what he sometimes calls the Free World and sometimes our National Interests.

Perhaps most alarming is the bland affirmation of clashing contradictories, as if people were already imbeciles. When we bomb hospitals and burn villages, the President is bound to make an unusually tender announcement about cerebral palsy (and the marines give out candy). When we allot 1.7 billions for a new space weapon, our astronauts are at once sent on a world tour for peace.

The theory of the Great Society is obvious enough. Lyndon Johnson came in during an unparalleled prosperity, with a consensus of businessmen and liberals and, seemingly, money for everything, including tax cuts to encourage investment. He made a fairly graceful capitulation for the Negro protest. Thus, the Great Society could re-invest unprecedented profits in new fields, including the public sector; could provide unskilled and semi-skilled jobs; and could consolidate the votes of the urban poor. But if we examine this happy formula, we find that money, power, and fear of change are the determinants. We do not find the magnanimity, disinterestedness, and imagination of a great society. Worse, it is less and less an American society. Instead of tackling the political puzzle of how to maintain democracy in a complex technology and among urban masses, it multiplies professional-client and patron-client relationships. Worst of all, if we watch, during ten minutes of television, the horrors of the world, the piggish commercials, and the nightly performance of the President, we do not see even a decent society. As the Connecticut Circuit Court recently put it succinctly, in clearing some tabloids of charges of obscenity: "Coarse and puerile these tabloids are, but so is much of our civilization. We doubt that they will pollute the social atmosphere."

The American Establishment

Nevertheless, the concept of a national mission cooked up by the past three Administrations is not merely a fraud. It is an ideology made necessary by contemporary history. In the first place, there has developed a dangerous vacuum of political-moral values, dangerous especially for the young. To give an important example: there must be *some* human use of our galloping high technology better than the infinite expansion of a hardware Gross National Product; affluence is no longer enough. One purpose of the big slogans has been to meet this moral demand and yet contain it, as we have seen, in the control of the same leaders and corporations. So far, the official moralists have not hit on anything believable, but that may come.

Secondly, however—and this, I think, is the essence—there must be some general ideology, whatever it is, to give a warrant to an amazing new grouping that has emerged in our society, the American Establishment. For this purpose, the Great Society might prove good enough, and it is virulent.

An Establishment is the clubbing together of the secular and moral leaders of society—in industry, the military, labor unions, the cities, sciences and arts, the universities, the church, and state—to determine not only the economy and policy but the standards and ideals of the nation. The role of an Establishment is to tell what is right, accredited, professional, British (German, Russian, etc.), and to rule out what is not (not *Kultur*, not Leninist, etc.). An important part of an Establishment is a large stable of mandarins to raise the tone, use correct scientific method, and invent rationalizations. Also, the literate mandarins write the speeches.

There is no doubt that such an interlocking accrediting club has attained enormous power in the United States. Its genius is to go round and round and be self-enclosed. The job in the want ads says "M.S. required," for industry respects the university; but meantime the university is getting contracted research from industry and the government. Cities or settlement houses will get funds from Washington if they employ accredited staff. (I am lay-ing stress on school credentials because education is probably the biggest business in the country; there has been no such class of monks since Henry the Eighth.) Retired generals become vice-presidents in charge of contracting; they know whom to talk to and how. A broadcaster seeks his license from the FCC [Federal Communications Commission], but the Administration has a healthy respect for the power of the broadcaster—hardly one license has been rescinded. Meantime, by FCC mandate, a commercial sponsor cannot censor the program he sponsors, but he does have the right to expect that it will not tarnish or jar the image of his firm. Tax-exempt foundations support what *is* art or research, as recommended by those who are accredited, and they will underwrite a pilot project if it is carried out by a proper institution. But woe to a project that has nothing to recommend it but that it is a good idea, and whose inventor carries his office under his hat. In principle such a project cannot exist, and soon it does not exist.

Now our country has had neither a traditional aristocracy nor a totalitarian dogma, so it is not easy for the American Establishment to find moral justification for so much omniscience and exclusive power. It has really thrived on quiet expansion and being taken for granted, like creeping socialism. It is not surprising that its ideology should be mere campaign slogans, future and hortatory, half public relations and half corny dreams.

But however hazy its justification, the personnel of the Establishment has specific properties: it must be rooted in the baronial institutions and it must be conspicuously idealistic. It was with uncanny precision—in fact, the candidates are preselected for him from 25,000 *vitae* by computer—that Johnson chose John Gardner as Secretary of Health, Education, and Welfare. Gardner was the head of the Carnegie Corporation, and he is the author of a book called *Excellence*.

Thus, the process of spelling out and implementing the vague national mission is as follows: From the Establishment, the President chooses task forces. The task forces think up programs and these are given for execution to those accredited by the Establishment. It is not astonishing, then, if a major function, if not purpose, of the Great Society is to aggrandize the Establishment, the education barons, the broadcasting barons, the automobile barons, the shopping center barons. In a youth employment project, more than three-quarters of the appropriation will go for (accredited) staff salaries and research; not much is left for wages for the kids. Of course, sometimes there is an hilarious exception, as when some SNCC [Student Nonviolent Coordinating Committee] youngsters I know got $90 a day as consultants at a conference on poverty in Washington.

So a practical definition of the Great Society is: to provide professional employment and other business for card-carrying members of the Establishment. *This* is not a fraud.

Of course, the Great Society is strictly for domestic consumption. Abroad, our friends are drifting away because we have lost our reputation; persuasion gives way to brute force. Thus, by a grim devolution, the Great Society turns out to be a liberal version of the old isolationism of Fortress America.

The Moral Vacuum

In conclusion, let me return to a thought mentioned above, the need to fill the moral vacuum. The technical, urban, and international premises of modern life have changed so rapidly and markedly that the old elites, who cling to their power, inevitably seem morally bankrupt, especially to the young. I have no doubt that this is the case everywhere—it has been persistently reported from the Soviet Union during the last ten years—but since ours is the most advanced country, we reveal the moral bankruptcy worst.

By the middle of the Administration of Eisenhower, it was impossible for a public spokesman to say "the American Way of Life" with a straight face. And there occurred the flood of social criticism, often devastating, which left us morally dank indeed. It was in this context that the President's Commission on National Goals made its report. But it was a feeble effort that influenced nobody, certainly not the young. The beat generation withdrew. And there began the spiritual defection of college youth from the corporations that has increased steadily. (In 1956, according to a survey by David Riesman, the great majority of collegians wanted to work for a big organization. Just now, at Harvard, more students want to go into the tiny Peace Corps than into business!)

John Kennedy hit on the Posture of Sacrifice, which was what young people wanted to hear, something to give meaning to the affluent society. But apart from the token of the Peace Corps— filled largely, as it turned out, by youth of the upper middle class—he could not produce anything to sacrifice *for*, not with so many credit cards around. Indeed, when they asked what they could do for their country, many of the best youth found that they wanted to serve precisely against the government, sometimes illegally, in the Negro movement and protesting against fall-out. And the majority of the returning Peace Corps itself have proved to be critical of the society they have come back to.

The Great Society, as we have seen, started with more moral ammunition: an electoral campaign against Black Reaction, a bill for Civil Rights, a war against poverty. Yet once again many of the best youth have remained unconverted. During the [1964 Democratic] nominating convention, the militants of the [Mississippi] Freedom Democratic Party rejected the Humphrey compromise [for limited participation]. Shortly after the electoral triumph of the Great Society, the students at [the University of California at] Berkeley raged in their thousands. This year, there have been student troubles on a hundred campuses, East, Middle West, and even South. The Students for a Democratic Society have thrown themselves into undermining precisely the War on Poverty, which they consider undemocratic and insincere. And both many students and many teachers seem to want to undermine even the war for the Free World in Vietnam. Some writers refused to go to the President's party.

The Youth Are Unpersuaded

In brief, as a moral incentive for youth, the Great Society, like its predecessors, is unpersuasive. It does not square with the obvious facts; it is too corrupt. Fatally, it avoids the deep problems that demand real changes. The political-moral problems that deeply interest youth are of the following kind: How to use high technology for human advantage? How to regain substantive democracy in modern cities and with mass-communications? How to get rid of the Bomb and the whole atmosphere of the Cold War? How to be educated without being processed? How to work at something worthwhile outside the rat race of an infinitely expanding GNP? How to avoid 1984?

The Establishment in America and its President do not cope with these questions because they *are* morally bankrupt.

II

Traditionally, we have understood politics to mean the clash of men independently organized with respect to their interests and ideologies; we have expected that policy would emerge out of public debate; we have believed that men in power require viable opposition; we have favored a system with dispersed centers of power. Instead, the Johnson consensus establishes the Democratic Party as *the* national party of the center—we no longer have a two-party system on the national level. This situation is facilitated by the inclusion of a large proportion of the business community in the Democratic Party coalition. This is where Mr. Johnson has particularly succeeded and where other Democratic Presidents failed—on the one hand, he has won full-fledged corporation participation in welfare-state policies; on the other hand, he has won wholehearted labor, liberal and ethnic group support for what is, in fact, a center-conservative government. Thus, "consensus" is a conveniently bland term which covers a new politics in America—the politics of what might be called "liberal corporatism."

A System of Deep Inequalities

Tom Hayden, one of the early founding members of Students for a Democratic Society (SDS), was sharply critical of much of the Great Society. The following paragraphs are excerpted from a 1966 article that was first published in Dissent.

The trend is *toward*, not away from, increased racial segregation and division, greater unemployment for Negroes than whites, worse educational facilities in the slums, less job security for whites, fewer doctors for nearly everyone: in essence, the richest society in all history places increasing pressures on its "have nots" despite all talk of the "welfare state" and "Great Society." The real subsidies go to the housebuilders, farmers, businessmen, scholars, while comparatively, there are only scraps for the poor. The welfare recipient who cannot purchase decent furniture will not take much comfort in knowing she is one of the "richest" poor people in the world. America's expanding affluence is still built on a system of deep inequalities. . . .

Seen in this context, the 1965 antipoverty program should evoke little optimism. The amount of money allotted is a pittance, and most of it is going to local politicians, school boards, welfare agencies, housing authorities, professional personnel and even the police; its main thrust is to shore up sagging organizational machinery, not to offer the poor a more equitable share of income and influence. Meaningful involvement of the poor is frustrated by the poverty planners' allegiance to existing local power centers. In reality, the poor only flavor the program. A few are co-opted into it, but only as atomized individuals. They do not have independent organizational strength, as do the machines and social agencies.

In both its rhetoric and its practice, liberal corporatism implies a political structure in which principal policy issues are worked out at the federal level, formulated with the active participation of experts, and ratified—not in the legislative arena—but through a process of consultation among a national elite representing those interests and institutions which now recognize each other as legitimate. Such a conception of government is "corporatist" in at least two ways: first, it involves the major corporations and other interest groups actively and directly in the governmental process; second, it models government structure and administrative style in the manner of modern corporation management. It is "liberal" in the sense that it includes the active participation of representatives of groups traditionally favoring liberal reform and democracy—particularly, for example, the unions. Liberal corporatism tends toward the *co-optation* of dissent and reform rather than their suppression.

It seems to me that the basic issue for the present national leadership is the preservation of a corporation economy while coping with the disastrous potentialities of a free competitive national and international system. Among such potentialities, of course, are economic slumps, intense labor-management conflict, internal political unrest and major war. Thus, the Johnson consensus seems to include a fundamental commitment by government to avoid such threats to the viability of the going system. The main way to do this, apparently, is to harness an extensive social welfare system to a centrally coordinated but privately controlled economy. So the Great Society program includes a commitment to the need for federal action to avoid economic recession and maintain adequate growth rates; for active government intervention in collective bargaining and the regulation of wages and prices; for large-scale public action to reduce the likelihood of unrest and violence in the slums and ghettoes of the cities; for welfare benefits which can maintain and expand popular support for the Democratic Party locally and nationally. . . .

Neglecting Egalitarian Goals

This full-scale, if belated and diluted, implementation of the New Deal promise does not necessarily imply that the Great Society will be a place of greater social justice and equality. For the current program is thoroughly circumscribed—it cannot seriously encroach on substantial corporate interests. Such interests include the maintenance of less than full employment, a decidedly impoverished public sector, a very strong emphasis on private consumption, and the use of public funds to subsidize private interests. Moreover, a more equitable distribution of wealth is unlikely because the Great Society consensus does not grant legitimate political voice to substantial sectors of the population. It took a century of bitter struggle for organized labor to win legitimacy; still millions of workers remain unorganized and voiceless. The voting rights law appears to guarantee, finally, the right of Southern Negroes to gain political voice; still, it will take further violent struggle before full enfranchisement is reached—and, still, it is not evident that the society is prepared to accept the right of Negroes to organize and exercise power in their own interest. The absence of the poor from the Great Society Barbecue keeps the consensus stable—and explains why it neglects egalitarian goals.

I do not know if liberal corporatism can indefinitely continue to maintain private control of the economy while preventing slump and dampening discontent. But it is a source of wonderment that so many who profess commitment to liberal and democratic traditions seem so complacently at home within the Johnsonian consensus. For the centralization of power, its grossly unequal distribution among interest groups and constituencies, and the techniques of control now available to authority present a situation which ought to be inherently antithetical to the committed Democrat. But the consequences of liberal corporatism for America are as appalling as its intrinsically undemocratic structure.

Problems of Liberal Corporatism

First, the centralization of power, information and interests is taking place in the most powerful nation-state in human history.

This state has the technological capacity to destroy civilization; hence it appears to have the military power to impose its will on all small, weak countries, and, within the limits of its rationality, on strong nations as well. The most immediately frightening thing about the Johnson consensus is that it is eroding any effective internal check on the use of that power; it is permitting the acquiescence of the public to any use of American power which the predominant interests deem desirable. And it is creating a situation in which the *capability* to use this power is becoming synonymous with the *desirability* of using it. When attempts by a government to justify its overseas adventures are no longer in moral terms—then it seems to me we have clear evidence that the popular will is no longer relevant. If the American elite has a commanding sense of its power to preserve its international interests intact, and no longer feels particularly responsible even to its own people—then I think humanity has a right to shudder.

Second, the predominance of corporate interests and the underrepresentation of the poor, the black, the old, the young, etc. lead to a glaringly inhumane allocation of resources and priorities in the society. It means, for instance, the continued allocation of public funds and technical manpower toward military and space technology—not simply because of Cold War necessity, but because the vast aerospace corporations cannot be sustained in any other way. Or, for another instance, it means the huge outlay of public funds for interstate highway construction (without public debate) and the consequent impoverishment of public transportation—not because this is the most efficient, safest, most comfortable way to travel, but because of the power of the auto lobby. And, for a final instance, it means that our cities are sinking into ungovernable chaos—not simply because their problems are so complex, but because no one is willing to govern them in behalf of the human beings who inhabit them. As long as corporate in-

77

terests dominate, as long as power is so badly skewed, every public venture becomes a subsidy for special interests, every regulatory agency becomes a lobby for the industry it regulates, every social reform is twisted and diluted to avoid jeopardizing private greeds, and so even the very air and water and land are made spoiled and dangerous for human use.

A final consequence of liberal corporatism is that it *requires* mass apathy. Since decisions are made centrally and at an elite level, policy formulation can only work when constituencies are immobilized. For if institutional leaders and organizational spokesmen were responsible and responsive to actively involved publics, then the bargaining away of popular rights and interests and the ritual devotion to public welfare which is the very substance of consensus politics would no longer be possible. Further, the preferred technique of social control—namely the exchange of benefits for acquiescence—instructs the people well as to the virtues of elite management and personal withdrawal from citizenly activity. Such management and such withdrawal occur not only in the sphere of national politics, but also in the arenas of decision-making to which people are more routinely related—in the cities and towns, the neighborhoods, the voluntary associations, the school systems, etc. It is my view that the system now emerging requires the end of citizenship as we have understood and hoped for it; therefore, it signifies an abortion of the possibilities for authentic community and meaningful individuality in American life.

Having said all this, I should stress that I do not think an American version of *1984* is inevitable, but I think it can be averted only through a radical reconstruction of the way we live and act now. What our country needs first of all is a restoration of democratic consciousness and democratic action.

Building a Democratic Society

Such a restoration can only come in the process of building a large-scale grass-roots movement for a democratic society. Such a movement would have on its agenda the following:

• It would insist on first-class citizenship for every person in the society. This means, for example, that it would actively engage in the task of organizing the politically disenfranchised and voiceless so that they can independently and effectively pursue their interests and rights in the political arena. It means, too, the development of a concept of citizenship which extends beyond the conventional political sphere to all the institutions of the society—the workplace, the school, the corporation, the neighborhoods, the welfare bureaucracies. The idea that men are citizens with respect to all exercise of authority, that each man has responsibility for the actions of the institution in which he is imbedded, that all authority should be responsible to those "under" it, that men ought not to be infantalized in their relations with each other, that they should have a voice in decisions which determine their fate—this view of man would be a core operating value of the movement for a democratic society.

• It would actively challenge the legitimacy of anti-democratic authority, laws and institutions in the society. The civil rights movement challenges the legitimacy of racist politicians, racist laws and racist practices. Similarly, I think we may be seeing the emergence of an antiwar movement which has begun to challenge the scope of military authority and influence in the society. A movement for a democratic society would extend these challenges to all instances of bureaucratic encroachment, special privilege and elite domination, in a permanent revolution against overweening power.

Expanding Democratic Consciousness

Each effort to achieve first-class citizenship and to undermine undemocratic authority represents an effort to redistribute power, a step away from overcentralization, and a challenge to corporatist ideology and practice. But it is clear that the organization of such activity is not sufficient; in addition, people need a vision of the possibilities for citizenship, democracy and community which would represent a concrete alternative to the present. Consequently, a third item on the agenda of the developing movement would be the expansion of democratic consciousness through the formulation of substantial models of a democratic future. I do not know what such models might look like. I am sure, however, that they will contain at their center such ideas as the decentralizing of decision-making, the development of diverse loci of power, the breaking up of gargantuan organizations, the use of technology to eliminate demeaning labor, the development of new definitions of work and status based on humanistic criteria. The need for serious intellectual work on the problem of democracy and culture in a society of our sort is extremely urgent.

My point then is this: liberals and radicals have spent their greatest energy in arduous campaigns for social reform and against reaction; they have succeeded in helping to construct a version of the welfare state. The task for authentic democrats now, however, is not to continue to "modernize" American politics so as to make the state more efficient or correct the flaws in the present system. Instead, we must restore democracy—and to do that we must find and build constituencies at the grass roots, we must challenge the encroachments of anti-democratic authority and ideology, we must announce a democratic vision which is concretely relevant to the technology of the future and the troubles and discontents of the people.

There is, I think, hope that this can be done. For a new generation is here, unburdened by the irrelevancies of the past, and imbued with a quest for idealism and a disdain for authority and status by their experience of growing up in liberal and affluent homes. Already, in their efforts to organize the poor and dispossessed, in their growing campaign to democratize the universities, in their intensifying campaign against militarism and cold-war ideology, and in their posture of plain honesty, they are providing the framework for the democratic revival.

Opposing President Johnson

Two years ago [in 1964], the main issues were between a President perceived as "left" and his right-wing opposition. Today, increasingly, the terms of debate are shifting—the President is becoming defined as a conservative and is having to cope with opposition to his left. Well, the President *is* a conservative, the nation *needs* a left opposition, the issues coming into focus through the action of the new generation are the real ones for 1966 and beyond. The time for democrats to choose between sustaining their own values and supporting a conservative Administration is coming upon us. Do we dare hope that liberals will strike out on their own?

CHAPTER 2

Vietnam and the Antiwar Movement

Chapter Preface

Between his November 1960 election and his January 1961 inauguration, John F. Kennedy met with outgoing president Dwight D. Eisenhower to be briefed on potential and actual foreign policy crises facing the nation. The situation in Vietnam, Kennedy recalled later, was never discussed. This omission proved to be ironic; in a decade full of significant global events that impacted America—including the 1961 Berlin Wall confrontation, the 1962 Cuban missile crisis, and the 1967 Arab-Israeli War—the Vietnam War stands out as the development that affected the United States more than any other.

Vietnam had been a site of war since the end of World War II, when Vietnamese nationalists clashed with French forces trying to regain colonial control of the country. Following France's defeat and withdrawal in 1954, the country was divided into two regions: North Vietnam, led by Ho Chi Minh, a communist who sought to unite the country under his rule, and South Vietnam, led by Ngo Dinh Diem, whose regime was supported by the United States. At the beginning of the 1960s America's official involvement in Vietnam was limited to several hundred military advisers sent by Eisenhower to assist the South Vietnamese regime. Few members of the general public were deeply informed about Vietnam and America's policy there. As late as 1964 only 8 percent of poll respondents expressed opposition to U.S. policy in Vietnam. However, by the end of the decade approximately half a million U.S. soldiers were stationed in Vietnam. They were fighting and dying in a seemingly endless conflict that had thoroughly polarized America, had inspired massive demonstrations and widespread draft resistance, and had claimed the lives of thousands of Americans and hundreds of thousands of Vietnamese. The war in Vietnam and the public controversy it caused affected many of the developments of the decade, including campus unrest, growing public distrust of government, and the surprising withdrawal of President Lyndon B. Johnson from the 1968 presidential race.

The reasoning behind America's military intervention in Vietnam was rooted in America's Cold War struggle against communism. Many viewed the successful communist revolutions in China in 1949 and Cuba in 1959 as significant defeats for the United States, and both Presidents Kennedy and Johnson were motivated by the desire not to "lose" any other nation to communist revolution. Vietnam was but one of many places in Asia, Latin America, and Africa that Kennedy and other American leaders believed were key to winning the Cold War between the "free world" and the communist nations led by China and the Soviet Union. The desire to build up South Vietnam as a viable alternative to communism and to demonstrate America's willingness to do whatever it took to successfully prevent another communist takeover prompted Kennedy to increase the number of U.S. troops in Vietnam to 16,000 during his brief presidency. These goals also led Johnson to begin extensive bombing campaigns against North Vietnam in early 1965 and to increase the number of U.S. troops deployed there to 267,000 by 1966. An American withdrawal from Vietnam, many believed, would help communism spread to neighboring regions and would irreparably damage American prestige abroad.

Beginning around 1965, however, when colleges staged several "teach-ins" to analyze and critique America's Vietnam policy, a movement to protest and resist the war in Vietnam started to spread. The antiwar movement consisted of diverse elements, including young men resisting the draft by burning draft cards and going to prison or fleeing to Canada, members of Congress objecting to the fact that war was never officially declared, respected moral and intellectual figures such as civil rights leader Martin Luther King Jr., and ordinary citizens disturbed by images of war on the nightly television news.

The antiwar movement itself divided the United States as President Johnson and others accused dissenters of sapping American morale and hampering American efforts to win the war. Some people viewed protesters as traitors for refusing to support America in a time of war. Organizations such as the American Legion and Young Americans for Freedom staged rallies backing the American effort in Vietnam and opposing the withdrawal of U.S. forces. Even though many Americans grew increasingly discouraged by the lack of progress in Vietnam, they did not necessarily support the tactics and ideas of the antiwar movement, especially those of its most radical elements. By 1969 the majority of Americans considered the war in Vietnam a "mistake," but 69 percent of respondents to a national public opinion poll still viewed antiwar protesters as "harmful to American life."

America did not withdraw from Vietnam until 1973; by 1975 South Vietnam had fallen to North Vietnam. Vietnam thus became America's first war defeat—a development some people have blamed on the antiwar movement. The viewpoints in this chapter provide a sampling of perspectives on both the Vietnam War and the antiwar movement.

VIEWPOINT 1

"To leave Viet-Nam to its fate would shake the confidence of [the world's] people in the value of an American commitment and in the value of America's word."

Americans Should Support the Vietnam War

Lyndon B. Johnson (1908–1973)

Lyndon B. Johnson became president of the United States in November 1963, following the assassination of John F. Kennedy. During the 1964 election campaign, he presented himself as the peace candidate in contrast with his Republican opponent, Barry Goldwater, who advocated bombing North Vietnam and otherwise escalating America's military involvement in the region. But Johnson was also determined, as he said privately hours after he took office in 1963, that he was "not going to lose Vietnam. I am not going to be the first president who saw Southeast Asia go the way China went." In early 1965, following his easy election victory over Goldwater, Johnson made several key decisions that escalated American involvement in the conflict. In February he began a sustained bombing campaign of North Vietnam. In March he secretly began sending regular combat troops to Vietnam (soldiers had already been sent to Vietnam as military "advisers" who were kept from official combat roles). The escalation of U.S. involvement prompted protest actions on college campuses and elsewhere, and Vietnam quickly became one of the dominant controversies of Johnson's presidency.

The following viewpoint is taken from a speech Johnson delivered at Johns Hopkins University on April 7, 1965. Johnson defends America's actions in Vietnam, arguing that communists in

From Lyndon B. Johnson's speech at Johns Hopkins University, April 7, 1965, in *Public Papers of the Presidents: Lyndon B. Johnson, 1965*, vol. 2 (Washington, DC: Government Printing Office, 1966).

Vietnam are being supported by the communist regime in China and that American involvement is necessary to fight communism in that area of the world.

Tonight Americans and Asians are dying for a world where each people may choose its own path to change.

This is the principle for which our ancestors fought in the valleys of Pennsylvania. It is the principle for which our sons fight tonight in the jungles of Viet-Nam.

Viet-Nam is far away from this quiet campus. We have no territory there, nor do we seek any. The war is dirty and brutal and difficult. And some 400 young men, born into an America that is bursting with opportunity and promise, have ended their lives on Viet-Nam's steaming soil.

Why must we take this painful road?

Why must this Nation hazard its ease, and its interest, and its power for the sake of a people so far away?

We fight because we must fight if we are to live in a world where every country can shape its own destiny. And only in such a world will our own freedom be finally secure.

This kind of world will never be built by bombs or bullets. Yet the infirmities of man are such that force must often precede reason, and the waste of war, the works of peace.

We wish that this were not so. But we must deal with the world as it is, if it is ever to be as we wish.

The world as it is in Asia is not a serene or peaceful place.

The first reality is that North Viet-Nam has attacked the independent nation of South Viet-Nam. Its object is total conquest.

Of course, some of the people of South Viet-Nam are participating in attack on their own government. But trained men and supplies, orders and arms, flow in a constant stream from north to south. This support is the heartbeat of the war.

And it is a war of unparalleled brutality. Simple farmers are the targets of assassination and kidnapping. Women and children are strangled in the night because their men are loyal to their government. And helpless villages are ravaged by sneak attacks. Large-scale raids are conducted on towns, and terror strikes in the heart of cities.

The confused nature of this conflict cannot mask the fact that it is the new face of an old enemy.

Over this war—and all Asia—is another reality: the deepening shadow of Communist China. The rulers in Hanoi are urged on by Peking. This is a regime which has destroyed freedom in Tibet, which has attacked India, and has been condemned by the United Nations for aggression in Korea. It is a nation which is helping the forces of violence in almost every continent. The contest in Viet-Nam is part of a wider pattern of aggressive purposes.

Why are these realities our concern? Why are we in South Viet-Nam?

An American Promise

We are there because we have a promise to keep. Since 1954 every American President has offered support to the people of South Viet-Nam. We have helped to build, and we have helped to defend. Thus, over many years, we have made a national pledge to help South Viet-Nam defend its independence.

And I intend to keep that promise.

To dishonor that pledge, to abandon this small and brave nation to its enemies, and to the terror that must follow, would be an unforgivable wrong.

We're also there to strengthen world order. Around the globe, from Berlin to Thailand, are people whose well-being rests, in part, on the belief that they can count on us if they are attacked. To leave Viet-Nam to its fate would shake the confidence of all these people in the value of an American commitment and in the value of America's word. The result would be increased unrest and instability, and even wider war.

We are also there because there are great stakes in the balance. Let no one think for a moment that retreat from Viet-Nam would bring an end to conflict. The battle would be renewed in one country and then another. The central lesson of our time is that the appetite of aggression is never satisfied. To withdraw from one battlefield means only to prepare for the next. We must say in southeast Asia—as we did in Europe—in the words of the Bible: "Hitherto shalt thou come, but no further."

There are those who say that all our effort there will be futile—that China's power is such that it is bound to dominate all southeast Asia. But there is no end to that argument until all of the nations of Asia are swallowed up.

There are those who wonder why we have a responsibility there. Well, we have it there for the same reason that we have a responsibility for the defense of Europe. World War II was fought in both Europe and Asia, and when it ended we found ourselves with continued responsibility for the defense of freedom.

Our objective is the independence of South Viet-Nam, and its freedom from attack. We want nothing for ourselves—only that the people of South Viet-Nam be allowed to guide their own country in their own way.

We will do everything necessary to reach that objective. And we will do only what is absolutely necessary.

American War and Peace Aims

A January 1966 editorial in Fortune *expresses support for President Johnson's military escalation in Vietnam the previous year, arguing that the conflict in Vietnam is part of a larger struggle to contain communism and the influence of the People's Republic of China in Asia.*

Quite suddenly, the American people are becoming aware of the depth of the U.S. military commitment in Vietnam. And, quite understandably, the shock of recognition has brought a tremor of uneasiness. Not only has the U.S. commitment grown enormously in a stunningly short time; it is rising toward levels that recently would have seemed unimaginable. The Johnson Administration is to be strongly commended for its resolute response to last spring's Communist buildup that threatened to overwhelm South Vietnam. But even as the war expands and slowly turns in our favor, uneasiness at home will persist—until the nation clarifies its reasons for fighting and its vision of the peace that should follow victory.

American war and peace aims are inextricably bound together. The minimum acceptable military outcome of the war, as Washington has repeatedly declared, is the withdrawal of invading Communist forces from South Vietnam and the cessation of Hanoi's attempts forcibly to determine its neighbor's future. No one knows how long the fighting may continue, or precisely how victory ultimately will be achieved: perhaps as the result of further escalation, including extension of the war in new forms to North Vietnam; perhaps as the result of negotiations proceeding from Communist acceptance of minimum U.S. conditions; perhaps through collapse of the enemy's rear and withdrawal of Red forces, denied their lifeline; or perhaps, as with much else in this strange war, by an improbable conjunction of events.

Regardless of how victory on the battlefield is finally won, American war aims—and peace aims—must certainly demand far more. It should be clear by now—after Korea, the battle of Taiwan Strait, Malaysia, and the attempted Communist coup in Indonesia—that Peking's brand of Communism intends to fasten its hold on all of Asia and to throw Western influence out. In fighting in Vietnam we are fighting on just one more front of that continuing war.

In recent months attacks on South Viet-Nam were stepped up. Thus, it became necessary for us to increase our response and to make attacks by air. This is not a change of purpose. It is a change in what we believe that purpose requires.

We do this in order to slow down an aggression.

We do this to increase the confidence of the brave people of South Viet-Nam who have bravely borne this brutal battle for so many years with so many casualties.

And we do this to convince the leaders of North Viet-Nam—and all who seek to share their conquest—of a very simple fact:

We will not be defeated.

We will not grow tired.

We will not withdraw, either openly or under the cloak of a meaningless agreement.

We know that air attacks alone will not accomplish all of these purposes. But it is our best and prayerful judgment that they are a necessary part of the surest road to peace. . . .

Because we fight for values and we fight for principles, rather than territory or colonies, our patience and our determination are unending.

Once this is clear, then it should also be clear that the only path for reasonable men is the path of peaceful settlement.

Such peace demands an independent South Viet-Nam—securely guaranteed and able to shape its own relationships to all others—free from outside interference—tied to no alliance—a military base for no other country.

These are the essentials of any final settlement.

We will never be second in the search for such a peaceful settlement in Viet-Nam.

There may be many ways to this kind of peace: in discussion or negotiation with the governments concerned; in large groups or in small ones; in the reaffirmation of old agreements or the strengthening with new ones.

We have stated this position over and over again, fifty times and more, to friend and foe alike. And we remain ready, with this purpose, for unconditional discussions. . . .

These countries of southeast Asia are homes for millions of impoverished people. Each day these people rise at dawn and struggle through until the night to wrestle existence from the soil. They are often wracked by disease, plagued by hunger, and death comes at the early age of 40.

Stability and peace do not come easily in such a land. Neither independence nor human dignity will ever be won, though, by arms alone. It also requires the work of peace. The American people have helped generously in times past in these works. Now there must be a much more massive effort to improve the life of man in that conflict-torn corner of our world.

Economic Development

The first step is for the countries of southeast Asia to associate themselves in a greatly expanded cooperative effort for development. We would hope that North Viet-Nam would take its place in the common effort just as soon as peaceful cooperation is possible.

The United Nations is already actively engaged in development in this area. As far back as 1961 I conferred with our authorities in Viet-Nam in connection with their work there. And I would hope tonight that the Secretary General of the United Nations could use the prestige of his great office, and his deep knowledge of Asia, to initiate, as soon as possible, with the countries of that area, a plan for cooperation in increased development.

For our part I will ask the Congress to join in a billion dollar American investment in this effort as soon as it is underway.

And I would hope that all other industrialized countries, including the Soviet Union, will join in this effort to replace despair with hope, and terror with progress. . . .

I also intend to expand and speed up a program to make available our farm surpluses to assist in feeding and clothing the needy in Asia. We should not allow people to go hungry and wear rags while our own warehouses overflow with an abundance of wheat and corn, rice and cotton.

So I will very shortly name a special team of outstanding, patriotic, distinguished Americans to inaugurate our participation in these programs. This team will be headed by Mr. Eugene Black, the very able former President of the World Bank.

In areas that are still ripped by conflict, of course, development will not be easy. Peace will be necessary for final success. But we cannot and must not wait for peace to begin this job. . . .

We often say how impressive power is. But I do not find it impressive at all. The guns and the bombs, the rockets and the warships, are all symbols of human failure. They are necessary symbols. They protect what we cherish. But they are witness to human folly.

A dam built across a great river is impressive.

In the countryside where I was born, and where I live, I have seen the night illuminated, and the kitchens warmed, and the homes heated, where once the cheerless night and the ceaseless cold held sway. And all this happened because electricity came to our area along the humming wires of the REA Electrification of the countryside—yes, that, too, is impressive. . . .

Every night before I turn out the lights to sleep I ask myself this question: Have I done everything that I can do to unite this country? Have I done everything I can to help unite the world, to try to bring peace and hope to all the peoples of the world? Have I done enough?

Ask yourselves that question in your homes—and in this hall tonight. Have we, each of us, all done all we could? Have we done enough?

We Must Choose

We may well be living in the time foretold many years ago when it was said: "I call heaven and earth to record this day against you, that I have set before you life and death, blessing and cursing: therefore choose life, that both thou and thy seed may live."

This generation of the world must choose: destroy or build, kill or aid, hate or understand.

We can do all these things on a scale never dreamed of before.

Well, we will choose life. In so doing we will prevail over the enemies within man, and over the natural enemies of all mankind.

VIEWPOINT 2

"In order to atone for our sins and errors in Vietnam, we should take the initiative in bringing the war to a halt."

Americans Should Oppose the Vietnam War

Martin Luther King Jr. (1929–1968)

As American involvement in Vietnam escalated, so did an organized movement of protest and resistance against the war. Thomas Cornell, a member of the Catholic Worker Movement, held the first protest against American involvement in Vietnam in 1963. He formed the Catholic Peace Fellowship the following year with, among others, Roman Catholic priests Daniel and Philip Berrigan. In 1965, antiwar activity increased on college campuses and a national protest at the Washington Monument drew more than twenty thousand people. Within the next few years the number and size of antiwar protests grew, as did the number of young men who resisted the military draft.

In April 1967, Martin Luther King Jr., a 1964 Nobel Peace Prize winner and a famous advocate of nonviolence as a means to address civil rights issues, broke his previous public silence on Vietnam and came out against the war. In a sermon, excerpted here, delivered at Riverside Church in New York City, King states his reasons for opposing U.S. involvement in Vietnam. King maintains that the United States bears primary responsibility for starting and prolonging the conflict and thus is responsible for making peace. He also links the civil rights cause to the antiwar movement by arguing that the Vietnam War is adversely affecting America's minorities. King's speech was bitterly criticized by many, including Vice President Hubert H. Humphrey and other members of the Johnson administration. It does, however, provide an expressive articulation of the concerns that motivated many antiwar protesters of the 1960s.

———————————

I come to this platform to make a passionate plea to my beloved nation. . . .

I wish not to speak with Hanoi and the NLF [National Liberation Front], but rather to my fellow Americans who, with me, bear the greatest responsibility in ending a conflict that has exacted a heavy price on both continents.

Vietnam and the War on Poverty

Since I am a preacher by trade, I suppose it is not surprising that I have seven major reasons for bringing Vietnam into the field of my moral vision. There is at the outset a very obvious and almost facile connection between the war in Vietnam and the struggle I, and others, have been waging in America. A few years ago there was a shining moment in that struggle. It seemed as if there was a real promise of hope for the poor—both black and white—through the Poverty Program. Then came the build-up in Vietnam, and I watched the program broken and eviscerated as if it were some idle political plaything of a society gone mad on war, and I knew that America would never invest the necessary funds or energies in rehabilitation of its poor so long as Vietnam continued to draw men and skills and money like some demonic, destructive suction tube. So I was increasingly compelled to see the war as an enemy of the poor and to attack it as such.

Perhaps the more tragic recognition of reality took place when it became clear to me that the war was doing far more than devastating the hopes of the poor at home. It was sending their sons and their brothers and their husbands to fight and to die in extraordinarily high proportions relative to the rest of the population. We were taking the young black men who had been crippled by our society and sending them 8000 miles away to guarantee liberties in Southeast Asia which they had not found in Southwest Georgia and East Harlem. So we have been repeatedly faced with the cruel irony of watching Negro and white boys on TV screens as they kill and die together for a nation that has been unable to seat them together in the same schools. So we watch them in brutal solidarity burning the huts of a poor village, but we realize that they would never live on the same block in Detroit. I could not be silent in the face of such cruel manipulation of the poor.

My third reason grows out of my experience in the ghettos of the North over the last three years—especially the last three summers. As I have walked among the desperate, rejected, and angry young men, I have told them that Molotov cocktails and rifles would not solve their problems. I have tried to offer them my deepest compassion while maintaining my conviction that social change comes most meaningfully through nonviolent action. But, they asked, what about Vietnam? They asked if our own nation wasn't using massive doses of violence to solve its problems, to bring about the changes it wanted. Their questions hit home, and I knew that I could never again raise my voice against the violence of the oppressed in the ghettos without having first spoken clearly to the greatest purveyor of violence in the world today—my own government.

Saving America's Soul

For those who ask the question, "Aren't you a civil rights leader?" and thereby mean to exclude me from the movement for peace, I have this further answer. In 1957 when a group of us formed the Southern Christian Leadership Conference, we chose as our motto: "To save the soul of America." We were convinced that we could not limit our vision to certain rights for black people, but instead affirmed the conviction that America would never be free or saved from itself unless the descendants of its slaves were loosed from the shackles they still wear.

Now it should be incandescently clear that no one who has any concern for the integrity and life of America today can ignore the present war. If America's soul becomes totally poisoned, part of the autopsy must read "Vietnam." It can never be saved so long as it destroys the deepest hopes of men the world over.

And as I ponder the madness of Vietnam, my mind goes constantly to the people of that peninsula. I speak now not of the soldiers of each side, not of the junta in Saigon, but simply of the people who have been living under the curse of war for almost three continuous decades. I think of them, too, because it is clear to me that there will be no meaningful solution there until some attempt is made to know them and their broken cries.

The Struggle for Vietnamese Independence

They must see Americans as strange liberators. The Vietnamese proclaimed their own independence in 1945 after a combined French and Japanese occupation and before the communist revolution in China. Even though they quoted the American Declaration of Independence in their own document of freedom, we refused to recognize them. Instead, we decided to support France in its re-conquest of her former colony.

America Is Not Fighting for Democracy

The Vietnam Day Committee (VDC) sponsored a major antiwar protest and "teach-in" at the University of California at Berkeley in May 1965. It subsequently became an antiwar organization that drew much support from student radicals in northern California. The following passage is excerpted from a 1965 pamphlet produced by the VDC and distributed to army inductees, encouraging them to oppose the war.

Your job as a soldier is supposed to be "to win the people of South Vietnam." Win them to what—democracy? No, we keep military dictators in power. What then? The American way of life? But why should they care any more about our way of life than we care about theirs? We can't speak their language or even pronounce their names. We don't know anything about their religion or even what it is. We never even heard of Vietnam until Washington decided to run it.

You are supposed to be fighting "to save the Vietnamese people from Communism." Certainly Communist influence is very strong in the National Liberation Front [NLF], the rebel government. Yet most of the people support the NLF. Why? Many of the same people who now lead the NLF led the Vietnamese independence movement against the Japanese during World War II, and then went on to fight against French colonial rule. Most Vietnamese think of the NLF leaders as their country's outstanding patriots. In fact, many anti-Communists have joined the guerrilla forces in the belief that the most important thing is to get rid of foreign domination and military dictators. On the other hand, very few Vietnamese support the official [South Vietnam] government of General [Nguyen Cao] Ky. His army has low morale and a high desertion rate.

Our government felt then that the Vietnamese people were not "ready" for independence, and we again fell victim to the deadly Western arrogance that has poisoned the internal atmosphere for so long. With that tragic decision, we rejected a revolutionary government seeking self-determination, and a government that had been established not by China (for whom the Vietnamese have no great love) but by clearly indigenous forces that included some communists. For the peasants, this new government meant real land reform, one of the most important needs in their lives.

For nine years following 1945 we denied the people of Vietnam the right of independence. For nine years we vigorously supported the French in their abortive effort to re-colonize Vietnam.

Before the end of the war we were meeting 80 per cent of the French war costs. Even before the French were defeated at Dien Bien Phu, they began to despair of their reckless action, but we did not. We encouraged them with our huge financial and military supplies to continue the war even after they had lost the will to do so.

After the French were defeated it looked as if independence and land reform would come again through the Geneva agreements. But instead there came the United States, determined that Ho [Chi Minh] should not unify the temporarily divided nation, and the peasants watched again as we supported one of the most vicious modern dictators—our chosen man, Premier [Ngo Dinh] Diem. The peasants watched and cringed as Diem ruthlessly routed out all opposition, supported their extortionist landlords and refused even to discuss reunification with the North. The peasants watched as all this was presided over by U.S. influence and then by increasing numbers of U.S. troops who came to help quell the insurgency that Diem's methods had aroused. When Diem was overthrown they may have been happy, but the long line of military dictatorships seemed to offer no real change—especially in terms of their need for land and peace.

The only change came from America as we increased our troop commitments in support of governments which were singularly corrupt, inept and without popular support. All the while, the people read our leaflets and received regular promises of peace and democracy—and land reform.

Now they languish under our bombs and consider us—not their fellow Vietnamese—the real enemy. They move sadly and apathetically as we herd them off the land of their fathers into concentration camps where minimal social needs are rarely met. They know they must move or be destroyed by our bombs. So they go.

They watch as we poison their water, as we kill a million acres of their crops. They must weep as the bulldozers destroy their precious trees. They wander into the hospitals, with at least 20 casualties from American firepower for each Viet Cong–inflicted injury. So far we may have killed a million of them—mostly children.

What do the peasants think as we ally ourselves with the landlords and as we refuse to put any action into our many words concerning land reform? What do they think as we test out our latest weapons on them, just as the Germans tested out new medicines and new tortures in the concentration camps of Europe? Where are the roots of the independent Vietnam we claim to be building?

Now there is little left to build on—save bitterness. Soon the only solid physical foundations remaining will be found at our military bases and in the concrete of the concentration camps we call "fortified hamlets." The peasants may well wonder if we plan to build our new Vietnam on such grounds as these. Could we blame them for such thoughts? We must speak for them and raise the questions they cannot raise. These too are our brothers.

Speaking for America's Enemies

Perhaps the more difficult but no less necessary task is to speak for those who have been designated as our enemies. What of the NLF—that strangely anonymous group we call VC or communists? What must they think of us in America when they realize that we permitted the repression and cruelty of Diem which helped to bring them into being as a resistance group in the South? How can they believe in our integrity when now we speak of "aggression from the North" as if there were nothing more essential to the war? How can they trust us when now we charge *them* with violence while we pour new weapons of death into their land?

How do they judge us when our officials know that their membership is less than 25 per cent communist and yet insist on giving them a blanket name?

Here is the true meaning and value of compassion and nonviolence—when it helps us to see the enemy's point of view, to hear his questions, to know his assessment of ourselves. For from his view we may indeed see the basic weaknesses of our own condition, and if we are mature, we may learn and grow and profit from the wisdom of the brothers who are called the opposition.

So, too, with Hanoi. In the North, where our bombs now pummel the land, and our mines endanger the waterways, we are met by a deep but understandable mistrust. In Hanoi there are men who led the nation to independence against the Japanese and the French, the men who sought membership in the French commonwealth and were betrayed by the weakness of Paris and the willfulness of the colonial armies. It was they who led a second struggle against French domination at tremendous costs, and then were persuaded at Geneva to give up, as a temporary measure, the land they controlled between the 13th and 17th parallels. After 1954 they watched us conspire with Diem to prevent elections which would have surely brought Ho Chi Minh to power over a united Vietnam, and they realized they had been betrayed again.

Ho Chi Minh has watched as America has spoken of peace and has built up its forces, and now he has surely heard the increasing international rumors of American plans for an invasion of the North. Perhaps only his sense of humor and irony can save him when he hears the most powerful nation of the world speaking of aggression as it drops thousands of bombs on a poor, weak nation more than 8000 miles from its shores.

At this point, I should make it clear that while I have tried here to give a voice to the voiceless of Vietnam and to understand the arguments of those who are called enemy, I am as deeply concerned about our own troops there as anything else. For it occurs to me that what we are submitting them to in Vietnam is not simply the brutalizing process that goes on in any war where armies face each other and seek to destroy. We are adding cynicism to the process of death, for our troops must know after a short period there that none of the things we claim to be fighting for are really involved. Before long they must know that their government has sent them into a struggle among Vietnamese, and the more sophisticated surely realize that we are on the side of the wealthy and the secure while we create a hell for the poor.

We Must Stop the War

Somehow this madness must cease. I speak as a child of God and brother to the suffering poor of Vietnam and the poor of America who are paying the double price of smashed hopes at home and death and corruption in Vietnam. I speak as a citizen of the world, for the world as it stands aghast at the path we have taken. I speak as an American to the leaders of my own nation. The great initiative in this war is ours. The initiative to stop must be ours.

This is the message of the great Buddhist leaders of Vietnam. Recently, one of them wrote these words: "Each day the war goes on the hatred increases in the hearts of the Vietnamese and in the hearts of those of humanitarian instinct. The Americans are forcing even their friends into becoming their enemies. It is curious that the Americans, who calculate so carefully on the possibilities of military victory, do not realize that in the process they are incurring deep psychological and political defeat. The image of America will never again be the image of revolution, freedom and democracy, but the image of violence and militarism."

If we continue, there will be no doubt in my mind and in the mind of the world that we have no honorable intentions in Vietnam. It will become clear that our minimal expectation is to occupy it as an American colony, and men will not refrain from thinking that our maximum hope is to goad China into a war so that we may bomb her nuclear installations.

The world now demands a maturity of America that we may not be able to achieve. It demands that we admit that we have been wrong from the beginning of our adventure in Vietnam, that we have been detrimental to the life of her people.

In order to atone for our sins and errors in Vietnam, we should take the initiative in bringing the war to a halt.

"Our youth are showing that they still believe in the American dream, and their protests attest to its continuing vitality."

Vietnam War Dissenters Are Helping America

J. William Fulbright (1905–1995)

As the number of U.S. soldiers in Vietnam grew from around 60,000 in mid-1965 to 485,000 by the end of 1967, the political movement against the war also grew. College students led rallies, marches, and protests; a rally in front of the Pentagon in October 1967 drew 50,000 people. By that time the antiwar movement had spread beyond college campuses. Organizations ranging from the Federation of American Scientists to the International Ladies' Garment Union took positions against the war, and new organizations representing religious leaders (Clergy and Laity Concerned), businesspeople (Business Executives Move for Vietnam Peace), and women (Women Strike for Peace, Another Mother for Peace) were formed to protest against the Vietnam War.

Opposition to the Vietnam War was also growing in Congress, especially the Senate. One of the most prominent senators to emerge as a critic of America's Vietnam policy during the 1960s was J. William Fulbright, an Arkansas Democrat and chairman of the Senate's Committee on Foreign Relations. In 1966 he held committee hearings on Vietnam that became a prominent and legitimizing platform for critics of the war.

The following viewpoint is taken from an August 1967 article in which Fulbright examines the connections between the Vietnam War and America's domestic problems, particularly the wave of violent riots that were wreaking havoc in Detroit, Michigan, and other cities. Fulbright contends that the war in Vietnam is an at-

J. William Fulbright, "The Great Society Is a Sick Society," *New York Times Magazine*, August 20, 1967. Copyright © 1967 by The New York Times Company. Reprinted by permission.

tempt to maintain an overseas "empire" and is contrary to traditional American values. The conflict, he asserts, is condemning President Lyndon B. Johnson's efforts to create a Great Society through government programs to failure. He concludes that rather than weakening the country, dissenters are in fact "regenerating" America by opposing the destructive war in Vietnam and advocating traditional American values of freedom and democracy.

Standing in the smoke and rubble of Detroit, a Negro veteran said: "I just got back from Vietnam a few months ago, but you know, I think the war is here."

There are in fact two wars going on. One is the war of power politics which our soldiers are fighting in the jungles of Southeast Asia. The other is a war for America's soul which is being fought in the streets of Newark and Detroit and in the halls of Congress, in churches and protest meetings and on college campuses, and in the hearts and minds of silent Americans from Maine to Hawaii. I believe that the two wars have something to do with each other, not in the direct, tangibly causal way that bureaucrats require as proof of a connection between two things, but in a subtler moral and qualitative way that is no less real for being intangible. Each of these wars might well be going on in the absence of the other, but neither, I suspect, standing alone, would seem so hopeless and demoralizing.

The connection between Vietnam and Detroit is in their conflicting and incompatible demands upon traditional American values. The one demands that they be set aside, the other that they be fulfilled. The one demands the acceptance by America of an imperial role in the world, or of what our policymakers like to call the "responsibilities of power," or of what I have called the "arrogance of power." The other demands freedom and social justice at home, an end to poverty, the fulfillment of our flawed democracy and an effort to create a role for ourselves in the world which is compatible with our traditional values. The question, it should be emphasized, is not whether it is *possible* to engage in traditional power politics abroad and at the same time to perfect democracy at home, but whether it is possible for *us Americans*, with our particular history and national character, to combine morally incompatible roles.

Vietnam and the Great Society

Administration officials tell us that we can indeed afford both Vietnam and the Great Society, and they produce impressive statistics of the gross national product to prove it. The statistics show financial capacity, but they do not show moral and psychological capacity. They do not show how a President preoccupied with bombing missions over North and South Vietnam can provide strong and consistent leadership for the renewal of our cities. They do not show how a Congress burdened with war costs and war measures, with emergency briefings and an endless series of dramatic appeals, with anxious constituents and a mounting anxiety of their own, can tend to the workaday business of studying social problems and legislating programs to meet them. Nor do the statistics tell how an anxious and puzzled people, bombarded by press and television with the bad news of American deaths in Vietnam, the "good news" of enemy deaths—and with vividly horrifying pictures to illustrate them—can be expected to support neighborhood antipoverty projects and national programs for urban renewal, employment and education. Anxiety about war does not breed compassion for one's neighbors nor do constant reminders of the cheapness of life abroad strengthen our faith in its sanctity at home. In these ways the war in Vietnam is poisoning and brutalizing our domestic life. Psychological incompatibility has proven to be more controlling than financial feasibility; and the Great Society has become a sick society.

When he visited America a hundred years ago, Thomas Huxley wrote: "I cannot say that I am in the slightest degree impressed by your bigness, or your material resources, as such. Size is not grandeur, and territory does not make a nation. The great issue, about which hangs the terror of overhanging fate, is what are you going to do with all these things?"

The question is still with us, and we seem to have come to a time of historical crisis when its answer can no longer be deferred. Before the Second World War our world role was a potential role; we were important in the world for what we *could* do with our power, for the leadership we *might* provide, for the example we *might* set. Now the choices are almost gone: we are, almost, the world's self-appointed policeman; we are, almost, the world defender of the status quo. We are well on our way to becoming a traditional great power—an imperial nation if you will—engaged in the exercise of power for its own sake, exercising it to the limit of our capacity and beyond, filling every vacuum and extending the American "presence" to the farthest reaches of the earth. And, as with the great empires of the past, as the power grows, it is becoming an end in itself, separated except by ritual incantation from its initial motives, governed, it would seem, by its own mystique, power without philosophy or purpose.

That describes what we have *almost* become, but we have not become a traditional empire yet. The old values remain—the populism and the optimism, the individualism and the rough-hewn equality, the friendliness and the good humor, the inventiveness and the zest for life, the caring about people and the sympathy for the underdog, and the idea, which goes back to the American Revolution, that maybe—just maybe—we can set an example of democracy and human dignity for the world.

That is something which none of the great empires of the past has ever done, or tried to do, or wanted to do, but we were bold enough—or presumptuous enough—to think that we might be able to do it. And there are a great many Americans who still think we can do it, or at least they want to try.

That, I believe, is what all the hue and cry is about—the dissent in the Senate and the protest marches in the cities, the letters to the President from the student leaders and former Peace Corps Volunteers, the lonely searching of conscience by a student facing the draft and the letter to a Senator from a soldier in the field who can no longer accept the official explanations of why he has been sent to fight in the jungles of Vietnam. All believe that their country was cut out for something more ennobling than imperial destiny. Our youth are showing that they still believe in the American dream, and their protests attest to its continuing vitality.

American Values

There appeared in a recent issue of the journal *Foreign Affairs* a curious little article complaining about the failure of many American intellectuals to support what the author regards as America's unavoidable "imperial role" in the world. The article took my attention because it seems a faithful statement of the governing philosophy of American foreign policy while also suggesting how little the makers of that policy appreciate the significance of the issue between themselves and their critics. It is taken for granted—not set forth as a hypothesis to be proven—that any great power, in the author's words, "is entangled in a web of responsibilities from which there is no hope of escape," and that "there is no way the United States, as the world's mightiest power, can avoid such an imperial role. . . ." The author's displeasure with the "intellectuals" (he uses the word more or less to describe people who disagree with the Administration's policy) is that, in the face of this alleged historical inevitability, they are putting up a disruptive, irritating and futile resistance. They are doing this, he believes, because they are believers in "ideology"—the better word would be "values" or "ideals"—and this causes their thinking to be "irrelevant" to foreign policy.

Here, inadvertently, the writer puts his finger on the nub of the current crisis. The students and churchmen and professors who are protesting the Vietnam war do not accept the notion that foreign policy is a matter of expedients to which values are irrelevant. They reject this notion because they understand, as some of our policymakers do not understand, that it is ultimately self-defeating to "fight fire with fire," that you cannot defend your values in a manner that does violence to those values without destroying the very thing you are trying to defend. They understand, as our policymakers do not, that when American soldiers are sent, in the name of freedom, to sustain corrupt dictators in a civil war, . . . damage—perhaps irreparable damage—is being done to the very values that are meant to be defended. The critics

understand, as our policymakers do not, that, through the undemocratic expedients we have adopted for the defense of American democracy, we are weakening it to a degree that is beyond the resources of our bitterest enemies.

Nor do the dissenters accept the romantic view that a nation is powerless to choose the role it will play in the world, that some mystic force of history or destiny requires a powerful nation to be an imperial nation. . . . They do not accept the view that, because other great nations have pursued power for its own sake—a pursuit which invariably has ended in decline or disaster—America must do the same. They think we have some choice about our own future and that the best basis for exercising that choice is the values on which this republic was founded. . . .

Even the most ardent advocates of an imperial role for the United States would probably agree that the proper objective of our foreign policy is the fostering of a world environment in which we can, with reasonable security, devote our main energies to the realization of the values of our own society. This does not require the adoption or imposition of these values on anybody, but it does require us so to conduct ourselves that our society does not seem hateful and repugnant to others.

At the present, much of the world is repelled by America and what America seems to stand for. Both in our foreign affairs and in our domestic life we convey an image of violence; I do not care very much about images as distinguished from the things they reflect, but this image is rooted in reality. Abroad we are engaged in a savage and unsuccessful war against poor people in a small and backward nation. At home—largely because of the neglect resulting from twenty-five years of preoccupation with foreign involvements—our cities are exploding in violent protest against generations of social injustice. America, which only a few years ago seemed to the world to be a model of democracy and social justice, has become a symbol of violence and undisciplined power. . . .

Moral Leadership

Far from building a safe world environment for American values, our war in Vietnam and the domestic deterioration which it has aggravated are creating a most uncongenial world atmosphere for American ideas and values. The world has no need, in this age of nationalism and nuclear weapons, for a new imperial power, but there is a great need of moral leadership—by which I mean the leadership of decent example. That role could be ours but we have vacated the field, and all that has kept the Russians from filling it is their own lack of imagination.

At the same time, as we have noted, and of even greater fundamental importance, our purposeless and undisciplined use of power is causing a profound controversy in our own society. This in a way is something to be proud of. We have sickened but not succumbed, and just as a healthy body fights disease, we are fighting the alien concept which is being thrust upon us, not by history but by our policymakers in the Department of State and the Pentagon. We are proving the strength of the American dream by resisting the dream of an imperial destiny. We are demonstrating the validity of our traditional values by the difficulty we are having in betraying them.

The principal defenders of these values are our remarkable younger generation, something of whose spirit is expressed in a letter which I received from an American soldier in Vietnam. Speaking of the phony propaganda on both sides, and then of the savagery of the war, of the people he describes as the "real casualties"—"the farmers and their families in the Delta mangled by air strikes, and the villagers here killed and burned out by our friendly Korean mercenaries"—this young soldier then asks ". . . whatever has become of our dream? Where is that America that opposed tyrannies at every turn, without inquiring first whether some particular forms of tyranny might be of use to us? Of the three rights which men have, the first, as I recall, was the right to life. How, then, have we come to be killing so many in such a dubious cause?". . .

An unnecessary and immoral war deserves in its own right to be liquidated; when its effect in addition is the aggravation of grave problems and the corrosion of values in our own society, its liquidation under terms of reasonable and honorable compromise is doubly imperative. Our country is being weakened by a grotesque inversion of priorities, the effects of which are becoming clear to more and more Americans—in the Congress, in the press and in the country at large. . . .

The Younger Generation

While the country sickens for lack of moral leadership, a most remarkable younger generation has taken up the standard of American idealism. Unlike so many of their elders, they have perceived the fraud and sham in American life and are unequivocally rejecting it. Some, the hippies, have simply withdrawn; and while we may regret the loss of their energies and their sense of decency, we can hardly gainsay their evaluation of the state of society. Others of our youth are sardonic and skeptical, not, I think, because they do not want ideals but because they want the genuine article and will not tolerate fraud. Others—students who wrestle with their consciences about the draft, soldiers who wrestle with their consciences about the war, Peace Corps Volunteers who strive to light the spark of human dignity among the poor of India or Brazil and VISTA [Volunteers in Service to America] volunteers who try to do the same for our own poor in Harlem or Appalachia—are striving to keep alive the traditional values of American democracy.

They are not really radical, these young idealists, no more radical, that is, than Jefferson's idea of freedom, Lincoln's idea of equality or Wilson's idea of a peaceful community of nations. Some of them, it is true, are taking what many regard as radical action, but they are doing it in defense of traditional values and in protest against the radical departure from those values embodied in the idea of an imperial destiny for America.

The focus of their protest is the war in Vietnam, and the measure of their integrity is the fortitude with which they refuse to be deceived about it. By striking contrast with the young Germans, who accepted the Nazi evil because the values of their society had disintegrated and they had no moral frame of reference, these young Americans are demonstrating the vitality of American values. They are demonstrating that, while their country is capable of acting falsely to itself, it cannot do so without internal disruption, without calling forth the regenerative counterforce of protest from Americans who are willing to act in defense of the principles they were brought up to believe in.

The spirit of this regenerative generation has been richly demonstrated to me in letters from student leaders, from former Peace Corps Volunteers and from soldiers fighting in Vietnam. I quoted from one earlier. Another letter that is both striking and representative was written by an officer still in Vietnam. He wrote:

> For eleven years I was, before this war, a Regular commissioned officer—a professional military man in name and spirit; now—in name only. To fight well (as do the VC), a soldier must believe in his leadership. I, and many I have met, have lost faith in ours. Since I hold that duty to conscience is higher than duty to the Administration (not "country" as cry the nationalists), I declined a promotion and have resigned my commission. I am to be discharged on my return, at which time I hope to contribute in some way to the search for peace in Vietnam.

Some years ago Archibald MacLeish characterized the American people as follows:

> Races didn't bother the Americans. They were something a lot better than any race. They were a People. They were the first self-constituted, self-declared, self-created People in the history of the world. And their manners were their own business. And so were their politics. And so, but ten times so, were their souls.

Now the possession of their souls is being challenged by the false and dangerous dream of an imperial destiny. It may be that the challenge will succeed, that America will succumb to becoming a traditional empire and will reign for a time over what must surely be a moral if not a physical wasteland, and then, like the great empires of the past, will decline or fall. Or it may be that the effort to create so grotesque an anachronism will go up in flames of nuclear holocaust. But if I had to bet my money on what is going to happen, I would bet on this younger generation—this generation of young men and women who reject the inhumanity of war in a poor and distant land, who reject the poverty and sham in their own country, who are telling their elders what their elders ought to have known—that the price of empire is America's soul and that the price is too high.

VIEWPOINT 4

"It is improper, and I think unpatriotic, to voice dissent in such a way that it encourages our enemies to believe we have lost the capacity to make a national decision and act on it."

Vietnam War Dissenters Are Weakening America

Dwight D. Eisenhower (1890–1969)

Sixty-nine percent of respondents to a 1969 poll said that anti-war protesters were "harmful to American life." Some Americans accused antiwar protesters of being traitors to their country and of prolonging the Vietnam War by giving North Vietnam encouragement. Many were particularly incensed by such actions as Stop the Draft Week, an October 1967 campaign organized by Students for a Democratic Society in which protesters harassed military recruiters, burned draft cards, and engaged in other confrontational activities.

The following viewpoint is taken from a 1968 article by Dwight D. Eisenhower, World War II hero and president of the United States from 1953 to 1961. During Eisenhower's presidency the United States had aided France's effort to maintain colonial control of Vietnam. Following the defeat of France in 1954, the United States helped create and aided a South Vietnamese regime in order to prevent the whole country from falling under the control of the communist Vietnamese leader Ho Chi Minh. Among the reasons Eisenhower gave for these actions was the "domino theory"—the idea that if Vietnam came under communist rule, other countries in the region would soon follow.

By the time this article was first published in April 1968, seven years after Eisenhower left office, America had stationed about a

Dwight D. Eisenhower, "Let's Close Ranks on the Home Front," *Reader's Digest*, April 1968. Copyright 1968, Dwight D. Eisenhower. Reprinted by permission of John Eisenhower.

half-million troops in South Vietnam. A growing number of Americans were actively opposed to the war, a vocal minority of whom openly expressed wishes for a North Vietnamese victory. In the essay, Eisenhower compares the Vietnam War to World War II, in which he was a leading general, and argues that America must regain the unity it had shown in the prior conflict in order to succeed in Vietnam. He criticizes the tactics and actions of antiwar activists, including congressional opponents, intellectual critics, and antiwar demonstrators, contending that many have gone beyond the boundaries of responsible dissent and are aiding America's enemies.

In a long life of service to my country, I have never encountered a situation more depressing than the present spectacle of an America deeply divided over a war—a war to which we have committed so much in treasure, in honor and in the lives of our young men. What has become of our courage? What has become of our loyalty to others? What has become of a noble concept called patriotism, which in former times of crisis has carried us through to victory and peace?

World War II

If in the desperate days of World War II we had been torn by this kind of discord, I doubt that we and our allies could have won. Looking back, I think how disheartening it would have been to those of us who commanded forces in the field if we had been called home to make speeches and hold press conferences—to shore up a wavering solidarity on the home front. Nothing of the sort happened then. But it is happening now. And how the enemies of freedom throughout the world—from Hanoi to Moscow—must be rejoicing!

In our war against the Axis powers a quarter of a century ago, we were fighting for the cause of freedom and human dignity, just as we are now. And in the long-range sense, we were also fighting for our own salvation, for a way of life we hold dear, just as we are now. In that war the American people understood this, and it was inspiring to see the single-minded way this country faced up to the job of fighting two first-rate military powers simultaneously.

We had a few slackers and draft dodgers, of course, but they were objects of scorn. We grumbled a bit about rationing and sometimes accused our draft boards of partiality, but these minor irrationalities were mostly a way of letting off steam. Essentially, we were united, and nearly everyone found some way of helping in the war effort. As a nation, we were dedicated to the job of winning completely and swiftly. And we did win—at least a year earlier than the most optimistic military timetables had forecast.

As commander of the Allied armies in Europe, I can testify that this solidarity, this upsurge of patriotism on the home front was a wonderfully encouraging thing. Neither I nor any other military leader had to lie awake nights wondering whether the folks back home would stick with us to the end. It never occurred to us that they might not. We knew that the American spirit had rallied to the cause, and this knowledge buoyed us up immeasurably—all of us, right down to the private in the ranks.

Today the reverse is true. We have "chosen up sides," as youngsters say in lining up their ball teams, and we call ourselves hawks and doves. This terminology in itself is inaccurate and ridiculous. A hawk is a bird of prey, a dove the helpless victim of predators. We are neither. We covet nobody's territory or property, want no dominion over others. On the other hand, we have always shown ourselves capable of self-defense. I trust we always shall.

Beyond Honorable Dissent

No one who believes in our democratic process can object to honorable dissent. This is part of the American credo, part of our birthright. There are those who now sincerely believe that we have no business being in Vietnam. I think they are terribly and dangerously wrong, but they have the right to state their views.

The current raucous confrontation, however, goes far beyond honorable dissent. Public men and private citizens alike take a stance and defend their positions angrily and unreasonably, often substituting emotion for logic and facts.

Not long ago, for example, a young U.S. Senator was quoted as saying that if we are fighting in Vietnam to protect ourselves, then we must concede that we are being selfishly immoral. To me this seems the height of tortured reasoning, if not worse. Certainly, we are fighting to defend ourselves and other free nations against the eventual domination of communism. In my opinion it would be grossly immoral *not* to resist a tyranny whose openly avowed purpose is to subjugate the earth—and particularly the United States of America. The Senator was indulging in sophistry, and I suspect his purpose was political rather than patriotic.

A ludicrous, and dangerous, aspect of this bitter quarrel is the large number of public men who regard themselves as military experts. One large defeatist group proclaims loudly and positively that "we can never win the Vietnam war." Others insist,

Against Both the War and the Protests

In a May 22, 1967, speech, Mark Arnold, a student at Oberlin College in Ohio, asserts that the United States should end its involvement in Vietnam. However, he also calls for an end to antiwar protests, arguing that they will actually prolong the war by giving the North Vietnamese hope that they can win the conflict.

I am opposed to the war in Vietnam. I consider it to be, like all wars, wasteful, destructive of human life, and immoral. . . .

I believe it imperative for the United States to withdraw from South Vietnam as soon as it possibly can. And it is for that reason that I today urge you and your fellow students to end the antiwar demonstrations. I repeat, I urge you and your fellow students to end the anti-war demonstrations.

To resolve this seeming paradox, we must consider both the efficacy of these forms of protest in achieving their intended goals and the effect of such actions upon our enemies in Vietnam. For, unlike those who demonstrate against the war, I take cognizance of one basic fact: the United States will not withdraw from Vietnam until it has obtained a settlement which it considers equitable. Thus I oppose demonstrations calling for an end to the American involvement in Vietnam because they have not had and will not have the slightest chances of forcing Johnson to end the war. The only thing these demonstrations can accomplish is to prolong unduly the United States involvement in Vietnam because they provide the Viet Cong with one last desperate hope of victory.

It is obvious that the anti-war protests in the past have failed to end the war or even to prevent its escalation. Since the peace marches and sit-ins first began on a major scale in late 1963, there have been over 5000 organized protests against the American involvement in Vietnam. Yet also since 1963, the total United States commitment has risen from a few thousand advisors to over 430,000 combat troops, and both Naval and Air Force planes have commenced bombing attacks against North and South Vietnam. The demonstrations were hardly effective. . . .

What do they accomplish? The only thing they do in the United States was admitted to me by one of the most militant anti-war students at Oberlin. In his words, "About the only thing the demonstrations do is to vent the spleens of some of us." But isn't this sort of self-gratification in itself immoral?

I believe that it is, the more so since these anti-war demonstrations have the unquestionably harmful effect of prolonging the American involvement in Vietnam.

contrary to the best military judgment and to clear evidence, that our air strikes "do no good" and we must cease all bombing of targets in the North. Still others want our troops to sit down in "defensive enclaves" and drop all offensive action—presumably until a tough enemy gets tired of looking at our military might and goes quietly home.

Instead of giving faith and backing to the men who are responsible for the conduct of the war, these armchair strategists snipe at every aspect of the conflict. Moreover, they never seem to lack a rostrum for their pronouncements. They are quoted endlessly and prominently in the press and on the airwaves, and of course their words give aid and comfort to the enemy and thus prolong the war.

A tactic of some dissenters—and this alarms me more than all the empty shouting—is their resort to force in open defiance of the laws of the land. They try to prevent recruiting officers from doing their job, and sometimes succeed. They try to halt the work of personnel recruiters from industries which manufacture war matériel. They lie down on the pavement in front of draft-induction centers; they jeer at the inductees and try to keep them from answering their call to service.

Some young Americans publicly burn their draft cards and state they will never go to war. The "peaceful" anti-war demonstrations frequently get out of hand and become bloodily violent. Dissenters of this type insist on their own right to free speech, but are unwilling to grant the same right to others. How often lately we have been subjected to the shocking spectacle of some distinguished speaker being smuggled in the back door of a lecture hall to avoid physical harm from the demonstrators out front!

These militant peace-at-any-price groups are a small minority, but all too often they get away with such illegal actions—and also get away with the headlines. There is no reason to tolerate this arrogant flouting of the law. It could be stopped—and should be stopped—at once. Their action is not honorable dissent. It is rebellion, and it verges on treason.

In the midst of this disgraceful public uproar, the dissenters continue to demand that we negotiate. I am a firm believer in constructive negotiation, provided both sides come to the conference table with honest and reasonable intentions. Thus far, North Vietnam has made it emphatically clear that it wants no negotiation—except on terms which would mean our complete capitulation. Listening to all the anti-war sound and fury on our home front, Hanoi obviously prefers to wait it out in the hope that public opinion in the United States will eventually compel our withdrawal. It is probable that the behavior of the dissenters themselves is making honorable negotiation impossible.

Reasons for Staying in Vietnam

Those who oppose the Vietnam war and insist on our unilateral withdrawal have said over and over that the American people have never been given a sound reason for our presence there. If they believe this, it must be because they refuse to read or listen to anything they don't like. There are reasons why it is critically important to fight the communists in Vietnam, and they have been stated often.

The first and most immediate reason—so obvious that it shouldn't have to be explained—is that we are trying to save a brave little country, to which we have given our solemn promise of protection, from being swallowed by the communist tyranny. We want the people of South Vietnam to have their chance to live in freedom and prosperity, and even in the midst of a bitter war we are already doing much to help them build up their economy.

If anyone doubts the determination of the communists to subjugate this small country and take it over by sheer savagery, let him read the accounts of the Vietcong's impersonal butchery of whole villages of innocent people. The communists' tactic of conquest by terror, their callous disregard for human life, their philosophy that the end justifies the means—no matter how barbarous and immoral the means may be—are precisely the same in Vietnam as they have used in gobbling up other countries and other free peoples of the world. Their objectives have not changed or softened over the years. The only language they understand is force, or the threat of force.

There is a larger reason for our military presence in Vietnam—and that is the urgent need to keep all Southeast Asia from falling to the communists. Some of our self-appointed military experts discount the "domino theory"—which, as applied to Southeast Asia, simply means that if we abandon South Vietnam to communism, the other countries of that area will also topple. In my opinion, the domino theory is frighteningly correct. I suggest that the peace-at-any-price advocates who scoff at this threat study the behavior of communism over the past two decades.

Here at home, this is election year, and I hope we do not permit the Vietnam war to become a divisive political issue. It is right and proper to advocate a change of leadership and to discuss the conduct of the war. But it is improper, and I think unpatriotic, to voice dissent in such a way that it encourages our enemies to believe we have lost the capacity to make a national decision and act on it. Meanwhile, I state this unequivocally: *I will not personally support any peace-at-any-price candidate who advocates capitulation and the abandonment of South Vietnam.*

As any citizen does, I deeply regret the necessity of pouring the blood of our young men and our treasure into this faraway war for freedom. But it is a necessity. This is an hour of grave national emergency. It is time that we do more thinking and less shouting; that we put our faith in our democratic processes and cease the dangerous tactic of deciding which laws we will and will not obey.

We should also ponder the previous successes and sacrifices we made in checking the advance of communism: how we helped save Western Europe through the Marshall Plan; how we checked aggression in Korea, on the free Chinese islands of Quemoy and Matsu, in Lebanon and the Dominican Republic. How we saved Formosa, and are successfully helping the South American nations resist the Cuban conspirators. These things we must continue to do, even when we stand alone—even when so-called friendly nations criticize our actions.

The Civil War

Sometimes I find comfort in going back even further in history. At one time during the Civil War, a profound spirit of defeatism developed in the North. A considerable portion of the people, discouraged and fearful, cried: Let the South go its way; we can never win this horrible war. Abraham Lincoln was reviled; draft laws were defied; hundreds were killed in resisting recruiting agents. The pressure on the government to acknowledge defeat was intense.

Lincoln, however, saw two things clearly. He knew that the successful secession of the South would fragment America and deny it its great destiny. And with a clear-sighted evaluation of the manpower and resources of both sides, he also knew that the North could win. He stood steadfast, and before long the courage and common sense of the people revived, the defeatists subsided, and the Union was saved.

It is my hope and belief that history will now repeat itself. I still have abiding faith in the good sense of the great majority of the American people. It is unthinkable that the voices of defeat should triumph in our land.

CHAPTER 3

The Youth Revolt and the Counterculture

Chapter Preface

During the 1960s, the large number of Americans born in the years after World War II began to reach adolescence and young adulthood. Many of the members of this generation started to question certain tenets of American society. Their areas of concern ranged from nuclear weapons and the Cold War to rules forbidding male and female college students to live together, from poverty and racial discrimination to fears that their prescribed futures as American workers and citizens were too confined and dull. The sheer size of the "Baby Boom" generation (by 1965, 41 percent of Americans were under twenty years of age) ensured that their activities would have a significant impact on the 1960s.

Young people sought to change the society in which they were raised in several ways. Some attempted to improve the world by postponing career pursuits and volunteering for such programs as the Peace Corps, which was founded in 1962. Many were active in the antiwar movement and in presidential campaigns. Others were involved in conservative groups such as Young Americans for Freedom, founded in 1960. Still others eschewed political activism but rebelled against "the Establishment" in their clothing, hair length, sexual values, music, use of drugs, and other lifestyle choices.

Two of the most well known manifestations of the "youth revolt" of the 1960s were the group Students for a Democratic Society (SDS) and the cultural rebels known as "hippies." Both SDS and the hippie culture attracted much media and public attention; both rebelled against American society—albeit in very different ways.

SDS formed the core of the "New Left"—a term used to describe the new generation of radical student activists who were critical both of American capitalism and of older leftist groups and organizations. Originally founded in 1960 as a student wing of the League for Industrial Democracy (a socialist and anticommunist organization dating back to 1905), within a few years SDS had severed its ties to its parent organization.

SDS had a brief but dramatic life. In 1962, fifty-nine members created the Port Huron statement, an influential and idealistic political platform that criticized various aspects of American society, including the U.S. role in the Cold War, materialistic complacency among the middle class, and the absence of true "participatory democracy" in American life. The group sponsored endeavors such as the Economic Research and Action Project (in which college students went into poor city neighborhoods and slums to organize the poor) with mixed success. In 1965, SDS began to focus more of its efforts on protesting against the Vietnam War. Due in part to the war's escalation and the end of automatic student deferments from the military draft, by 1967 the organization claimed about three hundred campus chapters with as many as sixty thousand members and sympathizers. However, its growing fame and size also brought organizational chaos and factional divisions, and its newer members were increasingly intrigued by ideas of violent social revolution. By 1969 SDS had splintered into several ineffectual organizations, the most famous of which—the Weathermen—functioned for a short time as an underground revolutionary sect.

Hippies represented a different sort of revolution, which focused on cultural values rather than political institutions. A number of young people defied middle-class respectability by dropping out of school and work, taking drugs such as marijuana and LSD, growing long hair and beards, wearing unconventional clothing, and living in communes or other experimental social arrangements. By 1967 the mass media were running frequent stories about hippies in such places as the Haight-Ashbury district of San Francisco and New York City's East Village.

Some observers praised hippies for creating a new "counterculture" that freed people from stifling social inhibitions and caused them to question the materialism and artifice of American society. Scholars such as Theodore Roszak (who first popularized the term *counterculture*) argued that hippies formed the vanguard of a reaction against a sterile and oppressive society. These commentators applauded the hippies' exploration of consciousness, Eastern religions, and anarchism. Hippies were criticized by others, however, for being immature, apolitical, and immoral. Many Americans were offended by the hippies' rejection of traditional American values. Hippies often encountered public hostility and were sometimes harassed and beaten by the police.

The hippie movement was relatively short-lived. To some degree, it was a victim of the heavy media attention that inspired many "weekend hippies" and teenage runaway "flower children" to come to Haight-Ashbury and other hippie enclaves. The influx of newcomers hastened the degeneration of many hippie neighborhoods into youth slums beset with drug abuse and violence. Aspects of the hippie lifestyle—its music, clothing, and art—were quickly commercialized and absorbed by American society, much to the dismay of some counterculture purists.

Only a small percentage of the large Baby Boom contingent were full-fledged participants in either SDS or the counterculture. Both movements, however, left a permanent social legacy because they caused fundamental reappraisals of American values and goals. SDS and other radical political activists forced people to confront questions of war and racial injustice, while hippies emphasized developing one's inner potential rather than focusing on external tokens of success and social approval. The lasting changes brought about by these two groups continue to be felt and debated today.

VIEWPOINT 1

"Although mankind desperately needs revolutionary leadership, America rests in national stalemate, . . . its democratic system apathetic and manipulated rather than 'of, by, and for the people.'"

The Student Movement Is a Necessary Response to Problems in American Society

Students for a Democratic Society (SDS)

When the 1960s began, college students as a group were viewed as being apathetic and conformist. As the decade progressed, however, increasing numbers of students engaged in protests and political activities on issues ranging from civil rights to the Vietnam War. The organization Students for a Democratic Society (SDS) was behind many of the student actions during these years. Formed in 1960, it became the best-known organization of what was called the "New Left" before disintegrating toward the end of the decade.

The following viewpoint is excerpted from the Port Huron Statement, a manifesto adopted at an SDS meeting at Port Huron, Michigan, in 1962. Drafted largely by Tom Hayden, a University of Michigan student who was later elected president of SDS and became one of its most prominent spokesmen, this document influenced many 1960s political activists both within and outside the student organization. The statement expresses the grievances that Hayden and other SDS members held against American soci-

From the Students for a Democratic Society's "Port Huron Statement," 1962. Reprinted courtesy of Tom Hayden.

ety as it had evolved since World War II and argues that college students have the opportunity—and the obligation—to act against racism, nuclear weapons, and other perceived injustices. SDS organized various projects, both within and outside college campuses, in subsequent years in pursuit of its goal of "participatory democracy."

We are people of this generation, bred in at least modest comfort, housed now in universities, looking uncomfortably to the world we inherit.

When we were kids the United States was the wealthiest and strongest country in the world; the only one with the atom bomb, the least scarred by modern war, an initiator of the United Nations that we thought would distribute Western influence throughout the world. Freedom and equality for each individual, government of, by, and for the people—these American values we found good, principles by which we could live as men. Many of us began maturing in complacency.

As we grew, however, our comfort was penetrated by events too troubling to dismiss. First, the permeating and victimizing fact of human degradation, symbolized by the Southern struggle against racial bigotry, compelled most of us from silence to activism. Second, the enclosing fact of the Cold War, symbolized by the presence of the Bomb, brought awareness that we ourselves, and our friends, and millions of abstract "others" we knew more directly because of our common peril, might die at any time. We might deliberately ignore, or avoid, or fail to feel all other human problems, but not these two, for these were too immediate and crushing in their impact, too challenging in the demand that we as individuals take the responsibility for encounter and resolution.

Paradoxes of America

While these and other problems either directly oppressed us or rankled our consciences and became our own subjective concerns, we began to see complicated and disturbing paradoxes in our surrounding America. The declaration "all men are created equal . . ." rang hollow before the facts of Negro life in the South and the big cities of the North. The proclaimed peaceful intentions of the United States contradicted its economic and military investments in the Cold War status quo.

We witnessed, and continue to witness, other paradoxes. With nuclear energy whole cities can easily be powered, yet the dominant nation-states seem more likely to unleash destruction greater than that incurred in all wars of human history. Although our own technology is destroying old and creating new forms of social organization, men still tolerate meaningless work and idleness. While two-thirds of mankind suffers undernourishment, our own upper classes revel amidst superfluous abundance. Although world population is expected to double in forty years, the nations still tolerate anarchy as a major principle of international conduct and uncontrolled exploitation governs the sapping of the earth's physical resources. Although mankind desperately needs revolutionary leadership, America rests in national stalemate, its goals ambiguous and tradition-bound instead of informed and clear, its democratic system apathetic and manipulated rather than "of, by, and for the people."

Not only did tarnish appear on our image of American virtue, not only did disillusion occur when the hypocrisy of American ideals was discovered, but we began to sense that what we had originally seen as the American Golden Age was actually the decline of an era. The worldwide outbreak of revolution against colonialism and imperialism, the entrenchment of totalitarian states, the menace of war, overpopulation, international disorder, supertechnology—these trends were testing the tenacity of our own commitment to democracy and freedom and our abilities to visualize their application to a world in upheaval.

Our work is guided by the sense that we may be the last generation in the experiment with living. But we are a minority—the vast majority of our people regard the temporary equilibriums of our society and world as eternally-functional parts. In this is perhaps the outstanding paradox: we ourselves are imbued with urgency, yet the message of our society is that there is no viable alternative to the present. Beneath the reassuring tones of the politicians, beneath the common opinion that America will "muddle through," beneath the stagnation of those who have closed their minds to the future, is the pervading feeling that there simply are no alternatives, that our times have witnessed the exhaustion not only of Utopias, but of any new departures as well. Feeling the press of complexity upon the emptiness of life, people are fearful of the thought that at any moment things might thrust out of control. They fear change itself, since change might smash whatever invisible framework seems to hold back chaos for them now. For most Americans, all crusades are suspect, threatening. The fact that each individual sees apathy in his fellows perpetuates the common reluctance to organize for change. The dominant institutions are complex enough to blunt the minds of their potential critics, and entrenched enough to swiftly dissipate or entirely repel the energies of protest and reform, thus limiting human expectancies. Then, too, we are a materially improved society, and by our own improvements we seem to have weakened the case for further change.

Some would have us believe that Americans feel contentment amidst prosperity—but might it not better be called a glaze above deeply-felt anxieties about their role in the new world? And if these anxieties produce a developed indifference to human affairs, do they not as well produce a yearning to believe there *is* an alternative to the present, that something *can* be done to change circumstances in the schools, the workplaces, the bureaucracies, the government? It is to this latter yearning, at once the spark and engine of change, that we direct our present appeal. The search for truly democratic alternatives to the present, and a commitment to social experimentation with them, is a worthy and fulfilling human enterprise, one which moves us and, we hope, others today. On such a basis do we offer this document of our convictions and analysis: as an effort in understanding and changing the conditions of humanity in the late twentieth century, an effort rooted in the ancient, still unfulfilled conception of man attaining determining influence over his circumstances of life. . . .

Basic Principles

A first task of any social movement is to convince people that the search for orienting theories and the creation of human values is complex but worthwhile. We are aware that to avoid platitudes we must analyze the concrete conditions of social order. But to direct such an analysis we must use the guideposts of basic principles. Our own social values involve conceptions of human beings, human relationships, and social systems.

We regard *men* as infinitely precious and possessed of unfulfilled capacities for reason, freedom, and love. In affirming these principles we are aware of countering perhaps the dominant conceptions of man in the twentieth century: that he is a thing to be manipulated, and that he is inherently incapable of directing his own affairs. We oppose the depersonalization that reduces human beings to the status of things—if anything, the brutalities of the twentieth century teach that means and ends are intimately related, that vague appeals to "posterity" cannot justify the mutilations of the present. We oppose, too, the doctrine of human incompetence because it rests essentially on the modern fact that men have been "competently" manipulated into incompetence—we see little reason why men cannot meet with increasing skill the complexities and responsibilities of their situation, if society is organized not for minority, but for majority, participation in decision-making.

Men have unrealized potential for self-cultivation, self-direction, self-understanding, and creativity. It is this potential that we regard as crucial and to which we appeal, not to the human potentiality for violence, unreason, and submission to authority. The goal of man and society should be human independence: a concern not with image or popularity but with finding a meaning in life that is personally authentic; a quality of mind not compulsively driven by a sense of powerlessness, nor one which unthinkingly adopts status values, nor one which represses all threats to its habits, but one which has full, spontaneous access to present and past experiences, one which easily unites the fragmented parts of personal history, one which openly faces problems which are troubling and unresolved; one with an intuitive awareness of possibilities, an active sense of curiosity, an ability and willingness to learn.

Student Protest

Mario Savio was one of the leaders of the Free Speech Movement, a protest movement by students at the University of California at Berkeley. The California revolt against campus regulations limiting student political activity inspired similar student protests at other colleges and universities during the 1960s. In a 1964 essay Savio describes the emergence of a new generation of student activists.

The university is the place where people begin seriously to question the conditions of their existence and raise the issue of whether they can be committed to the society they have been born into. After a long period of apathy during the fifties, students have begun not only to question but, having arrived at answers, to act on those answers. This is part of a growing understanding among many people in America that history has not ended, that a better society is possible, and that it is worth dying for. . . .

The most exciting things going on in America today are movements to change America. America is becoming ever more the Utopia of sterilized, automated contentment. The "futures" and "careers" for which American students now prepare are for the most part intellectual and moral wastelands. This chrome-plated consumers paradise would have us grow up to be well-behaved children. But an important minority of men and women coming to the front today have shown that they will die rather than be standardized, replaceable and irrelevant.

This kind of independence does not mean egotistic individualism—the object is not to have one's way so much as it is to have a way that is one's own. Nor do we deify man—we merely have faith in his potential.

Human relationships should involve fraternity and honesty. Human interdependence is contemporary fact; human brotherhood must be willed, however, as a condition of future survival and as the most appropriate form of social relations. Personal links between man and man are needed, especially to go beyond the partial and fragmentary bonds of function that bind men only as worker to worker, employer to employee, teacher to student, American to Russian.

Loneliness, estrangement, isolation describe the vast distance between man and man today. These dominant tendencies cannot be overcome by better personnel management, nor by improved gadgets, but only when a love of man overcomes the idolatrous worship of things by man. As the individualism we affirm is not egoism, the selflessness we affirm is not self-elimination. On the contrary, we believe in generosity of a kind that imprints one's unique individual qualities in the relation to other men, and to all human activity. Further, to dislike isolation is not to favor the abolition of privacy; the latter differs from isolation in that it occurs or is abolished according to individual will.

Defining Participatory Democracy

We would replace power rooted in possession, privilege, or circumstance by power and uniqueness rooted in love, reflectiveness, reason, and creativity. As a *social system* we seek the establishment of a democracy of individual participation, governed by two central aims: that the individual share in those social decisions determining the quality and direction of his life; that society be organized to encourage independence in men and provide the media for their common participation.

In a participatory democracy, the political life would be based in several root principles:

that decision-making of basic social consequence be carried on by public groupings;

that politics be seen positively, as the art of collectively creating an acceptable pattern of social relations;

that politics has the function of bringing people out of isolation and into community, thus being a necessary, though not sufficient, means of finding meaning in personal life;

that the political order should serve to clarify problems in a way instrumental to their solution; it should provide outlets for the expression of personal grievance and aspiration; opposing views should be organized so as to illuminate choices and facilitate the attainment of goals; channels should be commonly available to relate men to knowledge and to power so that private problems—from bad recreation facilities to personal alienation—are formulated as general issues.

123

The economic sphere would have as its basis the principles:

that work should involve incentives worthier than money or survival. It should be educative, not stultifying; creative, not mechanical; self-directed, not manipulated, encouraging independence, a respect for others, a sense of dignity, and a willingness to accept social responsibility, since it is this experience that has crucial influence on habits, perceptions, and individual ethics;

that the economic experience is so personally decisive that the individual must share in its full determination;

that the economy itself is of such social importance that its major resources and means of production should be open to democratic participation and subject to democratic social regulation.

Like the political and economic ones, major social institutions—cultural, educational, rehabilitative, and others—should be generally organized with the well-being and dignity of man as the essential measure of success.

In social change or interchange, we find violence to be abhorrent because it requires generally the transformation of the target, be it a human being or a community of people, into a depersonalized object of hate. It is imperative that the means of violence be abolished and the institutions—local, national, international—that encourage non-violence as a condition of conflict be developed.

These are our central values, in skeletal form. . . .

The bridge to political power . . . will be built through genuine cooperation, locally, nationally, and internationally, between a new left of young people and an awakening community of allies. In each community we must look within the university and act with confidence that we can be powerful, but we must look outwards to the less exotic but more lasting struggles for justice.

To turn these possibilities into realities will involve national efforts at university reform by an alliance of students and faculty. They must wrest control of the educational process from the administrative bureaucracy. They must make fraternal and functional contact with allies in labor, civil rights, and other liberal forces outside the campus. They must import major public issues into the curriculum—research and teaching on problems of war and peace is an outstanding example. They must make debate and controversy, not dull pedantic cant, the common style for educational life. They must consciously build a base for their assault upon the loci of power.

As students for a democratic society, we are committed to stimulating this kind of social movement, this kind of vision and program in campus and community across the country. If we appear to seek the unattainable, as it has been said, then let it be known that we do so to avoid the unimaginable.

VIEWPOINT 2

"So many college students 'go left' for the same reason that so many high-school students 'go delinquent.' They are bored. *"*

The Student Movement Stems from Boredom and Rebelliousness

Irving Kristol (b. 1920)

During the 1950s college students were called the "silent generation" because they tended to be conformist and rarely became involved in political activism. Few would use that term to describe students in the 1960s, as a significant number of students participated in various protest movements.

The actions of college students in 1964 at the University of California at Berkeley marked an important watershed in the rise of student activism in the 1960s. Over a period of several months, students engaged in several acts of organized protest, including rallies and the nonviolent occupation of an administration building. The Free Speech Movement (FSM), as the uprising came to be known, focused originally against campus restrictions on student political activity but eventually included other issues concerning both university life and American society in general. It served as a model for other mass demonstrations, student strikes, and other political protests in college campuses across the country. Although such activities only involved a minority of students, they attracted much attention from the media and American public.

The following viewpoint is excerpted from a November 1965 *Atlantic Monthly* article by Irving Kristol. A radical activist himself in his student days, by 1965 Kristol was a noted writer of increasingly conservative views. In the same year he cofounded the

Irving Kristol, "What's Bugging the Students?" *Atlantic Monthly*, 1965. Reprinted by permission of the author.

Public Interest, a journal whose articles criticized many governmental programs and ideological currents of the 1960s. In his *Atlantic* article, Kristol examines the events at Berkeley and other places and compares the current generation of student activists with the "silent generation" of the 1950s. He asserts that they lack a specific program of political reforms or ideas. Instead, Kristol concludes, most of the student activists are motivated to rebel by boredom and a desire to be unlike their parents. Critiquing the concept of "participatory democracy" that was an important part of Students for a Democratic Society's influential Port Huron Statement, he faults radical students for criticizing America while ignoring the injustices occurring in communist nations.

No one, except perhaps a few college administrators, mourns the passing of "the silent generation." But it must be said in its favor that at least one knew what the American university students of the 1950s were silent about, and why. They were conformist for plain, indeed, obvious and traditional, conformist reasons. We may have been distressed and vexed by this conformism; we were not mystified by it; whereas we are very much mystified by the nonconformism of the students of the sixties.

Many of the same middle-aged critics who so fervently and eloquently condemned the silent generation are now considerably upset and puzzled at the way students are "misbehaving" these days. One wanted the young to be idealistic, perhaps even somewhat radical, possibly even a bit militant—but not like this! It used to be said that the revolution devours its children. It now appears that these children have devoured this revolution.

What is it all about? One thing is fairly clear: the teach-ins, the sit-ins, the lay-downs, the mass picketing, and all the rest are not *merely* about Vietnam, or civil rights, or the size of classes at Berkeley, or the recognition of Red China. They are about these issues surely, and most sincerely. But there is, transparently, a passion behind the protests that refuses to be satisfied by the various topics which incite it. This passion reaches far beyond politics, as we ordinarily understand that term. Anyone who believes the turbulence will subside once we reach a settlement in Vietnam is in for a rude surprise. Similarly, anyone who thinks of present-day campus radicalism as a kind of overzealous political liberalism, whose extremism derives from nothing more than youthful high spirits, is deceiving himself. What we are witnessing is an event *in* American politics, but not *of* it.

No Radical Platform

Indeed, one of the most striking features of the new radicalism on the campus is that it is, in one sense, so apolitical. It is a strange experience to see a radical mood in search of a radical program; it is usually very much the other way around. These young American radicals are in the historically unique position of not being able to demand *a single piece of legislation* from their government—their "platform" is literally without one legislative plank. Their passion for "freedom now" coexists with a remarkable indifference to everything the United States government is doing, or might do, in this direction.

If one read every campus leaflet published . . . and attended every campus or off-campus demonstration, and knew only what one learned from these sources, one would hardly be aware that the Johnson Administration had enacted in the area of civil rights the most far-reaching reforms in a century of legislative history. There has been no campus meeting to celebrate the passage of the Civil Rights Act or the Voting Rights Act. There has not even been any meeting criticizing these laws for "not going far enough." It's as if nothing had happened—or, to put it more precisely, as if whatever happens in Washington has nothing to do with the world the students live and act in.

The same sort of thing is to be seen with regard to the war on poverty, a topic upon which students will declaim passionately and with unquestionable sincerity. But it seems that their passion is so pure, their sensibility so fine, that these would be violated by a consideration of anything so vulgar as how to get more money into poor people's pockets. The recent increase in social security and the medicare bill made their way through Congress without the benefit of so much as a benevolent nod from the campuses. Whenever I have mentioned this legislation in conversation, I have received an icy stare of incomprehension and disdain, as if I were some kind of political idiot who actually believed what he read in the *New York Times*.

Even in the single area where one would most expect specific and tangible proposals of reform, the organization of the multiversity, these have not made their appearance. For an entire year the students of the University of California at Berkeley have given dramatic evidence of dissatisfaction with their university experience—and does anyone know specifically what they would like, by way of improvement? The university officials certainly don't know, nor do the regents, nor do the faculty. Some outsiders *think* they know. Berkeley is too large, they say, too anonymous; there is no possibility of a face-to-face community of scholars, young and old. This is true enough. But the Riverside branch of this same university is a small liberal arts college, with great intimacy and comfort, and for the past decade it has had much difficulty in attracting enough students. They all want to go to Berkeley, and the reason, they will explain, is: "That is where the action is."

From Free Speech to Filthy Speech

Ronald Reagan, elected governor of California in 1966, expressed the feelings of many in a 1968 radio address on student demonstrators.

The people of California founded and generously support what has become the finest system of public higher education in the land. . . .

Generations of Californians have pursued knowledge within the widest range of disciplines. They have sampled widely of man's knowledge of man, of the history of his ideas and what he knows of the world around him.

This is the role of higher education in California. At least this has been the case up until recently.

Within the past five or six years, something new has been added—a violent strident something that has disturbed all of us; a something whose admitted purpose is to destroy or to capture and use society's institutions for its own purpose. I say "whose admitted purpose" because the leadership minces no words. It is boastful, arrogant and threatening. . . .

From the capture of a police car and negotiations conducted in an atmosphere of intimidation, threats and fear; we went from free speech to filthy speech.

The movement spread to other campuses. There has been general incitement against properly constituted law enforcement authorities and general trampling of the will, the rights and freedom of movement of the majority by the organized, militant, and highly vocal minority.

Though the causes were cloaked in the dignity of academic and other freedoms, they are—in fact—a lusting for power. Some protesters even marched under banners that ranged from the black flag of anarchy, the red flag of revolution, to the flags of enemies engaged in killing young Americans—the North Vietnamese and the Viet Cong.

The denunciations of the multiversity suspiciously resemble the way New Yorkers excoriate "megalopolis"—having come there in the first place, and determinedly remaining there, for no other reason than that New York *is* a megalopolis. All Americans will always insist that they adore small towns and detest great cities, but the movement of population from towns to cities remains strangely unaffected. And Berkeley, even today, has far more student applications than it can handle; one might even say, *especially* today, for I understand that the number of applications has, in fact, slightly increased.

An Existential Revolution

No, the upsurge of left-wing sentiment and left-wing opinion on the American campus today is not the sort of thing progressive parents and educators had in mind ten years ago when they benevolently urged students to become "socially committed" and "more idealistic." They naïvely wished them to have intelligent discussions of Vietnam, not to hurl insults and epithets at [American envoy] Averell Harriman (as happened at Cornell), or tear up their draft cards, or laud the Viet Cong. They wished them to be urbane and tolerant about sex, not to carry placards with dirty words, or demand the sale of contraceptives in the college bookstore. They wished them to be concerned for civic and social equality for the Negro, not to denounce "white America" as a pious fraud, whose "integration" did not differ essentially from South Africa's apartheid, or express sympathy with a mindless (if occasionally eloquent) black nationalism. They wished—they wished, in short, that their children be just like them, only a wee bit bolder and more enlightened. Instead, these children are making it very clear that being just like their parents, progressive or not, is the fate they wish most desperately to avoid.

And this, I think, is the crux of the matter. The new student radicalism is so fundamentally at odds with our conventional political categories because it is, above all, an *existentialist* revolt. The term is unfortunately chic, and ambiguous, too. But in this context it has a fairly definite meaning: the students are in rebellion, not so much because things are bad for them, or for others, but because things are what they are for them and for others.

Clues to the meaning of this rebellion may be found in two phrases that now appear ever more commonly in the left-wing campus vocabulary. The first is "organized America." The second is "participatory democracy."

Organized America

"Organized America" is, quite simply, America, and not, as one might think, some transient bureaucratic excrescence on the body of America. As a matter of fact, today's students are immensely skillful in coping with bureaucracies and their paper work. They fill out forms and applications with a briskness and competence that startle the middle-aged observer. (I would guess that no one over the age of forty could properly fill out a college application form unless he received guidance from some kindly youngster.) What bugs the students is not these trivia but the society they em-

anate from—the affluent society, welfare state and all. The liberalism (and the radicalism, too) of the 1930s and 1940s has borne its
fruit, and it tastes bitter to the children, setting their teeth on
edge. That is why American students, amidst reasonably general
prosperity and under a liberal Administration that is expanding
the welfare state more aggressively and successfully than anyone
had thought possible, feel more "alienated" than ever before. So
many college students "go left" for the same reason that so many
high-school students "go delinquent." *They are bored.* They see
their lives laid out neatly before them; they see themselves moving ahead sedately and more or less inexorably in their professional careers; they know that with a college degree even "failure" in their careers will represent no harsh punishment; they
know "it's all laid on"—and they react against this bourgeois
utopia their parents so ardently strove for.

One of the unforeseen consequences of the welfare state is that it
leaves so little room for personal idealism; another is that it mutes
the challenge to self-definition. All this is but another way of saying that it satisfies the anxieties of the middle-aged while stifling
the creative energies of the young. Practically every college student
these days understands what is meant by an "identity crisis": it is
one of the clichés of the sixties. It is not, perhaps, too much to say
that mass picketing on the campus is one of the last, conclusive
twitches of a slowly expiring American individualism.

American youth, however, has had one grand idealistic experience: the civil rights movement. This has been the formative experience for the activists of the 1960s; it is this movement that
gave them a sense of personal power and personal purpose; and
it is the civil rights movement which instructed them in the tactics of civil disobedience that are now resorted to at the drop of a
hat. Unfortunately, the civil rights movement has had one great
drawback: so far from being a proper "dissenting" movement, it
had behind it the President, Congress, the courts, the laws of the
land, and a majority of public opinion. This fact helps explain
why the younger militants have constantly pushed the movement toward "extremes"—for example, demanding utter, complete, and immediate *equality of condition* for the Negro, as against
mere equality of opportunity. Such equality of condition is what
"freedom now" has come to mean. And since this demand cannot
be fulfilled without repealing three centuries of history . . . there
is some satisfaction in such a maneuver. The trouble is that the
students do not know how to fulfill this demand either, and are
even running out of extremist slogans; which is why so many of
them are receptive to the idea of switching their attention to Vietnam, where they can be more splendidly, less ambiguously, in
"the opposition."

Participatory Democracy

A second theme of student radicalism today . . . is the idea of "participatory democracy." This is a vague notion, but a dynamic one. It expresses a profound hostility toward, and proposes an alternative to, everything that is impersonal, manipulative, "organized" in the American political process. Indeed, many of these students simply dismiss American democracy as a sham, a game played by the "power structure" for its own amusement and in its own interests. *True* democracy, they insist, can only mean direct democracy, where the people's will is expressed and legislated by the people themselves rather than by elected representatives, most of whom achieve office by deceit and retain office through the substantial support offered them by the vested interests.

One is reminded by this of nothing so much as the Russian Narodniki ("populists," our textbooks call them) of the end of the nineteenth century. They, too, were largely middle-class students who selflessly turned their backs on the careers the Czarist bureaucracy offered them. They, too, "returned to the people," leaving the fleshpots of Petrograd for the villages of the interior, much as our students leave their comfortable homes in New York or Chicago for Southern ghettos and slums. And they, too, were hostile to the nascent liberal institutions of their day, seeing political salvation only in a transformed and redeemed people rather than in improvements in any kind of system of representative government. It is also interesting to recall that, though they were as individuals the gentlest and most humane of their time, they nevertheless believed in the justice and efficacy of terrorism against the status quo and assassination against its spokesmen.

The analogy is, of course, very superficial: the United States today is not Czarist Russia of yesterday. But it is nevertheless illuminating, because it helps reveal the inner logic of the idea of "participatory democracy," a logic which proceeds from the most exemplary democratic premises to the most illiberal conclusions. Though few students these days learn it in their social studies course, the Founding Fathers of the American republic were exceedingly familiar with the idea of "participatory democracy"; as a matter of fact, this was what the word "democracy" usually meant prior to 1789. They rejected "participatory democracy" (they called it "direct democracy") in favor of "representative government" for two reasons. First, they didn't see how it could work in so large and complex a nation, as against a small city-state. Second, and more important, they thought it inconsistent with the idea of free government—that is, a government that respected the liberties of the individual. For participatory democracy requires that all people be fit to govern; and this in turn requires that all people *be made* fit to govern, by rigid and uniform educational training, constant public indoctrination, close supervision of private morals and beliefs, and so forth. No legislator can be as free as a private citizen, and to make all the people legislators is willy-nilly to abolish the category of private citizen altogether.

This, of course, is exactly what the Communists do, after their own fashion. They claim to exemplify a truer, more "direct," more "participatory," more "popular" democracy than is to be found in the representative institutions of the bourgeois West. The claim has a certain plausibility, in that regimes established by mass movements and mass revolutions certainly "involve the people" more than does any merely elected government. The semblance of "involvement" is perpetuated, as we know, through the mass organizations of the Communist state, and the fact that it is done under compulsion, and becomes more of a farce with every passing Communist year, is one of the inner contradictions both of the Communist system and of the myth of direct democracy itself.

These contradictions our left-wing students are not entirely unaware of. Though many of them are, to one degree or another, either pro-Communist or belligerently "neutralist," theirs is a very qualified and unconventional version of this attitude; which is why conventional anti-Communist propaganda tends to pass them by. They are, for instance, extraordinarily uninterested in the Soviet Union, and they become ever less interested to the degree that the Soviet Union liberalizes its regime—that is to say, to the extent that the Soviet Union becomes merely another "organized" system of rule.

What they seek is a pure and self-perpetuating popular revolution, not a "planned economy" or anything like that. And this is why they are so attracted to Castro's Cuba and Mao's China, countries where the popular revolution has not yet become "bourgeoisified." As for mass terror in Cuba and China—well, this actually may be taken as a kind of testimony to the ardor and authenticity of the regime's revolutionary fervor. Our radical students, like other radical students before them, find it possible to be genuinely heartsick at the injustices and brutalities of American society, while blandly approving of injustice and brutality committed elsewhere in the name of "the revolution."

Like other radical student generations before them, they are going to discover one day that their revolution, too, has been betrayed, that "organized society" is what revolutions establish as well as destroy. One hopes they will not be made too miserable by their disillusionment. One also hopes, it must be added, that they won't make *us* too miserable before that day arrives.

VIEWPOINT 3

"The hippies or the flower people . . . are nothing but people who've dropped these [societal] hangups."

Hippies Are Creating a Desirable Social Revolution

Sonny, interviewed by Lewis Yablonsky (b. 1925)

"Hippies," "freaks," and "flower children" were all names used to describe the young people who rejected traditional American values and lifestyles in regard to work, drugs, sex, money, and material goods. Young people living in counterculture enclaves during the 1960s shared a lifestyle that included drug experimentation, casual living and work arrangements, rock music, organic and macrobiotic foods, and "be-ins," which were celebratory gatherings or concerts held in parks and other public places. By 1967 hippies had become the focus of mass media scrutiny and, in some places, a tourist attraction.

Lewis Yablonsky was one of several social researchers to assess the counterculture and what it revealed about young Americans and their country. To research his 1968 book *The Hippie Trip*, the sociologist and professor at San Fernando Valley (California) State College observed the hippie scene firsthand. He spent several months in 1967 traveling to New York City's East Village, the Haight-Ashbury district of San Francisco, the Morningstar commune near Sebastopol, California, and other hippie strongholds, talking with many hippies and sharing their everyday life.

The following viewpoint is excerpted from an interview Yablonsky conducted with Sonny, one of several hippies he met while researching the counterculture in New York City. The viewpoint begins with Yablonsky introducing Sonny and setting the

From *The Hippie Trip* by Lewis Yablonsky (New York: Pegasus, 1968). Copyright 1968 by Lewis Yablonsky. Reprinted by permission of the author.

scene for the interview; the remainder consists of Sonny's answers to Yablonsky's questions about hippies and their values. Sonny argues that hippies are rejecting the repressive mainstream values of "square" American society and in doing so are creating a new way of life based on sharing, love, and openness.

In the crevices of the hippie movement are many unsung heroes. Stars who are not yet as glamorous and famous as Tim Leary has become in the popular mass media or Gridley Wright [a hippie who became a hero to many while on trial for marijuana possession] in the underground press. These lesser-known hippie high priests influence the novitiates and teenyboppers enormously. Their "rap" is delivered at all hours and in all hippie locales to youths seeking "the way" that they have found.

One young man of twenty-two who represents this significant role in the hippie movement was Sonny. . . . Sonny was introduced to me by my hippie guide Chuck as "a truly beautiful religious cat." After a brief discussion with him, I decided it would be important for me to get his "rap."

Sonny grew up in a wealthy eastern suburban town. His father was a $50,000-a-year executive. "My father is a proper super-straight cat who belongs to the right country club, drinks his share of the liquor on Saturday night, and is very taciturn, particularly when it comes to talking with his wife." His mother was "a standard hysterically square broad who pampered me to death." (Sonny, I later found out, prior to turning on to LSD and his hippie way of life, had attempted suicide around twenty times.)

Sonny seemed older than his twenty-two years, and was handsome by classic Hollywood standards in the image of Marlon Brando. He had a brilliant smile that he flashed on me many times during our brief but intense encounter. He had long black hair, wore a walrus mustache, and was properly festooned with beads, bells, and rough leather boots.

I interviewed Sonny in the Village pad of one of his disciples. He was enormously turned-on by some "great pot" he had recently smoked. Sonny's "rap" was for me a remarkably good summary of the hip philosophical sounds I had heard in many corners of [New York City's] East Village. Although some of what he says is a "repeat," the totality of his dialogue is a coherent statement of the hip life style and viewpoint in the East Village and other urban centers of the hippie world.

The Interview

S: I was a super-straight young man from respectable parents in a middle-class Roman Catholic home. We, of course, belonged to the country club. My eyes were on the commercial stars of America. I had a nice little sports car—the whole scene. Well, for a good period of time, I thought I'd be a marine biologist and I always had an interest in writing. It was kind of a toss-up between the two. I was going to be something very earth-shattering, very noble, very respected.

LY: What kind of hangups did you have? What things bugged you?

S: Oh, I had the typical hangups caused by psycho-repression and everything that every young person in America has—religious hangups, family hangups. I guess it would be easier to list the hangups I didn't have. I had the whole gamut of frustrations and indecisions that most young people in this country face. Most young people go through a period of indecision, doubt, rebellion, etc., and then figure, "Okay, fuck it. I'll accept everything."

LY: Did you ever get tangled up with any psychiatry?

S: Oh yeah, I had an out-of-sight psychiatrist! After the second time I quit college. My psychiatrist was probably the most neurotic man I ever met in my life. If you can picture a psychiatrist's office with a cross and crossed American flags underneath it, you get some idea of this man. To me he seemed very sick. I was fine when I came in, but he convinced me that I was out of my mind. I guess at the time I was going through a rather traumatic period where I still had the kind of held-over guilt feelings that are fostered from having a rather dogmatic world view pushed upon you. I still had emotional ties to that world view that had been drummed into me ever since I could begin to understand and comprehend. There was a very real conflict going on between, you know, my mind, my conscious mind and my subconscious mind . . . if you want to call it something like that. I'd get extremely uptight. I could see nothing but the hostility and anger that the people I cared for, my parents, were experiencing.

I had a very dark view of the world. I had already dropped out of college. My principal interest at that time had been philosophy and I traced Western philosophy to the point where I had absolutely smashed any positive view of the religious thing that I could have. I became wrapped up in despair and I suppose it became a kind of despair I liked. It became sort of an ever-present thing. It got to be too much and, you know, I slashed my arms and wrists. (I noticed around twenty slash-mark scars on his arms.)

LY: How many times did you try suicide?

S: Oh, I have absolutely no idea. I had the main hassle of our time.

My refusal to accept the life that my parents picked for me. Most parents within the society are doing something they don't really want to do. You know, there's always some dream that they always wanted, yet they can't do it. And they're caught up in a very materialized sort of game structure. And they excuse this or they rationalize that by saying, "Well, we're going through this so our children can have a better life." That's the excuse that every parent uses, you know, when he isn't leading the type of life that he'd like. And so, when a child grows up and decides that he doesn't want what they've had in their mind for him for all these years, they kind of forget that perhaps he has the right to decide his own form of life. And so you get into a real conflict with them and yourself at that point.

The whole society's based on a very egocentric form of game structure. All the games within the society are ego games. Of prime importance within this society is the self-image and the image presented to others. It just becomes a very paramount thing in everybody's life. It's influenced by movies. People try and be a movie star like John Wayne or somebody like that. They stroll down the street looking tough. They grab onto certain concepts of masculinity and femininity which have nothing to do with what's masculine at all . . . it's just a facade. This allows the self, or ego, to dominate feelings and true expressions. So you become not really yourself, but just kind of a shallow mirror image of some originally false idea. The games would break down if the people became aware that they are games. . . .

LSD

LY: When did you have your first LSD experience?

S: I guess it was about a year and a half ago.

LY: What did it do for you?

S: When I first began to take acid, I wasn't really ready. I was still in a kind of depressed, masochistic stage and it intensified that quite a bit. But eventually there came a period where I began to understand what acid was about and began to use it properly. The first thing it should be used for is to go through your own mind. To look at yourself from outside of yourself to see what kind of things are working in you that are fucking you up, that are making you a manic-depressive, or whatever form your insanity takes.

LY: Did you find anything specific you could put your finger on or was it a general reaction when you began to explore your own, I guess, inner space?

S: Well, I think the most specific thing I thought was that I'd been blind all my life to what is beautiful. You're surrounded so much in this society with what is ugly that it becomes almost the only aesthetic value you can judge. You can see the ugly. You can always see the ugly. If you want to you can get upset by it. People aren't raised to be willing to see the beautiful and I began to see the beautiful. I began to know things such as good karma. I began to be able to sit in the woods and feel a part of it . . . feel a part of nature . . . feel the oneness that is possible. I began to understand what love and beauty are all about.

The Hippie Movement

LY: In your opinion how did the hippie movement start?

S: The hippie movement, if you want to call it that, is a natural outgrowth of the 50's beatnik movement plus the important extra ingredient—acid.

Beat people like [Jack] Kerouac, [Henry] Miller, Gregory Corso, Allen Ginsburg are still with us. These are people who have become dissatisfied with American society and the American way of life. At that point, they were beginning to see the ridiculousness of it. That's pretty much all they were seeing. They were looking at the negative side of society and they weren't reacting really by trying to change anything positive. They were associated, of course, with the left. The beatnik movement of the 50's was basically just a commentary movement. A group of people expressing themselves principally through the arts. They said, "This is ridiculous, fuck it; we want no part of it."

Their rallying cry, if they had any, was the sexual revolution. Probably their best spokesman was Henry Miller. Their movement, if you want to judge it by the sexual revolution, was fairly successful—at least in this country. There's been a very definite change in sexual mores, particularly among young people.

That period is pretty much passed now. The junction point between what you might call the hippie world and the beatnik world of the previous generation was the introduction of LSD and other psychedelic drugs. Probably people became aware of it at first through [Aldous] Huxley's essays. LSD, mescaline, grass, have been on the scene almost forever but it's spreading now. And I would say that if the hippie movement has a rallying cry it would have to be the psychedelic-drug revolution.

Instead of people saying everything is shit and walking around with their eyes to the ground, kicking stones, mumbling curses under their breath, and adopting a very superior attitude, like "We know where it's at and nobody else does, and you people are too far gone to even approach it," you have, well, things like we just saw in Tompkins Square Park [in the East Village]— people with flowers on . . . you know, running around ringing bells. They're kind of happy.

It's been going on in small groups since the time of . . . Christ. It's nothing, I think, but people becoming aware of their humanness. People dropping off all the hangups and the frustrations that society has foisted upon them. Society exists, I think, almost as a third thing—as an entity in itself. For its own self-preservation and perpetuation it has to install certain attitudes within the people who are in it. These attitudes may be fine for maintaining *that* form of society and keeping *that* form of society alive and functioning. But it has a very real tendency to fuck up the personalities and the minds of the people within it.

The hippies or the flower people or whatever you want to call 'em are nothing but people who've dropped these hangups. People who can behave as children when they want to, unashamedly. And I don't think there is any human being alive who wouldn't want to just run and skip in the streets like a kid. Swing from light posts, climb trees. People who aren't afraid of loving each other. People who aren't suspicious.

Sharing

Friendship no longer becomes a thing of dominance, you know, where one friend dominates the other or where you're always suspicious that maybe someone's out to get you or knife you in the back. It's . . . it's just open. It's dropping all the false trappings of society.

If you need money or anything, you ask somebody for it. If you want to, people turn you on free. I went to three different places last night. Every place I went, I got stoned. I had some grass this morning so I found some people in the park and came up here and got nicely stoned. . . .

The concept now is to try and get away from trading and bartering. I kind of feel that everybody has one thing which they like to do. Sometimes more than one thing. One function that makes them happy. And to a lot of people that are here in the Village the only reason that they got the courage to come here is because that thing is in the arts. If you're serious about art, you can't really exist in this society because there's just no way to live. This society isn't geared for serious poets, artists, painters.

The people here have their thing. But there are also other people. For example, people down on Wall Street—maybe they would really dig being farmers. Nothing would make them more happy than to till the land, till the soil. To other people, they have a thing like they keep building things. All the frustrated little fix-it shops out in suburbia. Those people would really be happy if they could make something beautiful. And although it isn't very practical in this society now, or in the very near future, it's plausible to envision a society where everybody could just go out and "do their thing." The only way that that could work, each one doing his own thing, is if you do away with the whole concept of pay.

These ideas are working now. It's working down here and it's working in the communities and tribes out in the country. When you do your thing. If you dig farming, you give the food away, except for what you need to eat. If you're making things—chairs, tables, or anything like that—you give them away to those who need it. And if you need help on something, you just ask somebody, "Hey, I'm doing this today," and so they come and help you. It's sort of a total sharing.

I don't think it's a socialistic idea at all. I think it's more a humanist idea. And it will work 'cause it works down here. If you're hungry now, I'd tell you where to go where people have food. You just walk in the door and they'd give you a plate of food. If you wanted to get stoned now, I could tell you where to go.

LY: What you're talking about now has only really come about in the last six months or a year.

S: I'd say last year. This whole thing, we'll call it a movement, has grown so much in the last year it's unbelievable.

I've been traveling through college towns. The academic atmosphere is nice to visit every once in a while. The number of college students who are turning on to dope, love, and beauty is unbelievable! I can see it in the schools. The school I went to a year ago and returned to again last year has changed. It was textbooks before, now it's flowers and love.

LY: Do you think it's a real love?

S: Oh, well, speaking on a general basis is ridiculous. I can only take you out and show you people that I know. I undoubtedly have sort of surrounded myself with friends that have the same sort of ideas and feelings that I do.

The Reaction of Squares

LY: What is it that you see? How do you think square middle-class Mr. Jones is going to react to the hip movement?

S: It's not only Mr. Jones. Puerto Rican Mr. Gonzales is carrying a knife. I think that his reaction to it right now is one of basic hostility and anger. It stems a great deal from envy. I think a great deal of the hostility is because they're seeing people who are happy doing things that they've been told all their life will never make them happy. People in this society have been told you have to work eight hours a day or you won't eat. And there are people down here who are just happy in doing their thing. People who are not working for anybody in the Establishment are staying alive and they're eating.

They've been told that promiscuous sex is bad, so they have filled themselves with sexual frustration. They have all kinds of hangups and probably the most warped sexual fantasies that you could imagine. I know from some of the chicks down here who

139

get weird propositions from straight cats all the time.

LY: What do they come on with?

S: That whole thing is very negative and it's not really worth going into.

LY: You mean they're perverse sexual propositions?

S: Sure, perverse propositions. Their attitude of sex is basically a very sick one. Sex in this country is such a fantastically important thing. It's put on an unattainable pedestal and it has so many ties. It's a confused thing. It's almost designed to bring guilt. Most people don't enjoy it. They don't know what they're doing. They can't really have sex and be a part of it. Sex is a very human thing and it should be a very natural thing and a very beautiful

---

A Yearning for Love

Sociologist Lewis Yablonsky, in the concluding section of his 1968 book The Hippie Trip, *argues that hippies are perhaps the inevitable result of a society that has failed to provide a sense of meaning for many young Americans.*

The hippie movement beneath the surface carnival is a valiant attempt by a segment of American youths to achieve an intense condition of human creativity and LOVE. That their aspirations fall far short of their lofty goals may be more of a commentary on the spiritual poverty of the society in which the effort is taking place than on the feeble attempts at love acted out by the young affluent participants in the movement.

To freely paraphrase Voltaire: "If the hippies did not exist, we would invent them." The fact of the movement's existence reflects at least two conditions. One is that American society has failed to hold the life-style attention of a sizable number of youths who, although they have access to most of its material opportunities, remain frustrated and uncommitted. The other condition is that the hippie movement fills a spiritual and religious vacuum for its adherents and fellow travelers not satisfied by the overall social structure. Here Tim Leary's flippant comment on American religiosity is pertinent: "Religion is not a bunch of people getting up on Sunday morning, going down to a mortgaged building, and staring at the back of somebody's neck." The deeper human relationships of tribes, families, and friends are, in his viewpoint, more fundamental religious situations.

America might invent a hippie movement if it did not exist because apparently the yearning for creativity, humanism, and love, no matter how deeply buried in the plastic heart of the most robot-like psychopathic American, is a Homo sapiens trait that cannot be extinguished. There is a surge in this direction found in every record of society in human history. And the hippie movement may signal the beginning of a new American Renaissance of humanism.

thing which, for the most part in this society, it is not.

I don't mean sex in the sense of going out and getting laid—or going down to a bar, getting drunk, and then driving some chick out in your Chevrolet and, you know, screwing her in the back seat. Sex is a very beautiful thing, but in this society it isn't.

LY: Is it beautiful in hippie society?

S: For the most part, it is. It's free. It's natural. Nobody makes a big deal of it. It's not a big deal. It isn't the big, you know, all-important question. If a group of hippie males get together they really don't talk about some broad's bust size or who got laid last night. You know what locker-room conversation is like. I don't know whether you've ever played football and that, but the all-important questions are drinking and sex.

I'd like to go back to one question. You said, "What do you think the reaction of Mr. Jones will be?" And I think that's completely dependent on how the hippie attitude or the hippie movement, if you want to call it that, is expressed in the arts. It hasn't been expressed well, yet. The only way that people are going to understand what's happening is if they can understand the people who are a part of this. What they see now are bearded freaks.

They assume that all the bearded freaks take drugs. They don't differentiate between LSD, grass, cocaine, or cough medicine. They put them all in the same category and then imagine that we're all out to beat them, steal their color TV sets, and rape their daughters. So you know they're antagonistic.

A large number of people in the hippie movement are in the arts. Most of them are very bad, but most artists of any period are very bad. You only get a few very good ones. If artistically these ideas that are happening now, if the feelings that people are beginning to get now can be expressed, and expressed in such a way that not only other hippies will understand it but the straight people will understand it too, then perhaps there can be a meeting of minds. Perhaps if the harsh edge of hostility toward hippies by Mr. Jones was taken away, then when a hip person went through Ohio these people could see more than bearded freaks. If they can see people who are happy then the power of the movement is expressed to them.

The power of the movement is through artistic expression and through just being. That's what the Be-In concept is. The whole idea of a Be-In is just to have a whole bunch of hippies, or people who feel like this, in a group—happy and doing their thing. When straight people go by and see somebody else happy when they themselves aren't, maybe they'll begin to question why they aren't. . . .

LY: To go back to the community reaction thing—why do you think middle-class people are so hostile toward hippies?

S: Mr. Jones is hostile in large part because he sees joy and happiness where joy and happiness shouldn't be. He isn't so much worried about it for himself, but he's worried about it for his sons and daughters. Because Mr. Jones is basically not a happy person. Mr. Jones comes home at night, he's tired—he has a beer, he watches TV, and goes to bed. He gets up the next morning and goes through the same thing. Mr. Jones is caught up in a very depressing sort of life and he knows that his children would say that he is not basically a happy man. Mr. Jones drinks too much. He gets pissed off a lot. He grumbles and complains a lot.

And then he sees these people out there having fun. Mr. Jones doesn't believe, because he's very skeptical, that they're really happy. But he's afraid that his sons and daughters will see "the flower children" and believe that they really are happy. Perhaps his children do not want to grow up and be grumbling and mumbling like Mr. Jones. They may want to go out dancing in the streets and do what they want to do.

Right here on the East Side, if you want to speak about a very local matter, we're living in what basically is a ghetto. Predominantly Negro, Ukrainian, Puerto Rican, and hippie. Next to the hippies, the Puerto Ricans are the latest arrivals, so they're the poorest. And the ones with the most frustrations to take out on someone. They're pretty well boxed in and they don't have too much of a chance.

The hippies have been condemned by society, particularly since the [May 30, 1967] Tompkins Square incident [in which police beat hippies gathered at Tompkins Square Park]. That kind of showed the Puerto Ricans down here that the Establishment police say it's all right to hit a hippie. The hippies are bad. It's giving them a scapegoat. They can hit without getting hit back. There are no gangs of hippies walking the streets with switchblades who are going to, you know, get revenge. And now that they've seen that the police can beat hippies, they've found out that the law probably won't get after them for beating up a hippie or two—or cutting them. That's how you get this natural violent reaction.

LY: Where do you see the movement heading?

S: I see a lot of people coming to the rather obvious conclusion that cities are an unnatural place to live. Cities breed hostility. Cities as a human environment are architecturally negative. I think a lot of hip people are coming to the conclusion that the cities, for them at least, are a very unnatural way to live. And people who have the kind of ideas I've been telling you about have decided to get out into small tribes, find an open area of open land or woods somewhere, do their thing, and live in the country.

VIEWPOINT 4

"The hippies will not change America because change means pain, and the hippie subculture is rooted in the pleasure principle."

Hippies Are Not Creating a Desirable Social Revolution

Jack Newfield (b. 1939) and the Communications Company

The hippies of the 1960s engendered diverse reactions from the rest of America. Some viewed hippies as incisive social critics, while others considered them to be harmless young people making a spectacle of themselves. Others criticized hippies on a variety of counts. Many "squares" were affronted by the hippies' appearance and behavior; numerous Americans concurred with conservative California governor Ronald Reagan's description of a hippie: "His hair was cut like Tarzan, and he acted like Jane, and he smelled like Cheetah." However, hippies also received criticism from sources far less conservative than Reagan, as the following two-part viewpoint indicates.

Part I is taken from a 1967 article in the *Nation*, a periodical of the political left. The author is Jack Newfield, an early member of Students for a Democratic Society (SDS) and then an assistant editor of the *Village Voice*, a New York weekly liberal/radical newspaper. Newfield expresses some agreement with hippies and their views on American society, but he faults them for being politically inactive and for eschewing any effort to improve America. Transforming American society requires organized political work, such as that being done by SDS, he argues.

Part I: Jack Newfield, "One Cheer for the Hippies," *Nation*, June 26, 1967. Reprinted with permission from the *Nation* magazine; © The Nation Company, L.P. Part II: Communications Company, "Uncle Tim'$ Children," undated handbill distributed in the late sixties in the Haight-Ashbury district of San Francisco.

143

Part II of the viewpoint is taken from a leaflet distributed in the Haight-Ashbury district of San Francisco, the largest and most famous of the hippie enclaves. Among the institutions that made Haight-Ashbury a mecca for many hippies were the Diggers, a small anarchist group that provided free food, clothing, and medical care; the Psychedelic Shop, a store that sold incense, posters, and drug paraphernalia; and the *Oracle*, an underground newspaper noted for its colorful covers and its counterculture articles on drugs, politics, rock music, and mysticism.

Due in part to mass media coverage, Haight-Ashbury became a magnet for many teenage runaways, drug addicts and dealers, and curious onlookers during the 1967 "Summer of Love." The new arrivals were the primary target audience of a 1967 leaflet published by the Communications Company, an underground news organization that produced handbills on topics ranging from poetry to where to get free food. The leaflet reprinted here paints a bleak description of the conditions of Haight-Ashbury and severely criticizes the *Oracle* and LSD advocate Timothy Leary for spreading myths about the attractiveness of drug use and hippie life.

I

The hippies are happening. Ed Sanders of the [rock group] Fugs is on a cover of *Life*. Tulsa, Okla., which went for [Republican] Barry Goldwater by 30,000 votes [in the 1964 presidential election], recently had its first love-in. Gray Line sight-seeing buses detour through Haight-Ashbury to display the local "freaks" to the Babbitts. Squares (not hippies) pay $4 to see the psychedelic Billy Graham—Dr. Timothy Leary—preach his "turn on, tune in, dropout" sermons. . . . And the folk-rock group, Jefferson Airplane, has recorded a commercial for white Levi denims—even as 460 of that company's employees strike in Blue Ridge, Ga., against the chronically exploitive conditions of Southern textile mills.

Individually, the hippies are beautiful. They know a lot of things the squares don't. They know that marijuana is mildly pleasant and doesn't give you lung cancer; that Bob Dylan, John Lennon and Leonard Cohen are authentic poetic voices for all those who have grown up absurd; that it is better to make love than war; that most things taught in college must be unlearned later in life; that it is healthier to be spontaneous, communal and tolerant than repressed, materialistic and bigoted; and that it is groovy to read Herman Hesse, Snoopy and Allen Ginsberg.

All this being eagerly granted, the point must now be made that the hippies have been overrated. Their ultimate vision is in no way superior to that of the New Left, of [Norman] Mailer, [Albert] Camus or [Thomas] Pynchon. The hippies will not change America because change means pain, and the hippie subculture is rooted in the pleasure principle. They have an intellectual flabbiness that permits them to equate an original talent like Kenneth Anger with a put-on like Andy Warhol. For this reason they are vulnerable to the kind of exploitation symbolized by the Jefferson Airplane commercial. They lack the energy, stability and private pain to serve as the "new proletariat" that some in the New Left perceive them to be. Bananas, incense and pointing love rays toward the Pentagon have nothing to do with redeeming and renovating America; Leary's call to "drop out" is really a call to cop out.

The whole hippie contagion seems to be a recoil from the idea of politics itself; it is not merely apolitical but anti-political. "Civil rights is a game for squares," one hippie told me. "Why should I demonstrate to get the spades all the things I'm rejecting?" And the *Berkeley Barb*, one of the best of the dozen underground weeklies, scorned the April 15 [1967] anti-war Mobilization for being "deadly serious, militant and political."

Beats and the New Left

The hippies, in fact, have more in common with the nihilism of the 1950 beats than with the activism of their generational comrades in the New Left. The beats opted out of a repressive, materialistic society because they felt impotent to change it. Ike [President Dwight D. Eisenhower], McCarthyism, Korea, Madison Avenue, the cold war, the [electoral] defeats of [Adlai] Stevenson made politics appear impossible to the alienated young of the 1950s. Without hope, they sought escape by withdrawing into Eastern religions, sex, jazz, drugs and madness. It required foreign examples of effective student radicalism–in Korea, Japan, Cuba and Turkey, all in 1959—to inspire the young here.

The New Left took root in 1960 and 1961 because social change through political activism suddenly seemed possible with the election of John Kennedy. There were sit-ins, and lunch counters were desegregated. There were freedom rides, and bus terminals were desegregated. There were heroism and death in the Deep South, and a Civil Rights Act was drafted. There was a free-speech movement at Berkeley, and educational reform of the dehumanizing multiversity became a fashionable symposium topic.

145

SDS [Students for a Democratic Society] organized around the ideal of participatory democracy, and the "maximum feasible participation of the poor" clause was written into the [federal government's] anti-poverty program. For a time there appeared to be in Washington a higher moral authority which would respond humanely to protest.

But just as the beats did not develop in a vacuum, neither have the hippies; their growth has been in direct correlation to the country's drift to the right since the [1964] Gulf of Tonkin "incident" [that resulted in U.S. escalation in Vietnam] and the [1965] Watts "rebellion." The young who once idolized JFK perceive his successor—correctly, I think—as an anti-democratic manipulator who has stultified the possibility of change through dissenting politics. [President Lyndon B.] Johnson has become a depressing Ike figure and Vietnam the monstrously swollen equivalent of the Korean police action. In 1963 Bob Dylan sang of changes "blowin' in the wind"; today he chants: "Although the masters make the rules/for the wise men and the fools/I've got nothing Ma, to live up to." In 1962 more Harvard seniors wanted to volunteer for the Peace Corps than wanted to work for a large corporation; this is no longer the case. The Haight-Ashbury scene jumped into national prominence in the same month that the voters were sanctioning [conservative governors Ronald] Reagan, [George] Wallace and [Lester] Maddox, and the Vietnamese War turned a corner into its present open-ended escalation. Suddenly, it seemed more possible to change private reality with LSD than America's reality with SDS.

The Problems with Hippies

My own quarrel with the hippie ethic can be summarized in five arguments.

The first is that I don't think it will be permanently impossible to alter America through radical political action. The hippies seem to side with [French author Marquis de] Sade when he says: "And why should you care about the world outside? For me the only reality is imagination, the world inside myself. The revolution no longer interests me." But the New Left is closer to [French revolutionary Jean Paul] Marat, who answers in [playwright] Peter Weiss's *Marat/Sade*: "Against nature's silence I use action. . . . I don't watch unmoved; I intervene and say this and this are wrong, and I work to alter and improve them. The important thing is to pull yourself up by your own hair, to turn yourself inside out, and see the whole world with fresh eyes."

What the hippies forget is how unlikely social change seemed in 1957 and 1958. It took a new generation of kids, who had not read *On the Road*, to prove that America had not congealed into a static cage. Reform will become possible again, especially once the Vietnamese War ends. What the pleasure-oriented hippies can't accept is that political action is a painful, Sisyphean task that includes sacrifice, boredom and defeat.

My second point against the hippies is that precisely because they are *not a real threat to anything* they are used to goose a lifeless middle class, and are even widely imitated. Thus they create the illusion of influence when the jet set adopts their fashions, slang and music. But it is huckster America that profits by merchandising everything from "psychedelic salami" to "psychedelic earrings."

Hip Culture Oppresses Women

The Lower East Side Women's Liberation Collective, which consisted of thirteen women who were part of the counterculture in New York City's East Village, produced an essay in 1970 arguing that the hip scene retains traditional sexist role expectations for women.

Hip culture: be natural, be free, do your own thing, get rid of your middle class hang-ups, turn on, drop out. Groovy? But for who? Middle class white men can sometimes find individual solutions, but oppressed people can't. Women can't find individual solutions.

In the context of this society, escape is an illusion for both sexes. Dropping out is a game open only to middle class men—they can play at an alternative while still maintaining their class privilege in a class society. Oppressed people don't have the chips required to play and the deck is clearly stacked against women. In a society such as ours, run by a wealthy few, and based on the control, division and systematic oppression of all other people, doing your *own* thing changes nothing and in fact supports that society by default. Hippy culture is not revolutionary even though that is the packaging it's sold in.

Straight society—the Amerikan Death Trap—is a drag. Middle class values, morals and attitudes are repressive. Women as well as men do try to drop out, but for us it's different. We gain superficial freedoms—we can go without make-up or bras, we can smoke dope and act "unladylike." But our real situation is basically unchanged and in some cases worsened. In a society based on male domination the balance of power does not change just because the style of dress does. Basic male-female role definitions remain the same.

Third, the hippies think their vision of a drug-induced, homogenized love is an original panacea. One hippie even told me: "Man, I love everything. That fire hydrant, LBJ, Wallace, all them cats."

America is surely short of love, but the love the hippies invoke is so generalized and impersonal as to be meaningless. And as an observer I don't detect any greater love content in relations within the hippie subculture; they are just as exploitive and ego-centered and neurotic as the rest of us.

Fourth, the philosophical rationale the hippies cite for dropping out is that life is essentially absurd anyway, and since it has no meaning, it is pointless to try to change events. It is better, they say, again echoing Sade, to savor all possible personal experience instead.

Evidence certainly mounts to support an absurdist interpretation of recent history, beginning with the [Kennedy] assassination in Dallas, through the CIA's secret life, up to Byron de la Beckwith [the man accused of killing civil rights leader Medgar Evers] now running for lieutenant governor of Mississippi. Yet both [Jean-Paul] Sartre and Camus accepted—and then transcended— absurdity, and were able to embrace an even deeper engagement and commitment. Sartre and Camus did not "turn on and drop out" when the Nazis marched across France; they both joined the underground.

Finally, there is the dilemma of LSD. I have read several research papers and find much of the evidence is contradictory. Clearly, LSD has been useful, in a therapeutic sense, in treating problems like homosexuality, impotence and alcoholism. But LSD has also caused plenty of mental damage, recurring hallucinations, freak-outs and visits to hospital emergency wards by teeny-boppers who think they are giraffes. And, in general, the effect of acid on activists is to make them fugitives from the system, instead of insurgents against the system. Acid-heads tend to withdraw from politics (as Dr. Leary recommends), pursue private or politically unrealistic goals, and become disruptive if they remain inside activist organizations. They lack the patience and stability for the drudgery of organizing and scholarship.

The Alternative to Hippies

The alternative to the hippies remains the New Left, which, contrary to some reports, seems still to be growing. The spring semester indicated how deep the roots of student discontent have penetrated, with major campus rebellions at Long Island University, Texas, Drew University, Catholic University, Howard, Jackson State and Oklahoma. In May, card-carrying SDS members were freely elected student body presidents at Indiana and Northwestern. More than 350 students have signed an ad in the *Harvard Crimson* asserting that they will defy the draft. Vietnam Summer claims to have 2,000 organizers in the field.

Undeniably, the hippies represent an important break with the past and have considerable merit. Their musical innovations will, I suspect, ultimately prove as rich as the bop revolution forged . . . in the 1940s. The diggers, who run the indigenous mission halls for their hippie brethren, are closer to St. Francis than to Cardinal [Francis] Spellman.

But, finally, Dylan, pot and bright colors are the *hippies'* liberation. The poor, the voteless, the manipulated, the spiritually undernourished—they are oppressed by injustice that is crystallized in institutions. Only a radical political movement can liberate *them*. I want to save the squares too.

II

Pretty little 16-year-old middle-class chick comes to the Haight to see what it's all about and gets picked up by a 17-year-old street dealer who spends all day shooting her full of speed again and again, then feeds her 3000 mikes [micrograms of LSD] and raffles her temporarily unemployed body for the biggest Haight Street gang bang since night before last.

The politics and ethics of ecstasy.

Rape is as common as bullshit on Haight Street.

The Love Generation never sleeps.

The Oracle [a San Francisco underground newspaper] continues to recruit for this summer's Human Shit-In, but the psychedelic plastic flower and god's eye merchants, shocked by the discovery that increased population doesn't necessarily guarantee increased profits at all, have invented the Council for a Summer of Love to keep us all from interfering with commerce.

People Are Dying

Kids are starving on The Street. Minds and bodies are being maimed as we watch, a scale model of Vietnam. There are people—our people—dying hideous long deaths among us and the Council is planning alternative activities. Haight Street is ugly shitdeath and Alan Watts [a philosopher whose writings on Eastern philosophy were influential in the counterculture] suggests more elegant attire. . . .

The HIP Merchants—the cats who have sold our lovely little psychedelic community to the mass media, to the world, to you— are blithely & sincerely unaware of what they have done. They're as innocent as a busy-fingered blind man in a nudist colony. They don't see hunger, hip brutality, rape, gangbangs, gonorrhea, syphilis, theft, hunger, filth. They walk in their own beauty down Haight Street & if they see the shit at all, they deplore it & say that Somebody should do something about it. Sometimes they complain about shoplifting.

They do not realize that they & Uncle Timothy [Leary] have lured an army of children into a ghastly trap from which there is no visible escape. They do not see that they are destroying a whole generation of American youth. . . .

The Oracle, I admit, *has* done something to ease life on Haight Street; it's hired street kids to peddle the paper. Having with brilliant graphics and sophomoric prose urged millions of kids to Drop Out of school and jobs it now offers its dropouts menial jobs. That's hypocritical and shitty, but it's something. It means that a few dozen kids who can meet the Oracle's requirements can avert starvation whenever the Oracle comes out.

Groovy.

And why hasn't the man who *really* did it to us done something about the problem he has created? Why doesn't Doctor Timothy Leary help the Diggers? He's now at work on yet another Psychedelic Circus at $3.50 a head, presumably to raise enough cash to keep himself out of jail, and there isn't even a rumor that he's contributed any of the fortune he made with the last circus toward alleviating the misery of the psychedelphia he created.

Tune in, turn on, drop dead? One wonders. Are Leary and [Richard] Alpert and the Oracle all in the same greedy place? Does acid still have to be sold as hard as Madison Avenue still sells sex? What do these nice people mean by "Love"? . . .

Are you aware that Haight Street is just as bad as the squares say it is? Have you heard of the killings we've had on Haight Street? Have you seen dozens of hippies watching passively while some burly square beats another hippy to a psychedelic red pulp? Have you walked down Haight Street at dawn and seen and talked with the survivors?

The trouble is probably that the HIP shopkeepers have believed their own bullshit lies. They believe that acid is the answer & neither know nor care what the question is. They think dope is the easy road to God.

"Have you ever been raped?" they say. "Take acid & everything'll be groovy.

"Are you ill? Take acid & find inner health.

"Are you cold, sleeping in doorways at night? Take acid & discover your own inner warmth.

"Are you hungry? Take acid & transcend those mundane needs.

"You can't afford acid? Pardon me, I think I hear somebody calling me."

VIEWPOINT 5

"This was the true happening at Woodstock—the realization by . . . [those] who think of themselves as the first generation in a new age of peace, that they have a voice, a viable style, a community of trust."

Woodstock Proves the Viability of Countercultural Ideals

Margaret Mead (1901–1978)

Beginning with the "be-in" at San Francisco's Golden Gate Park in 1967, outdoor rock music festivals were, according to historian Timothy Miller, "the definitive gatherings of the countercultural faithful." The largest of these gatherings was Woodstock, a three-day event held in August 1969 on a farm in rural New York, close to the town of Bethel. The festival featured many famous rock bands and musicians of the time and drew approximately 400,000 people, many of whom gathered not only to hear the music but also to be with peers in a setting where counterculture values regarding drugs, sex, nudity, property, community, and other matters prevailed.

The significance of Woodstock in evaluating the future of the counterculture and America's youth was much debated in the nation's media. In the following viewpoint, published several months after the festival, noted anthropologist Margaret Mead reflects on the meaning of Woodstock. She maintains that the Woodstock festival was a positive achievement that signaled the emergence of a new generation of Americans whose differing values should not be condemned by others. Mead, whose research in the South Pacific and other places examined the question of how culture affects personality, was a prolific lecturer and commentator on social and gender issues.

Friday, August 15, 1969, was a hot, clear summer day. Even before the sun rose, long lines of cars—new cars and old cars painted with slogans, sports cars, Volkswagens, pickup trucks, jeeps, trailers, almost anything on wheels—converged on Route 17B, the road leading to Bethel, New York, where, on Max Yasgur's dairy farm, the stage was set for "three days of peace and music." Some 70,000 young people from all over the United States had paid $18 in advance to hear rock music at the Woodstock Music and Art Festival. Perhaps twice that number were expected in the course of the weekend.

The earliest arrivals on Friday discovered that they were not the firstcomers. Far and wide, fields and pastures already were dotted with tents and improvised arrangements for living in that green and smiling countryside. By seven o'clock in the morning every approach was clogged. The cars slowed, stopped, started and ground to a final halt. Now the only way into the festival was on foot. Four miles . . . eight miles . . . ten miles. Toting sleeping bags, knapsacks, shopping bags, hibachis, soft drinks, a bag of doughnuts, a can of beans, a couple of apples, the endless stream of boys and girls poured into the festival area and, always moving closer together, settled on the ground in the amphitheater.

The crew of technicians still was struggling with the massive sound system on the improvised stage. The gates intended to control admittance never were put up and the attempt to collect or sell tickets broke down almost at once. By noon the young producers accepted reality. The festival, they announced, was free and open to everyone there. The crowd cheered.

The first scheduled performers, caught in the jam, had to be airlifted in. (It was the helicopters that ensured mobility. Three had been planned for; eventually 12 were pressed into service.) And still the crowd poured in. No one knows what the total festival population was. The best-informed guess was about 400,000. And no one has even tried to guess how many thousands more were turned back on the crowded roads, far beyond walking distance.

Overnight, the young people told one another, a whole city, the third largest in New York State, had come into being—a fantastic city in which everything was improvised, drugs were omnipresent and anyone over 30 was out of place ("an uptight guy, you know, who wanted a drink"). Overnight, they said, almost as many came together there voluntarily as there were men involuntarily fighting the war in Vietnam. And while they sat through that first night, listening to the performers, rain poured down and the countryside was churned into a sea of red mud.

News Reports

The first news of the festival that reached Europe called it a catastrophe. I was in England, where the BBC was broadcasting harrowing accounts of the rioting going on in Northern Ireland between Catholics and Protestants. In almost the same tone of voice in which newscasters described that futile battle, in which some were killed and many were wounded, they told the listening world that a state of emergency had been declared in Bethel, where 300,000 (later half a million) young enthusiasts were in dire straits as a result of rain, lack of food, shelter and sanitation, rising disorder and the uncontrolled use of dangerous drugs.

It sounded extremely frightening. But the few pictures in the newspapers made me wonder. One, I remember, was of a young boy lying on the hood of a car—"out, asleep, drugged"—or perhaps just exhausted? Another photograph showed a young couple pushing a baby carriage across a field. Certainly the disaster—if it was a disaster—was happening in a universe very different from the one in which men could still murderously attack each other in the name of religion.

When I returned to New York three days later, the Woodstock story was being told and retold as young people, dazed and tired, drifted home. What might have been a disaster had turned instead into a kind of miracle. Listening to those who had been there, you heard wonder in their voices, saw it in their eyes, as they said, "We were all there together. It was beautiful."

No one denied the struggle merely to survive. That almost everyone did survive was part of the delight. Those who had been at Bethel talked freely about the lack of food and water. The mud. The breakdown of sanitation. The smell of garbage. The cuts and lacerations as thousands walked barefoot on the littered ground. The bad trips. And again the mud. ("Can you imagine my *parents* sitting on a wet sleeping bag for two nights and two days?") The crowds. ("They kept saying, 'Remember, the guy next to you is your brother,' and we did!") And when I asked what it meant to them, the answer was almost always: "We were there."

Like most other adults—the local people who sent in truckloads of food, the doctors who came in to look after the injured and the sick, the police who concentrated on keeping the roads open, the photographers who brought back their way-out pictures and those who only listened afterward—I was convinced. Something very good happened at Woodstock. In spite of everything, the young people achieved what they had gone there for—three days of peace and music. Even those who never heard the music.

When my contemporaries tried to say what it was all about, they were puzzled. Most people, of course, marveled at the absence of fighting, the almost total absence of any kind of violence in a situation in which, it would seem, the smallest incident might have touched off a riot. But putting it like this, negatively, somehow misses the point.

This is a generation that can be fierce and angry on behalf of others. They have marched in sympathy with the children in the ghettos, in protest against the war and the killing in Vietnam, to rouse others to the plight of children in Biafra. And when they are led to expect violence, they react violently. Excluded from planning that involves their lives, feared, scorned and provoked, the young strike back and shout words that in turn provoke and horrify.

On this occasion the extraordinary thing was their spontaneous gentleness. They had come of their own free will, because everyone who cared would be there and it was a way of showing one belonged. Strangers for the most part, they spoke the language of people who trust one another.

The sheer size of the crowd astonished everyone. But after all, such huge gatherings are not unknown. The best parallels are the great religious pilgrimages—the medieval Christian pilgrims who traveled from all parts of Europe to Santiago de Compostela, in northwestern Spain; or, today, the Moslems who, in enormous crowds, make the journey to Mecca; or the orthodox Hindus who go to bathe ceremonially in the Ganges River.

There is one very striking difference, however. In the case of religious pilgrimages, tradition sets the style of behavior in every detail. Hostels exist to receive the pilgrims and strict rules are enforced to protect their safety.

Crises and Improvisations

In contrast, at the Woodstock festival everyone was on his own and each crisis called for some new improvisation. Looked at superficially, the whole thing had the appearance of something created overnight. The emphasis on spontaneity, the lack of overt forms of organization and the unexpectedness of what happened blind us to the fact that there was a kind of structure, an image of what it was to be together. Because of it, people survived and the occasion had deep meaning for them.

True, the facilities originally provided turned out to be totally inadequate, but crises were met. Extra helicopters were found. Doctors and medical supplies were flown in. The roads were kept open; no one felt trapped. Members of the Hog Farm commune and others like them, only a little older and more experienced

A Coming Revolution

Andrew Kopkind, a journalist sympathetic to the New Left, wrote about Woodstock in Hard Times. *He contends that the festival dramatized the emergence of a "new culture of opposition" in America.*

Although the outside press saw only masses, inside the differentiation was more impressive. Maybe half the crowd was weekend-hip, out from Long Island for a quick dip in the compelling sea of freaks. The other half had longer been immersed. It was composed of tribes dedicated to whatever gods now seem effective and whatever myths produce the energy needed to survive: Meher Baba, Mother Earth, street-fighting man, Janis Joplin, Atlantis, Jimi Hendrix, Che. . . .

No one in this country in this century had ever seen a "society" so free of repression. Everyone swam nude in the lake, balling was easier than getting breakfast, and the "pigs" just smiled and passed out the oats. For people who had never glimpsed the intense communitarian closeness of a militant struggle—People's Park or Paris in the month of May or Cuba—Woodstock must always be their model of how good we will all feel after the revolution.

So it was an illusion and it wasn't. For all but the hard core, the ball and the balling is over; the hassles begin again. . . . The repression-free weekend was provided by promoters as a way to increase their take and it will not be repeated unless future profits are guaranteed. . . .

What is not illusionary is the reality of a new culture of opposition. It grows out of the disintegration of the old forms, the vinyl and aerosol institutions that carry all the inane and destructive values of privatism, competition, commercialism, profitability and elitism. The new culture has yet to produce its own institutions on a mass scale; it controls none of the resources to do so. For the moment, it must be content—or discontent—to feed the swinging sectors of the old system with new ideas, with rock and dope and love and openness. Then it all comes back, from Columbia Records or Hollywood or Bloomingdale's in perverted and degraded forms. But something will survive, because there's no drug on earth to dispel the nausea. It's not a "youth thing" now but a generational event; chronological age is only the current phase. Mass politics, it's clear, can't yet be organized around the nausea; political radicals have to see the cultural revolution as a sea in which they can swim, like black militants in "black culture." But the urges are roaming, and when the dope freaks and nude swimmers and loveniks and ecological cultists and music groovers find out that they have to fight for love, all fucking hell will break loose.

than most members of the audience, fed the hungry, counseled the distressed, helped care for the sick and those whose experiments with drugs miscarried.

Above all there were the voices, sometimes identified and sometimes anonymous, that rang out between performances, telling the lost where to find their friends and keeping everyone in communication.

This, it seems to me, provides a key to understanding why it was that the young who lived through it all could say, "It was beautiful." The planning, the improvisation, the stream of communication about what was happening, were part of the event itself. Those who carried the main responsibilities were also very young, and from this emerged the sense that everyone spoke the same intelligible language.

This was the true happening at Woodstock—the realization by these "Aquarians," who think of themselves as the first generation in a new age of peace, that they have a voice, a viable style, a community of trust.

What does this mean for the future?

It must be admitted that Woodstock might have been a disaster but for two things, one an accident and the other owing to the exercise of intelligence, that can be elaborated on. The accident was the rain. The young, in addition to being numerous and gentle, in search of music and peace, were drenched. Chilled, exhausted but still enthusiastic, they moved the hearts of everyone. Moreover, the rain kept away many of the television cameras (and so, also, hordes of merely curious sightseers) until it was all over. It was the kind of accident one cannot count on happening twice.

The second circumstance was that the responsibility for the festival was in the hands of young people who could think, respond and plan in the style of the audience. The very acuteness of the crisis also meant that they remained in responsible control. Their choice of a location, away from a large, settled community, turned out to be the only feasible one. Their choice of musicians drew the crowd. The choice of the Hog Farmers and others like them to act as intermediaries made sense to everyone. Their protective use of human resources probably saved the situation.

This is something others can build on, not only for other festivals but also for any event in which masses of young people are involved. With the responsibility in their own hands, they worked things out. It all made sense.

But it must also be admitted that there was tremendous inadvertent destruction of property. Farmers' fields were trampled, their fences burned for fuel, their crops looted and destroyed—all things that farmers do not take to kindly. The astonishing thing is that these very real losses caused so little rancor and led to almost no immediate reprisals. Instead, a very large number of people responded to trust on a massive scale with trust and friendliness. "They were such nice kids!"

In these circumstances most accidental destruction can be avoided. We have the technology to set up, if we will, the necessary facilities for caring for the needs of an enormous temporary "city." We have the human resources to protect the citizens of such a city and those among whom they come. If great gatherings of this kind are part of the style of living of present-day young people, we can ensure their safety.

But I believe we must differentiate between facilitation and exploitation. The crowds that gathered at this festival, part of an affluent generation that has seldom been cold or hungry except by choice, found the hardships exhilarating. The message they got was that this was a spontaneous, uncommercialized event. We must help them keep it so; to do otherwise would be to destroy what is at the heart of the event.

The Lesson of Woodstock

For older people the lesson of Woodstock is that such gatherings do have structure, however invisible it is to the eyes of members of another generation. But no outsider—who does not speak the language, who cannot set the pace, who does not move with the rhythm of those involved—can foresee what will be needed long ahead or from hour to hour. The responsibility must be in the hands of those who, as members of the whole generation group, are creating the new style as they all move together. This is the reality of a new kind of world that only a new generation can bring into being.

I do not think the Woodstock festival was a "miracle"—something that can happen only once. Nor do I think that those who took part in it established a tradition overnight—a way of doing things that sets the pattern of future events. It was confirmation that this generation has, and realizes that it has, its own identity.

No one can say what the outcome will be; it is too new. Responding to their gentleness, I think of the words "Consider the lilies of the field . . ." and hope that we—and they themselves—can continue to trust the community of feeling that made so many say of those three days, "It was beautiful."

*"Woodstock . . . was only a moment of glorious
innocence, and such moments happen only by accident,
and then not often."*

Woodstock Does Not
Prove the Viability of
Countercultural Ideals

Philip P. Ardery Jr. (dates unknown)

The Woodstock rock festival, which created an instant city of
400,000 people at a farm in New York for three days in August
1969, marked a symbolic high point of the 1960s counterculture.
Many participants and observers praised the festival as a realization of a nonviolent and attractive community based on counterculture values. Some, such as activist and writer Abbie Hoffman,
spoke of an emerging "Woodstock nation" of disaffected young
Americans.

In the following viewpoint, Philip P. Ardery Jr., then an editorial staff member of the conservative periodical *National Review*,
argues against such interpretations of the meaning of Woodstock.
Describing some of his own experiences while attending the festival, he maintains that the spirit of community found there was in
large measure the normal response of any people who need to cooperate to overcome predicaments such as food shortages and
rain. Ardery concludes that the Woodstock experience does not
indicate that a hippie counterculture is becoming a significant social force in America.

Philip P. Ardery Jr., "Upon a Time in Woodstock," *National Review*, September 9, 1969; © 1969
by National Review, Inc., 150 E. 35th St., New York, NY 10016. Reprinted by permission.

No stars that night over our outdoor city, and we, a half million of us, sat fitfully up in our amphitheater turned bog, hearing singers and guitars below but not really listening. Behind the stage, across a country road, a field stretched out, the fence around it laced with a string of red Christmas tree bulbs—our own, private constellation. The lights, blurred by rain, glowed eerily and took our attention, because sound was there too, a whipping whine, much louder than the music. A spotlight shot its bright cone earthward, a visible sign of something hovering, blowing up wet grass, and then, finally, touching down. Many in our city—who knows why?—suddenly broke into applause.

One young man, half-high on marijuana, offered a stoned reading of the scene: "You see, the Martians announced they would pay earth a visit, and all these people came out to greet them, and some bands got together to play a few songs of welcome." Far. Out. But then the scene, like other scenes during those three days, invited wild interpretations. The Woodstock Music and Art Fair fit no one's expectations, and we groped to give it form and purpose—and continued groping until the end.

True, the focus, the central interest of the weekend was not this landing on the helipad. But then—and this created our confusion—neither was it the music, the single attraction that had lured one of every seventy Americans from fifteen to 25 to an isolated New York farm. So many came to listen that we overwhelmed the performers, however well some of them played. Our cars, our tents and ourselves improvised a city, twenty-second largest in the United States, and the fact of this city, its weather, its privations, its confusion and its civility, dominated our senses. We shared a formless experience, one we had not prepared for, and it gratified immensely.

There are, really, only three groups of people who disapproved our pleasure. First, and justifiably, the farmers and townspeople of upstate New York, who did not engineer their own inconvenience. Our improvised city, without enough land, shelter, food, warmth or sanitation to sustain itself, took over their roads, parked its cars on their lawns, pitched its tents in their fields, rustled their crops, stole their fenceposts for firewood, used their creeks as garbage dumps and latrines. We wronged them. Eight thousand of us hung around on Monday to clean up, make amends.

The Political Left

The Left, too, hated the Fair, what it was supposed to be and what it actually was. The idea of holding it was an affront, a fantastic wager that the revolution of youth is far less political than cultural. Eight, maybe ten thousand people swept into Chicago last summer [1968] to see Hubert Humphrey and Richard Daley. Nowhere, New York, offered Jimi Hendrix and Janis Joplin, and the promoters needed 200,000 customers to break even on their investment. When the bet paid off too handsomely (our overlarge crowd broke down the gates, the ushers never sold or collected tickets, the promoters lost more than $1 million), and, swelled to city size, we transformed ourselves from an audience for music into participants in a muddy void, we filled that void not with rebellion and angry talk but with drugs and quiet friendship. Our uninvolvement, our frivolity maddened the Left. We did not even collect pennies for SANE [Committee for a SANE Nuclear Policy].

A Peaceful Mob

Some locals, the Left—and then many ordinary Americans disliked us too. Our city's drugs were illegal. Its citizens unkempt. And, worst of all, the city was a mob, the nemesis of all purposeful men, all believers in American individualism. But it was not planned that way. Most of us by far had come for music, to enjoy a one-to-one relationship with the stage, not to be lost in a muddy commune. Else why would we have chosen Woodstock? There have been other festivals this summer, and hundreds of "be-ins," but none drew close to our half million. None offered so many fine musicians.

We became a mob, but only because our extreme disorientation, our fear of being trapped there, the pleas to share, be cool, *it's the only way to make it*, forced a collective consciousness upon us. What made us a mob made us good, too, because our fears and needs pushed the limits of togetherness beyond our city of peers, to the gracious and generous police and townspeople. The worst of us learned that cops and rednecks are more angel than pig.

Our city depended on them, and they on us. We behaved well so that the squares could help us survive. Doctors healed wounds, treated illnesses, smoothed out rough "trips." Police helicopters flew in our food, flew out our sick. Farmers shared their produce. And the promoters, after having made the one gigantic mistake of conceiving the idea of Woodstock, spared no expense to make us less uncomfortable, even when they knew we had robbed them of their profit.

Hippies Reborn?

The few very hip ones among us came away from it all positively glowing. Had not the rest of us failed to find purpose in being there, had not we simply existed communally, and yet enjoyed it? It seemed to some that the ideal hippie, killed in San

Mass Infantilism

William A. Rusher, an editor for the National Review, *responded to Philip P. Ardery's article on the Woodstock festival with a column of his own, in which he criticized those who were at the festival for their immaturity.*

The truth is that what we saw at Bethel [Woodstock] was just the biggest expression to date of a phenomenon newly brought into being by America's rapid population growth, coupled with widespread affluence. The phenomenon is best described as "mass infantilism," for it is precisely that: the impulsive, simplistic drives of children, acted out on a far larger scale (and in many cases, I might add, by far older people) than we have ever seen before.

The young have always had, and probably will always have, a natural hankering for a less demanding, more accommodating world—a world in which the charms of irresponsibility are not so harshly penalized.

What has happened recently is that the absolute number of such young people (including a good many semipermanent "children" with impressive beards) has reached a critical mass at which these inchoate universal yearnings can be organized, up to certain low levels, and euphoniously articulated (if nobody very critical happens to be listening). The process has been aided very substantially indeed by the high level of prosperity reached in the American society. These youngsters have the time (either they are not working at all, or not working very hard); they have the money; they have the transportation. They have, in short, everything it takes to indulge themselves in one vast paroxysm of mass infantilism—leaving it to the squares, of course, to feed them when they hunger, and doctor them when they bleed, and nurse them back from "bad trips," and clean up after them when they're gone.

And they have one other thing, too, not quite so childlike: the quiet, smiling grace of the passive aggressor. No doubt Mr. Ardery is right when he protests that the *size* of the Bethel festival "wasn't planned." But you can be sure the confrontation was: the calculated affronting of square, stupid, old middle-class America with new and dubious values in far more than just music.

That is why there is a part of me that would cheerfully have salted a few of those tender young behinds with birdshot, if I had owned a farm in Sullivan County. But the rest of me is proud of the good burghers who chose, instead, to sweat it out gamely till they were gone, and then to pick up the threads of their own disregarded lives and go on with the serious business of living. Let's hope that next day, at the Bethel Post Office, there were some letters from sons and husbands in Vietnam that made it all seem worthwhile.

From William A. Rusher, "Mass Infantilism, Anyone?" *National Review*, October 7, 1969; © 1969 by National Review, Inc., 150 E. 35th St., New York, NY 10016. Reprinted by permission.

Francisco by methadrine and angry politics, had been reborn, and in such numbers that he might survive, multiply, maybe even prevail.

But that—the root of the individualist's fear—is making too much of Woodstock. It was only a moment of glorious innocence, and such moments happen only by accident, and then not often. Had everyone known we would be a city, there would have been more toilets, more food, more tents, more water, more comfort generally. And therefore less confusion and fear, less need to band together and be good. Had the East Coast known there would be a complete electrical failure on November 9, 1965, workers would have stayed at home, housewives would have stockpiled canned foods and candles, and no puzzled, gay and loving people would have flooded downtown streets.

And these accidental bursts of aimless solidarity do not last forever. America take heart. By Sunday afternoon, most of us had abandoned Woodstock, eager for a return to form, purpose and individuality. The same thousands who waved gaily from their cars, hardly creeping away from the mudpile, were driving furiously and honking horns by the time they got back to New York City.

CHAPTER 4

Social Unrest and Movements for Equality

Chapter Preface

The growth and evolution of the black civil rights movement was one of the key developments of the 1960s, not only for what it achieved for African Americans, but also for what it inspired among other minority groups in American society. During the 1960s many groups—blacks, women, Hispanics, American Indians, gays and lesbians, and others—took unprecedented steps to protest their exclusion from the American political mainstream and to demand respect and fair treatment. The activism of these groups contributed to the turbulent nature of the decade.

The civil rights movement was a response to institutionalized racial discrimination that blacks faced in most parts of the United States. In the South, well into the 1950s, an intricate system of legalized segregation (called Jim Crow) confined blacks to separate and inferior schools, public facilities, and neighborhoods. Although not subject to such blatant segregation, African Americans in other regions were often denied equal access to jobs, housing, education, and political power because of their race.

By the early 1960s the civil rights movement had succeeded in placing the condition of black Americans at the forefront of national attention. The movement by then had evolved into two distinct wings. The National Association for the Advancement of Colored People (NAACP), for decades the nation's preeminent civil rights group, sought to overturn segregation laws and attain civil rights through legal challenges and political lobbying. Newer organizations, including the Southern Christian Leadership Conference (SCLC), the Student Nonviolent Coordinating Committee (SNCC), and the Congress of Racial Equality (CORE), attracted more militant and impatient activists who utilized more direct and confrontational tactics, such as mass public protests and nonviolent civil disobedience of segregation laws. Despite their differences, the various civil rights organizations shared the same goal of a racially integrated society; toward that end, they included people of all races as members. Their work was essential in securing the passage of the 1964 Civil Rights Act (barring racial discrimination in employment and public facilities) and the 1965 Voting Rights Act (empowering the federal government to ensure that blacks were not denied their right to vote).

Despite the passage of these two historic laws, by the mid-1960s many blacks—both within and outside the civil rights movement—were unsatisfied with the progress of the civil rights cause. Some groups, including both SNCC and CORE, eventually rejected the goal of a racially integrated and color-blind society and expelled their white members. For many blacks, the separatist ideological goal of "black power" replaced the previous demand for racial inclusion as the best means for African Americans to control their own destinies and communities.

Both the civil rights movement and the subsequent cry for "black power" inspired other groups to engage in political and social activism. In California, for example, labor organizer Cesar Chavez led a strike and nationwide grape boycott to raise wages for Mexican-American farmworkers. Calling for "red power," American Indians engaged in militant protests and formed the National Indian Youth Council (NIYC) and the American Indian Movement (AIM). Gay men and lesbians became increasingly open about their sexual orientation and endeavored to secure their rights following the 1969 Stonewall riot in New York City (which was prompted by a police raid on a gay bar).

The civil rights movement also inspired the revitalization of the feminist movement, which had become almost inactive following its 1920 victory in securing women's right to vote. Despite gaining suffrage, women had continued to face significant discrimination in education, employment, and legal matters. In the 1960s, however, several developments—including the growing numbers of women in higher education, the availability of the birth-control pill, a decline in the birthrate, and the increasing numbers of women in the workforce—led many women to question the commonly held belief that women should be housewives and mothers. Many of these women had participated in the civil rights movement; their feminist activism was in part an extension of the civil rights movement's vision of equality and in part a reaction to the sexism women encountered within the movement.

As the feminist movement developed, it divided in a manner similar to the civil rights movement. The National Organization for Women (NOW) was formed in 1966 to litigate and lobby against gender discrimination and for equal rights under the law; it was in some respects the feminist equivalent of the NAACP. More radical "women's liberation" groups, which began to emerge toward the end of the 1960s, argued that NOW's focus on political change failed to take into account the way women were subordinated by traditional gender roles. Many sought to change or even abolish marriage, which they considered an oppressive and sexist institution. Some rejected male companionship entirely, arguing that all men were the source of women's oppression.

The feminist movement of the late 1960s and the civil rights movement of the early 1960s changed both laws and social attitudes in America, and in so doing created some of the most enduring legacies of that decade. Their achievements, controversial then, are still being debated today.

165

"I have a dream that one day this nation will rise up and live out the true meaning of its creed: 'We hold these truths to be self-evident; that all men are created equal.'"

The Civil Rights Struggle Brings Hope for Black Americans

Martin Luther King Jr. (1929–1968)

On August 28, 1963, more than two hundred thousand people gathered in front of the Lincoln Memorial in Washington, D.C., to demonstrate for civil rights. The event marked a high point for the civil rights movement—a campaign of nonviolent confrontations and protests staged by African Americans and their supporters to end laws and customs of racial discrimination and segregation. For many the most inspirational part of the demonstration—and the civil rights movement as a whole—was Martin Luther King Jr.'s "I Have a Dream" speech, reprinted here.

King, a Baptist minister, first came to national prominence in 1955 in Montgomery, Alabama, when he helped lead an organized boycott of the city's buses in protest of discriminatory seating rules. In numerous sermons, speeches, and writings over the next several years, King helped establish the basic philosophy of the civil rights movement. Among the ideas he stressed were the fundamental injustice of racial segregation, the necessity for civil disobedience to laws viewed as wrong, and the paramount importance of using nonviolent tactics when confronting an unjust society. All these elements can be found in King's speech, which in many ways epitomizes the optimistic spirit of the civil rights movement of the early 1960s. Although he recognizes that activists have undergone great hardships, King asserts that the just and racially inclusive America envisioned by the movement is indeed possible. For the rest of his life, King continued to work toward his vision of an inclusive America attained by nonviolent means; his assassination in 1968 shocked and saddened many Americans.

Five score years ago, a great American, in whose symbolic shadow we stand, signed the Emancipation Proclamation. This momentous decree came as a great beacon light of hope to millions of Negro slaves who had been seared in the flames of withering injustice. It came as a joyous daybreak to end the long night of captivity.

But one hundred years later, we must face the tragic fact that the Negro is still not free. One hundred years later, the life of the Negro is still sadly crippled by the manacles of segregation and the chains of discrimination. One hundred years later, the Negro lives on a lonely island of poverty in the midst of a vast ocean of material prosperity. One hundred years later, the Negro is still languished in the corners of American society and finds himself an exile in his own land. So we have come here today to dramatize an appalling condition.

In a sense we have come to our nation's Capital to cash a check. When the architects of our republic wrote the magnificent words of the Constitution and the Declaration of Independence, they were signing a promissory note to which every American was to fall heir. This note was a promise that all men would be guaranteed the unalienable rights of life, liberty, and the pursuit of happiness.

It is obvious today that America has defaulted on this promissory note insofar as her citizens of color are concerned. Instead of honoring this sacred obligation, America has given the Negro people a bad check; a check which has come back marked "insufficient funds." But we refuse to believe that the bank of justice is bankrupt. We refuse to believe that there are insufficient funds in the great vaults of opportunity of this nation. So we have come to cash this check—a check that will give us upon demand the riches of freedom and the security of justice. We have also come to this hallowed spot to remind America of the fierce urgency of *now*. This is no time to engage in the luxury of cooling off or to take the tranquilizing drug of gradualism. *Now* is the time to make real the promises of Democracy. *Now* is the time to rise from the dark and desolate valley of segregation to the sunlit path of racial justice.

Martin Luther King Jr.'s speech was one of the highlights of the 1963 March on Washington.

Now is the time to open the doors of opportunity to all of God's children. *Now* is the time to lift our nation from the quicksands of racial injustice to the solid rock of brotherhood.

The Negro's Legitimate Discontent

It would be fatal for the nation to overlook the urgency of the moment and to underestimate the determination of the Negro. This sweltering summer of the Negro's legitimate discontent will not pass until there is an invigorating autumn of freedom and equality. 1963 is not an end, but a beginning. Those who hope that the Negro needed to blow off steam and will now be content will have a rude awakening if the Nation returns to business as usual. There will be neither rest nor tranquility in America until the Negro is granted his citizenship rights. The whirlwinds of revolt will continue to shake the foundations of our Nation until the bright day of justice emerges.

But there is something that I must say to my people who stand on the warm threshold which leads into the palace of justice. In the process of gaining our rightful place we must not be guilty of wrongful deeds. Let us not seek to satisfy our thirst for freedom by drinking from the cup of bitterness and hatred. We must forever conduct our struggle on the high plane of dignity and discipline. We must not allow our creative protest to degenerate into physical violence. Again and again we must rise to the majestic heights of meeting physical force with soul force. The marvelous new militancy which has engulfed the Negro community must not lead us to a distrust of all white people, for many of our white brothers, as evidenced by their presence here today, have come to realize that their destiny is tied up with our destiny and their freedom is inextricably bound to our freedom. We cannot walk alone.

And as we walk, we must make the pledge that we shall march ahead. We cannot turn back. There are those who are asking the devotees of civil rights, "When will you be satisfied?" We can never be satisfied as long as the Negro is the victim of the unspeakable horrors of police brutality. We can never be satisfied as long as our bodies, heavy with the fatigue of travel, cannot gain lodging in the motels of the highways and the hotels of the cities. We cannot be satisfied as long as the Negro's basic mobility is from a smaller ghetto to a larger one. We can never be satisfied as long as a Negro in Mississippi cannot vote and a Negro in New York believes he has nothing for which to vote. No, no we are not satisfied, and we will not be satisfied until justice rolls down like waters and righteousness like a mighty stream.

I am not unmindful that some of you have come here out of great trials and tribulations. Some of you have come fresh from narrow jail cells. Some of you have come from areas where your quest for freedom left you battered by the storms of persecution and staggered by the winds of police brutality. You have been the veterans of creative suffering. Continue to work with the faith that unearned suffering is redemptive.

Go back to Mississippi, go back to Alabama, go back to South Carolina, go back to Georgia, go back to Louisiana, go back to the slums and ghettos of our modern cities, knowing that somehow this situation can and will be changed. Let us not wallow in the valley of despair.

I Have a Dream

I say to you today, my friends, that in spite of the difficulties and frustrations of the moment I still have a dream. It is a dream deeply rooted in the American dream.

I have a dream that one day this nation will rise up and live out the true meaning of its creed: "We hold these truths to be self-evident; that all men are created equal."

I have a dream that one day on the red hills of Georgia the sons of former slaves and the sons of former slaveowners will be able to sit down together at the table of brotherhood.

I have a dream that one day even the state of Mississippi, a desert state sweltering with the heat of injustice and oppression, will be transformed into an oasis of freedom and justice.

I have a dream that my four little children will one day live in a nation where they will not be judged by the color of their skin but by the content of their character.

I have a dream today.

I have a dream that one day the state of Alabama, whose governor's lips are presently dripping with the words of interposition and nullification, will be transformed into a situation where little black boys and black girls will be able to join hands with little white boys and white girls and walk together as sisters and brothers.

I have a dream today.

I have a dream that one day every valley shall be exalted, every hill and mountain shall be made low, the rough places will be made plain, and the crooked places will be made straight, and the glory of the Lord shall be revealed, and all flesh shall see it together.

This is our hope. This is the faith with which I return to the South. With this faith we will be able to hew out of the mountain of despair a stone of hope. With this faith we will be able to transform the jangling discords of our nation into a beautiful symphony of brotherhood. With this faith we will be able to work together, to pray together, to struggle together, to go to jail together, to stand up for freedom together, knowing that we will be free one day.

Let Freedom Ring

This will be the day when all of God's children will be able to sing with new meaning "My country 'tis of thee, sweet land of liberty, of thee I sing. Land where my fathers died, land of the pilgrim's pride, from every mountainside, let freedom ring."

And if America is to be a great nation this must become true. So let freedom ring from the prodigious hilltops of New Hampshire. Let freedom ring from the mighty mountains of New York. Let freedom ring from the heightening Alleghenies of Pennsylvania!

Let freedom ring from the snowcapped Rockies of Colorado!

Let freedom ring from the curvaceous peaks of California!

But not only that; let freedom ring from Stone Mountain of Georgia!

Let freedom ring from Lookout Mountain of Tennessee!

Let freedom ring from every hill and mole hill of Mississippi. From every mountainside, let freedom ring.

When we let freedom ring, when we let it ring from every village and every hamlet, from every state and every city, we will be able to speed up that day when all of God's children, black men and white men, Jews and Gentiles, Protestants and Catholics, will be able to join hands and sing in the words of the old Negro spiritual, "Free at last! free at last! thank God almighty, we are free at last!"

VIEWPOINT 2

"America's reaction to what the Negro considered just demands was a disillusioning experience."

The Civil Rights Struggle Has Brought Despair to Black Americans

Julius Lester (b. 1939)

The Civil Rights Act of 1964 banned racial and sexual discrimination in employment, education, and other areas of life. The Voting Rights Act of 1965 strengthened the power of the federal government to prevent discrimination in voting registration and elections by local authorities. These landmark legal victories for America's minorities came about largely because of the civil rights movement and the public support it had generated with its campaign of nonviolent resistance to racial discrimination and segregation. Although most public attention was focused on leaders such as Martin Luther King Jr., much of the legwork of the movement was performed by the Student Nonviolent Coordinating Committee (SNCC). Formed in 1960 by black and white college students to plan "sit-ins" of segregated facilities, SNCC also organized black communities and voter registration drives in the South. Members of SNCC, both black and white, often faced violent reprisals from local racist whites. Many activists were beaten and jailed; several were killed. They drew attention and sympathy for their cause by maintaining a philosophy of nonviolence despite such treatment.

However, by 1966 many blacks, including members of SNCC,

From Julius Lester, "The Angry Children of Malcolm X," in *Key List Mailing: Selected Documents of Current and Lasting Interest in the Civil Rights Movement*, published by the San Francisco Regional Office of SNCC, 1966. Reprinted by permission of Julius Lester.

were becoming disillusioned with the lack of progress being made by the civil rights movement. Some questioned whether the laws passed in 1964 and 1965 really made a difference. Others criticized King's leadership and his insistence on nonviolence. They questioned whether blacks should struggle for integration within American society, arguing that blacks should concentrate on improving their own condition without trying to placate white America.

The following viewpoint is taken from an essay written in 1966 by Julius Lester, a former field secretary of SNCC who later became a noted writer of fiction and nonfiction and a professor at the University of Massachusetts at Amherst. Lester provides a personal account of the evolution of the civil rights movement from around 1960, when black students first became heavily involved, to 1966, when students and other activists were losing faith with the progress and direction of the civil rights movement. He writes that many blacks were turning to the ideas of Malcolm X, a militant and confrontational black nationalist who was killed in 1965, and were considering violent retaliation to be a better option than passive resistance to continuing racial discrimination and division in America.

By 1966, SNCC, the new Black Panther Party, and other black organizations were rejecting the nonviolent and inclusive doctrines of Martin Luther King Jr.; the more militant slogan of "black power" was replacing the traditional civil rights motto "we shall overcome." The second half of the 1960s would be marked by growing divisions between militants and moderates within the black civil rights movement and by increasing racial polarization across America.

This is their message: *The days of singing freedom songs and the days of combatting bullets and billy clubs with love are over. "We Shall Overcome" sounds old, out-dated. "Man, the people are too busy getting ready to fight to bother with singing any more!"*

The world of the black American is different from that of the white American. This difference comes not only from the segregation imposed on the Black, but it also comes from the way of life he has evolved for himself under these conditions. Yet, America has always been uneasy with this separate world in its midst. Feeling most comfortable when the black man emulates the ways and manners of white Americans, America has, at the same time, been stolidly unwilling to let the black man be assimilated into the mainstream.

With its goal of assimilation on the basis of equality, the civil rights movement was once the great hope of black men and liberal whites. In 1960 and 1961 Negroes felt that if only Americans knew the wrongs and sufferings they had to endure, these wrongs would be righted and all would be well. If Americans saw well-dressed, well-mannered, clean Negroes on their television screen not retaliating to being beaten by white Southerners, they would not sit back and do nothing. *Amor vincit omnia!* and the Reverend Dr. Martin Luther King, Jr., was the knight going forth to prove to the father that he was worthy of becoming a member of the family. But there was something wrong with this attitude and young Negroes began to feel uneasy. Was this not another form of the bowing and scraping their grandparents had had to do to get what they wanted? Were they not acting once again as the white man wanted them to? And why should they have to be brutalized, physically and spiritually, for what every other American had at birth? But these were only timid questions in the mind for which no answer was waited. You simply put your body in the struggle and that meant entering the church in Albany, Danville, Birmingham, Greenwood, Nashville, or wherever you were, entering the church and listening to prayers, short sermons on your courage and the cause you were fighting, singing freedom songs—Ain't Gon' Let Nobody Turn Me Round and you would name names, the sheriff's, the Mayor's, the Governor's and whoever else you held responsible for the conditions and—always at the end—We Shall Overcome with arms crossed, holding hands of the person next to you and swaying gently from side to side, We Shall Overcome Someday someday but not today because you knew as you walked out of the church, two abreast, and started marching toward town that no matter how many times you sang about not letting anybody turn you around red-necks and po' white trash from four counties and some from across the state line were waiting with guns, tire chains, baseball bats, rocks, sticks, clubs and bottles, waiting as you turned the corner singing about This Little Light of Mine and how you were going to let it shine as that cop's billy club went upside your head shine shine shining as you fell to the pavement with someone's foot into your back until a cop dragged you away, threw you into the paddy wagon and off to the jail you and the others went, singing I Ain't Scared of Your Jail 'Cause I Want My Freedom. . . .

But a response did begin to come from the nation. All across the North young white kids held sympathy demonstrations and then with the Freedom Rides in 1961 whites came South to go to jail with Negroes—for Freedom. Those who came said integration was their fight, too, because they could never be whole men, either, in a segregated society. Some whites stayed after the Freedom Rides and moved into Negro communities to live and to work.

At that time there was a split between activists in the Movement. Some felt that more and more demonstrations were needed while others felt that the effect of demonstrations was limited. Power was what was needed and power came through having a say in the system. That came through the ballot. Once you had some say in government, you could have some say about jobs. After all, what was the point of desegregating a lunch counter if you didn't have the money to buy a hamburger?

So began the slow tedious work of going into a town, finding someone who wouldn't be afraid to have a civil rights worker living in his house and would help the worker become known in the community. The civil rights worker had to find a minister courageous enough to let his church be used for a mass meeting and then he had to go around the community asking people to come out to the meeting. At the mass meeting there was usually hymn singing and a prayer service first. Then the minister would make a few remarks before introducing the civil rights worker, who by that time, if he were a veteran, would've been through the sit'ins, the Freedom Rides, five or six different jails and a lot of hungry days. He had dropped out of college, or quit his job if he had never been to college to become a full-time organizer for SNCC [Student Nonviolent Coordinating Committee]. His job was simple: organize the community to march down to the courthouse to register to vote. In small Mississippi towns, though, he didn't even think of organizing the community. He would feel good if he could convince five people to go. If five went and if the inevitable happened (violence, arrests), he had a good chance of organizing the community. It was not important at that time if one name was put on the voter registration rolls. The most important thing was to get the people organized. . . .

There were still demonstrations, but now they were not aimed as much at public accommodations, the most obvious symbols of oppression. The picket line around the courthouse, the symbol of the seat of power, were the new targets. The immediate result was the same. Heads that had been beaten before were beaten again. Heads that had never been beaten were beaten. New bloody heads were on the six o'clock news alongside ones that still had scabs from the last head-whipping session. If you were a civil rights worker in Mississippi you learned many things quickly. Don't sleep by windows if possible. Don't answer a knock at the door in the middle of the night unless your caller showed you nothing less than his birth certificate. If you're on the highway at night, you learned to drive as if you were training to be an astronaut. . . . Each organizer had his own little techniques for staying alive. Non-violence might do something to the moral conscience of a nation, but a bullet didn't have morals and it was beginning to occur to more and more organizers that white folks had plenty more bullets than they did conscience.

Black People Are Fed Up

The black nationalist ideals of Malcolm X, founder of the Organization of Afro-American Unity, have remained highly influential among African Americans in the decades following his 1965 assassination. The following passage is excerpted from a speech Malcolm X gave in Cleveland in April 1964.

I'm not an American. I'm one of the 22 million black people who are the victims of Americanism. One of the 22 million black people who are the victims of democracy, nothing but disguised hypocrisy. So, I'm not standing here speaking to you as an American, or a patriot, or a flag-saluter, or a flag-waver—no, not I. I'm speaking as a victim of this American system. And I see America through the eyes of the victim. I don't see any American dream; I see an American nightmare. . . .

Black people are fed up with the dillydallying, pussyfooting, compromising approach that we've been using toward getting our freedom. We want freedom *now*, but we're not going to get it saying "We Shall Overcome." We've got to fight until we overcome. . . .

It's time for you and me to stop sitting in this country, letting some cracker senators, Northern crackers and Southern crackers, sit there in Washington, D.C., and come to a conclusion in their mind that you and I are supposed to have civil rights. There's no white man going to tell me anything about *my* rights. Brothers and sisters, always remember, if it doesn't take senators and congressmen and presidential proclamations to give freedom to the white man, it is not necessary for legislation or proclamation or Supreme Court decisions to give freedom to the black man. You let that white man know, if this is a country of freedom, let it be a country of freedom; and if it's not a country of freedom, change it.

We will work with anybody, anywhere, at any time, who is genuinely interested in tackling the problem head-on, nonviolently as long as the enemy is nonviolent, but violent when the enemy gets violent.

How naive, how idealistic they were then. They had honestly believed that once white people knew what segregation did, it would be abolished. But why shouldn't they have believed it? They had been fed the American Dream, too. They believed in Coca Cola and the American Government. "I dreamed I got my Freedom in a Maidenform Bra." They were in the Pepsi Generation, believing that the F.B.I. was God's personal emissary to uphold truth and punish evil.

That was before the countless demonstrations where the F.B.I. took notes standing next to cracker cops while they were wiping the nigger blood off their bill-clubs, and checking the batteries in their cattle-prods. . . . It was [the massive civil rights demonstration in Alabama at] Birmingham, '63 that finally forced the Image of Youth and Liberty, Jack Kennedy, into proposing a Civil Rights Bill. . . . [He] didn't like the idea of the [1963] march on Washington, but managed to turn it into a Kennedy victory and finally endorsing it as being in the American tradition, whatever that means. After the March, the American Monarch had the Big Six Negro Leaders over to the White House for tea and cookies and to chat with Jackie about the Riviera in the winter (it's a whole lot better than the Delta I hear). The Monarch, his face rugged from the spray of the wind-swept Atlantic, as thousands of eulogies have proclaimed since his swift demise, stood there smiling, feeling pretty good because all the liquor stores and bars in Washington had been closed for the day so there was no danger of a bunch of niggers getting ahold of some fire-water, forgetting that they weren't in Harlem, Buttermilk Bottom and all those other weird-named places niggers picked to live in. (The order forbidding the sale of alcoholic beverages is one of the biggest insults Negroes have ever had hurled at them. It would have been much easier to take if it had simply been said The Great White Father can't trust his pickaninnies if the bars and liquor stores are left open.) Jack could also stand there and smile because John Lewis of SNCC had had his speech censored by the more 'responsible' leaders, who threatened to withdraw from the march. Even censored, Lewis' speech raised pertinent questions—questions that had been on the mind of many. . . . But Jack could smile, because John Lewis had deleted from his speech the most pertinent question of all, "I want to know—which side is the Federal Government on?"

A lot of people wanted to know that, particularly after Lyndon Baines Johnson became President of the United States in a split second one Friday afternoon. When he asked for the nation's help and God's in that cracker drawl, Negroes began pulling out road maps, train schedules and brushing up on their Spanish. A lot of them had always wanted to see what Mexico was like anyway, and it looked as if the time to do that thing was near.

But Big Lyndon, despite his beagle hounds and daughters, fooled everybody. Not only did he strengthen the civil rights bill and support it fully, he started giving Martin Luther King competition as to who was going to lead "the movement." King lost.

With the push for the civil rights bill in Congress, there began talk of a white backlash in the '64 elections. It seemed that whites were getting a little tired of picking up the papers and seeing niggers all over the front page. Even if they were getting their heads kicked in half the time, four years of seeing that was about enough. The average white person didn't know what niggers wanted and didn't much care. By now they should have gotten whatever the hell it was they said they didn't have and if they hadn't gotten it by now, they either didn't deserve it or didn't need it.

The North and Civil Rights

What was really bothering Northern whites, however, was the fact that the Movement had come North. De Facto Segregation and De Facto Housing were new phrases meaning No Niggers Allowed in This School and You Damn Well Better Believe No Niggers Allowed in This Neighborhood. If you believed the liberal press, though, it wasn't as serious a problem as the one down South, because in the North segregation wasn't deliberate, it just sort of happened that way. Many Negroes never found out what De Facto meant, but they assumed it was the De Facto and not segregation they ran up against when they couldn't find an apartment to rent outside of Harlem. Soon, though, the mask fell from the North's face. In New York it happened when CORE [Congress of Racial Equality] threatened a stall-in on all of the city's express-ways the morning of the World's Fair opening. The threat alone was enough to make over three-fourths of the people who drove to work leave their cars in the garage and take the train or simply call in sick. The threat alone was enough to make New York liberal newspapers read as if they had acquired Southern accents over night. A few months later, an organization of whites arose in New York which called itself SPONGE—Society for the Prevention of Negroes Getting Everything. It was difficult to speak any longer of a North and a South. As Malcolm X once said, everything south of the Canadian border was South. There was only up South and down South now, and you found "cracker" both places.

While the North was being shocked into realizing that there were Negroes in its midst, the South was sympathizing with the assault that Mississippi was about to suffer. Almost a thousand white students were going into the State in June, 1964, to work in Freedom Schools, community centers and to register people in the Mississippi Freedom Democratic Party, a political party organized that winter which was going to challenge the state Democratic organization at the Democratic Convention in August. . . .

The Mississippi Summer Project . . . accomplished its purpose; the press came to Mississippi. . . . All summer the articles came about white boys and white girls living with poor Negroes in Mississippi. It didn't escape the attention of Negroes that seemingly no one cared about the Negro civil rights workers who have been living and working in Mississippi for the previous three years. Didn't anyone care about Willie Peacock, born and raised on a Mississippi plantation, who couldn't go back to his home town because he was an organizer for SNCC and the white people would kill him if he went to see his mother? Apparently not.

Mississippi was taken out of the headlines in July [1964], however, when Harlem held its own summer project, to protest the murder of a thirteen-year-old boy by a policeman. Summer projects, northern style, usually involve a southern coke bottle with gasoline, stuffing a rag down the neck and lighting it. *Things go better with coke.*—Harlem, Bedford-Stuyvesant, Rochester and Chicago sent coke after coke after coke that summer but the granddaddy of them all, Watts [Los Angeles, came] the following summer.

If the press had ever screamed as loudly for an end to segregation and discrimination as it screamed for law and order, segregation would be a vague memory today. Somehow, though, law and order becomes all important only when Negroes take to the streets and burn or wipe out a few of the white man's stores. Law and order is never so important to the press when the police is whuppin niggers' heads on the week-ends. It slowly began to dawn on Negroes that whites didn't care quite as much about helping them get their freedom as they did about law and order. "Law and order must prevail" has become the cliche of the '60's. Law and order have always prevailed—upside the Black man's head at every available opportunity.

The system was breaking down, but it was breaking in ways few had foreseen and fewer understood. The walls of segregation and discrimination were not crumbling and giving way to flowers of love and brotherhood. The walls were crumbling, but only to reveal a gigantic castle with walls ten times thicker than the walls of segregation. The castle was painted a brilliant white and lettered in bright red were the words Racism. What it meant to the Negro was simple. The white man only wanted you to have what he wanted you to have and you couldn't get it any other way except the way he said you could get it. Racism. It was the attitude that closed the bars and liquor stores on the day of the March. It was the attitude which made newspapers and government officials, even Big Lyndon Himself, say, "that if Negroes went about things in the wrong way, they would lose the friends they already had." It was the attitude that made the press continue to call Muhammad Ali, Cassius Clay even though that was no longer his name. But the movement was moving. It was no longer a Friendship Contest. It was becoming a War of Liberation.

Malcolm X

More than any other person Malcolm X was responsible for the new militancy that entered The Movement in 1965. Malcolm X said aloud those things which Negroes had been saying among themselves. He even said those things Negroes had been afraid to say to each other. His clear uncomplicated words cut through the chains on black minds like a giant blowtorch. His words were not spoken for the benefit of the press. He was not concerned with stirring the moral conscience of America, because he knew—America had no moral conscience. He spoke directly and eloquently to black men, analyzing their situation, their predicament, events as they happened, explaining what it all meant for a black man in America.

America's reaction to what the Negro considered just demands was a disillusioning experience. Where whites could try to attain the American Dream, Negroes always had had to dream themselves attaining The Dream. But The Dream was beginning to look like a nightmare and Negroes didn't have to dream themselves a nightmare. They had been living one a long time. They had hoped that America would respond to their needs and America had equivocated. Integration had once been an unquestioned goal that would be the proudest moment for Negro America. Now it was beginning to be questioned.

The New York school boycotts of 1964 pointed this up. Integration to the New York City Board of Education meant busing Negro children to white schools. This merely said to Negroes that whites were saying Negroes had nothing to offer. Integration has always been presented as a Godsend for Negroes and something to be endured for whites. When the Board of Education decided to bus white children to Negro schools the following year, the reaction was strangely similar to that of New Orleans and Little Rock. Today, whites in Chicago and New York chant at Negro demonstrators, "I wish I was an Alabama deputy, so I could kill a nigger legally."

Integration and Identity

When it became more and more apparent that integration was only designed to uplift Negroes and improve their lot, Negroes began wondering whose lot actually needed improving. Maybe the white folks weren't as well-educated and cultured as they thought they were. Thus, Negroes began cutting a path toward learning who they were. . . .

Identity has always been the key problem for Negroes. Many avoid their blackness as much as possible by trying to become assimilated. They remove all traces of blackness from their lives.

179

Their gestures, speech, habits, cuisine, walk, everything becomes as American Dream as possible. Generally, they are the 'responsible leaders,' the middle class, the undercover, button-down collar Uncle Toms, who front for the white man at a time of racial crisis, reassuring the nation that "responsible Negroes deplore the violence and looting and we ask that law and order be allowed to prevail." A small minority avoid the crux of their blackness by going to another extreme. They identify completely with Africa. Some go to the extent of wearing African clothes and speaking Swahili. They, however, are only unconsciously admitting that the white man is right when he says, Negroes don't have a thing of their own. . . .

Now the Negro is beginning to study his past, to learn those things that have been lost, to recreate what the white man destroyed in him and to destroy that which the white man put in its stead. He has stopped being a Negro and has become a black man in recognition of his new identity, his real identity. 'Negro' is an American invention which shut him off from those of the same color in Africa. He recognizes now that part of himself is in Africa. Some feel this in a deeply personal way, as did Mrs. Fannie Lou Hamer who cried when she was in Africa, because she knew she had relatives there and she would never be able to know them. Her past would always be partially closed.

Many things that have happened in the past six years have had little or no meaning for most whites, but have had vital meaning for Negroes. Wasn't it only a month after the March on Washington that four children were killed in a church bombing in Birmingham? Whites could feel morally outraged, but they couldn't know the futility, despair and anger that swept through the nation within a nation—Black America. There are limits to how much one people could endure and Birmingham Sunday possibly marked that limit. The enemy was not a system. It was an inhuman fiend who never slept, who never rested and no one would stop him. Those Northern protest rallies where Freedom Songs were sung and speeches speeched and applause applauded and afterwards telegrams and letters sent to the President and Congress—they began to look more and more like moral exercises. See, my hands are clean. I do not condone such a foul deed, they said, going back to their magazines, feeling purged because they had made their moral witness.

What was needed that Sunday was ol' John Brown to come riding into Birmingham as he had ridden into Lawrence, Kansas, burning every building that stood and killing every man, woman and child that ran from his onslaught. Killing, killing, killing, turning men into fountains of blood, spouting spouting spouting until Heaven itself drew back before the frothing red ocean.

180

But the Liberal and his Negro sycophants would've cried, Vengeance accomplishes nothing. You're only acting like your oppressor and such an act makes you no better than him. John Brown, his hand and wrists slick with blood, would have said oh so softly and so quietly, Mere Vengeance is folly. Purgation is necessity.

The Limits of Love

Now it is over. America has had chance after chance to show that it really meant "that all men are endowed with certain inalienable rights." America has had precious chances in this decade to make it come true. Now it is over. The days of singing freedom songs and the days of combating bullets and billy clubs with love. We Shall Overcome (and we have overcome our blindness) sounds old, out-dated. . . . As one SNCC veteran put it after the [1966] Mississippi March, "Man, the people are too busy getting ready to fight to bother with singing anymore." And as for Love? That's always been better done in bed than on the picket line and marches. Love is fragile and gentle and seeks a like response. They used to sing "I Love Everybody" as they ducked bricks and bottles. Now they sing:

Too much love,

Too much love,

Nothing kills a nigger like

Too much love.

They know, because they still get headaches from the beatings they took while love, love, loving. They know, because they died on those highways and in those jail cells, died from trying to change the hearts of men who had none. They know, the ones who have bleeding ulcers when they're twenty'tree and the ones who have to have the eye operations. They know that nothing kills a nigger like too much love.

At one time black people desperately wanted to be American, to communicate with whites, to live in the Beloved Community. Now that is irrelevant. They know that it can't be until whites want it to be and it is obvious now that whites don't want it.

VIEWPOINT 3

"It would be a grave mistake to charge off the recent riots to unredressed Negro grievances alone. To do so is to ignore . . . a major national problem: the deterioration of respect for the rule of law."

Rioters Should Be Condemned for Rejecting Law and Order

Richard Nixon (1913–1994)

Martin Luther King Jr.'s dream of a nonviolent revolution in American race relations was shattered by a series of urban riots in the mid-1960s. In Harlem, New York, in 1964; Watts, Los Angeles, in 1965; Chicago and Cleveland in 1966; Detroit and Newark in 1967; and in numerous other places, local residents confronted police, looted stores and businesses, and burned buildings; they in turn were fired upon by police and National Guard troops who were sent to restore order. Between 1964 and 1968, riots resulted in almost $200 million in destroyed property, forty thousand arrests, seven thousand injured, and around two hundred deaths.

Americans differed on the implications of these riots and how the country should respond to them. Some viewed them as "political rebellions" that were meant to draw attention to the harsh conditions many minorities faced in urban ghettos. The National Advisory Commission on Civil Disorders (the Kerner Commission), appointed by President Lyndon B. Johnson, implicated "white racism" for creating an "explosive mixture" of poverty, police brutality, and poor schools in the nation's cities. Its report called for significant government programs to help the urban poor.

Richard Nixon, "If Mob Rule Takes Hold in the U.S.—a Warning from Richard Nixon," *U.S. News & World Report*, August 15, 1966. Copyright 1966, U.S. News & World Report. Reprinted with permission.

In the following viewpoint, Richard Nixon provides a different explanation of the causes of urban violence. In a 1966 article in *U.S. News & World Report*, excerpted here, he argues that riots are being caused by a general breakdown of respect for law, which he attributes in part to the civil disobedience doctrines of the civil rights movement. Nixon, who lost the 1960 presidential race to John F. Kennedy and later lost the 1962 California gubernatorial election, was able to successfully utilize the theme of restoring "law and order" to make a political comeback and win the presidency in 1968.

The polls still place the war in Vietnam and the rising cost of living as the major political issues of 1966. But, from my own trips across the nation, I can affirm that private conversations and public concern are increasingly focusing upon the issues of disrespect for law and race turmoil.

The recent riots in Chicago, Cleveland, New York and Omaha have produced in the public dialogue too much heat and very little light. The extremists have held the floor for too long.

One extreme sees a simple remedy for rioting in a ruthless application of the truncheons and an earlier call to the National Guard.

The other extremists are more articulate, but their position is equally simplistic. To them, riots are to be excused upon the grounds that the participants have legitimate social grievances or seek justifiable social goals.

Declining Respect for Law

I believe it would be a grave mistake to charge off the recent riots to unredressed Negro grievances alone.

To do so is to ignore a prime reason and a major national problem: the deterioration of respect for the rule of law all across America.

That deterioration can be traced directly to the spread of the corrosive doctrine that every citizen possesses an inherent right to decide for himself which laws to disobey and when to disobey them.

The doctrine has become a contagious national disease, and its symptoms are manifest in more than just racial violence. We see them in the contempt among many of the young for the agents of the law—the police. We see them in the public burning of draft cards and the blocking of troop trains.

We saw those symptoms when citizens in Chicago took to the streets to block public commerce to force the firing of a city official. We saw them on a campus of the University of California, where students brought a great university to its knees in protest of the policies of its administration.

Who is responsible for the breakdown of law and order in this country? I think it both an injustice and oversimplification to lay blame at the feet of the sidewalk demagogues alone. For such a deterioration of respect for law to occur in so brief a time in so great a nation, we must look to more important collaborators and auxiliaries.

It is my belief that the seeds of civil anarchy would never have taken root in this nation had they not been nurtured by scores of respected Americans: public officials, educators, clergymen and civil rights leaders as well.

When the junior Senator from New York [Robert Kennedy] publicly declares that "there is no point in telling Negroes to obey the law," because to the Negro "the law is the enemy," then he has provided a rationale and justification for every Negro intent upon taking the law into his own hands. . . .

The agonies and indignities of urban slums are hard facts of life. Their elimination is properly among our highest national priorities, but within those slums, political phrases which are inflammatory are as wrong and dangerous as political promises which are irredeemable.

In this contest, men of intellectual and moral eminence who encourage public disobedience of the law are responsible for the acts of those who inevitably follow their counsel: the poor, the ignorant and the impressionable.

A Climate of Lawlessness

Such leaders are most often men of good will who do not condone violence and, perhaps even now, see no relation between the civil disobedience which they counsel and the riots and violence which have erupted. Yet, once the decision is made that laws need not be obeyed—whatever the rationale—a contribution is made to a climate of lawlessness.

To the professor objecting to de facto segregation, it may be crystal clear where civil disobedience may begin and where it must end. But the boundaries have become fluid to his students. And today they are all but invisible in the urban slums.

In this nation we raise our young to respect the law and public authority. What becomes of those lessons when teachers and leaders of the young themselves deliberately and publicly violate the laws?

There is a crucial difference between lawful demonstration and protests on the one hand—and illegal demonstrations and "civil disobedience" on the other.

I think it is time the doctrine of civil disobedience was analyzed and rejected as not only wrong but potentially disastrous.

If all have a right to engage in public disobedience to protest real or imagined wrongs, then the example set by the minority today will be followed by the majority tomorrow.

Issues then will no longer be decided upon merit by an impartial judge. Victory will go to the side which can muster the greater number of demonstrations in the streets. The rule of law will be replaced by the rule of the mob. And one may be sure that the majority's mob will prevail.

From mob rule it is but a single step to lynch law and the termination of the rights of the minority. This is why it is so paradoxical today to see minority groups engaging in civil disobedience; their greatest defense is the rule of law. . . .

Civil disobedience creates a climate of disrespect for law. In such a climate the first laws to be ignored will be social legislation that lacks universal public support. In short, if the rule of law goes, the civil-rights laws of recent vintage will be the first casualties.

Historic advances in civil rights have come through court decisions and federal laws in the last dozen years.

In addition to police and National Guard units, regular U.S. Army soldiers were sent to occupy and enforce curfew orders in areas of Detroit, Michigan, following riots in July 1967.

UPI/Corbis-Bettmann

Only the acceptances of those laws and the voluntary compliance of the people can transfer those advances from the statute books into the fabric of community life.

If indifference to the rule of law permeates the community, there will be no voluntary acceptance. A law is only as good as the will of the people to obey it. . . .

A Wall of Hate

Across this nation today, civil disobedience and racial disorders are building up a wall of hate between the races which, while less visible, is no less real than the wall that divides freedom and slavery in the [German] city of Berlin. . . . Continued racial violence and disorders in the cities of the nation will produce growing disenchantment with the cause of civil rights—even among its staunchest supporters.

It will encourage a disregard for civil rights laws and resistance to the legitimate demands of the Negro people.

Does anyone think that progress will be made in the hearts of men by riots and disobedience which trample upon the rights of those same men? But then is it not enough to simply demand that all laws be obeyed?

Edmund Burke once wrote concerning loyalty to a nation that "to make us love our country, our country ought to be lovely." There is an analogy in a commitment to the rule of law. For a law to be respected, it ought to be worthy of respect. It must be fair and it must be fairly enforced.

It certainly did nothing to prevent a riot when Negroes in Chicago learned that while water hydrants in their own area were being shut down, they were running free in white neighborhoods just blocks away.

Basic Dignity

Respect for the dignity of every individual is absolutely essential if there is to be respect for law.

The most common and justifiable complaint of Negroes and members of other minority groups is not that their constitutional rights have been denied, but that their personal dignity is repeatedly insulted.

As an American citizen, the American Negro is entitled to equality of rights, under the Constitution and the law, with every other citizen in the land. But, as important as this, the Negro has the right to be treated with the basic dignity and respect that belong to him as a human being.

Advocates of civil disobedience contend that a man's conscience should determine which law is to be obeyed and when a law can be ignored. But, to many men, conscience is no more than the enshrinement of their own prejudices. . . . But if every man is to decide for himself which to obey and which to ignore, the end result is anarchy.

The way to make good laws is not to break bad laws, but to change bad laws through legitimate means of protest within the constitutional process.

In the last analysis, the nation simply can no longer tolerate men who are above the law. For, as Lincoln said, "There is no grievance that is a fit object of redress by mob law."

VIEWPOINT 4

"Disobedience, disorder, and even violence must be risked as the only alternative to continuing slavery."

Riots Should Be Understood as Social Revolutions

Tom Hayden (b. 1939)

The arrest of a black taxi driver in July 1967 in Newark, New Jersey, which had the highest black unemployment rate as well as the highest maternal mortality rate of any city in America, set off five days of arson and looting; twenty-five blacks were killed by the police. The violence in Newark was but one of a series of riots that swept many American cities in the 1960s, including Watts, Los Angeles, in 1965 and Detroit in 1967.

Some people blamed the violence on the oppressive living conditions of the nation's black urban poor and asserted that the riots served as a warning to America that social change was necessary. Among those who argued for such an interpretation was Tom Hayden, a former president of Students for a Democratic Society (SDS). Hayden had been active in Newark since 1964 as part of SDS's Economic Research and Action Project (ERAP), an effort to sponsor community organizing and attain SDS's vision of "participatory democracy" in urban ghettos. He argues in the following viewpoint, excerpted from his 1967 book *Rebellion in Newark*, that because ordinary political and economic channels of change have been ineffective for blacks in urban ghettos, blacks are forced to resort to an "American form of guerrilla warfare" in order to force necessary social reforms.

Hayden, one of the most famous radical dissenters of the 1960s, also was involved in the protest movement against the Vietnam

War. In the 1980s, he became a California state legislator and wrote *Reunion*, a memoir of his experiences during the 1960s and after.

This country is experiencing its fourth year of urban revolt, yet the message from Newark is that America has learned almost nothing since Watts.

Of primary importance is the fact that no national program exists to deal with the social and economic questions black people are raising. Despite exhaustive hearings over the last five years on problems of manpower and unemployment, anti-poverty programs and the urban crisis, there is no apparent commitment from national power centers to do something constructive.

During the height of the rioting in Newark and Detroit, Congress discussed gun-control laws, voted down with chuckles a bill for rat extermination, and President Johnson set up a commission to do more investigating of the crisis. The main emphasis of governmental remedial programs seems likely to be on ending the riots rather than dealing with the racial and economic problem. President Johnson made this clear in his televised July 28 [1967] address on the "deeper questions" about the riots:

> Explanations may be offered, but nothing can excuse what [the rioters] have done. There will be attempts to interpret the events of the past few days, but when violence strikes, then those in public responsibility have an immediate and a very different job: *not to analyze but to end disorder.*

When it moves past riot-control to discussion of social programs, Congress is likely to lament the failure of past civil rights, welfare, and anti-poverty programs, rather than focus on the need for new ones. As with foreign aid, white politicians (and their voters) tend to view aid to Negroes as a form of "charity" to be trimmed wherever possible, or as a means of eliminating surplus food, or a way to enlarge urban patronage roles. Negroes more than likely will be instructed to "help themselves."

But unlike the Italians, Irish, and Jews, black Americans have always faced a shrinking structure of economic opportunity in which to "help themselves." If sheer effort were the answer, the black people who chopped cotton from dawn to sunset would today be millionaire suburban homeowners. Self-help does not build housing, hospitals, and schools. The cost of making cities livable and institutions responsive is greater than any sum this country has ever been willing to spend on domestic reform. In addition, the very act of spending such money would disrupt much of the status quo. Private interests, from the real estate lobby and the construction unions to the social work profession, would be threatened. Urban political machines would have to make space for black political power. Good intentions tend to collapse when faced with the necessity for massive spending and structural change.

This political bankruptcy leads directly to the use of military force. When citizens have no political way to deal with revolution, they become counter-revolutionary. The race issue becomes defined exclusively as one of maintaining white society. Holding this view forces the white community to adopt the "jungle attitudes" that they fear the Negroes hold. "Go kill them niggers," white crowds shouted to Guardsmen at 7 o'clock Friday morning as they rode into Newark. During the riot, a *New York Times* reporter was stopped at 2:30 A.M. in Mayor Addonizio's west side neighborhood by a pipe-smoking gentleman carrying (illegally) a shotgun. He explained that a protection society was formed in case "they" should come into the neighborhood. Rifle stores in white neighborhoods all over the east coast are selling out. In such way, the society becomes militarized.

Declaring War on Negroes

A police "takeover" of local government is not necessary to declare war on Negroes. All that is necessary is to instill in the white citizens the idea that only military force stands between them and black savages. The civilians merely turn over the problem to the troops, who define the problem in terms of using arms to maintain the racial status quo. A typical military attitude in the wake of the riots was offered in the July 29th *Times* by the commander of the New York State National Guard, who said that a greater commitment of force might have prevented rioting around the country. He recommended the use of heavy weapons including hand grenades, recoilless rifles and bazookas. He blamed indecisive civilian authority for making National Guard units operate "with one hand behind their backs" in riot areas.

This military orientation means that outright killing of people is condoned where those people cannot accept law and order as defined by the majority. The country is not moved by the deaths of twenty-five Negro "rioters."

News of a Negro's death is received at most as a tragedy, the inevitable result of looting and lawlessness. When a picture appears of a policeman over a fallen victim, the typical reaction is framed in the terms set by the majority: the dead man is a sniper, a looter, a burner, a criminal. If history is any guide, it is a foregone conclusion that no white policeman will be punished for murder in Newark.

Violence Is Necessary

H. Rap Brown, an outspoken civil rights activist and leader, caused much controversy in the late 1960s with his remarks justifying black violence. The following passage is excerpted from his 1969 book Die, Nigger, Die!

The question of violence has been cleared up. This country was born of violence. Violence is as american as cherry pie. Black people have always been violent, but our violence has always been directed toward each other. If nonviolence is to be practiced, then it should be practiced in our community and end there. Violence is a necessary part of revolutionary struggle. Nonviolence as it is advocated by negroes is merely a preparation for genocide. Some negroes are so sold on nonviolence that if they received a letter from the White House saying to report to concentration camps, they would not hesitate. They'd be there on time! If we examine what happened to the Jews, we find that it was not the Germans who first began to remove Jews. It was other Jews! We must be prepared to fight anyone who threatens our survival. Black and white. The rebellions taught Blacks the value of retaliatory violence. The most successful rebellion was held in Plainfield [New Jersey]. It was successful in the sense that white violence was minimized. The only death that occurred in Plainfield was that of a white racist cop. We know how sensitive america is about the killing of policemen—especially white policemen. But both National Guardsmen and local police were afraid to shoot up the Black community because the brothers had just stolen two crates of guns. Each one of these guns would shoot seven times before you load it, which makes it hard to hold it; eight times fore you cock it, and it takes a man to stop it. The very fact that white folks fear guns shows the value in being armed. Power, indeed, must come from the barrel of a gun.

Even many white sympathizers with the Negro cause, and Negro leaders themselves, believe that disorder must be stopped so that, in [NAACP leader] Roy Wilkins' words, "society can proceed." The question they do not ask is: whose society? They say that Negro rioting will create a backlash suppressing the liberties needed to organize for change. But this accurate prediction overlooks the fact that those very civil liberties have meant little protection for civil rights workers and ordinary black people in the South, and nearly as little for people in the ghettoes of the North. The freedom that middle-class people correctly feel are real to themselves have very little day-to-day meaning in the ghetto, which is more like a concentration camp than an open society for a large number of its residents. But in order to protect these liberties, many civil rights leaders take part in condemning the ghetto

191

to brutal occupation. Even where "excessive force" is deplored, as Roy Wilkins deplored it in Newark, the assumption still remains that there is a "proper" degree of force that should be used to maintain the status quo. Top officials welcome this liberal support, and agree that any "excessive" force is regrettable and will be investigated. Thus most of the society becomes involved in organizing and protecting murder.

However, the use of force can do nothing but create a demand for greater force. The Newark riot shows that troops cannot make a people surrender. The police had several advantages over the community, particularly in firepower and mechanical mobility. Their pent-up racism gave them a certain amount of energy and morale as well. But as events in the riot showed, the troops could not apply their methods to urban conditions. The problem of precision shooting—for example, at a sniper in a building with forty windows and escape routes through rooftop, alley, and doorway—is nearly as difficult in the urban jungle as precision bombing is in Vietnam. There is a lack of safe cover. There is no front line and no rear, no way to cordon an area completely. A block that is quiet when the troops are present can be the scene of an outbreak the moment the troops leave.

At the same time, the morale fueled by racism soon turns into anxiety. Because of racism, the troops are unfamiliar with both the people and structure of the ghetto. Patrol duty after dark becomes a frightening and exhausting experience, especially for men who want to return alive to their families and homes. A psychology of desperation leads to careless and indiscriminate violence toward the community, including reprisal killing, which inflames the people whom the troops were sent to pacify.

The situation thus contains certain built-in advantages for black people. The community is theirs. They know faces, corners, rooms, alleys. They know whom to trust and whom not to trust. They can switch in seconds from a fighting to a passive posture. It is impressive that state and local officials could not get takers for their offer of money and clemency to anyone turning in a sniper.

This is not a time for radical illusions about "revolution." Stagnancy and conservatism are essential facts of ghetto life. It undoubtedly is true that most Negroes desire the comforts and security that white people possess. There is little revolutionary consciousness or commitment to violence *per se* in the ghetto. Most people in the Newark riot were afraid, unorganized, and helpless when directly facing the automatic weapons. But the actions of white America toward the ghetto are showing black people, especially the young, that they must prepare to fight back.

Guerrilla Warfare

The conditions slowly are being created for an American form of guerrilla warfare based in the slums. The riot represents a signal of this fundamental change.

To the conservative mind the riot is essentially revolution against civilization. To the liberal mind it is an expression of helpless frustration. While the conservative is hostile and the liberal generous toward those who riot, both assume that the riot is a form of lawless, mob behavior. The liberal will turn conservative if polite methods fail to stem disorder. Against these two fundamentally similar concepts, a third one must be asserted, the concept that a riot represents people making history.

The riot is certainly an awkward, even primitive, form of history-making. But if people are barred from using the sophisticated instruments of the established order for their ends, they will find another way. Rocks and bottles are only a beginning, but they cause more attention than all the reports in Washington. To the people involved, the riot is far less lawless and far more representative than the system of arbitrary rules and prescribed channels which they confront every day. The riot is not a beautiful and romantic experience, but neither is the day-to-day slum life from which the riot springs. Riots will not go away if ignored, and will not be cordoned off. They will only disappear when their energy is absorbed into a more decisive and effective form of history-making.

Men are now appearing in the ghettoes who might turn the energy of the riot to a more organized and continuous revolutionary direction. Middle-class Negro intellectuals (especially students) and Negroes of the ghetto are joining forces. They have found channels closed, the rules of the game stacked, and American democracy a system that excludes them. They understand that the institutions of the white community are unreliable in the absence of black community power. They recognize that national civil-rights leaders will not secure the kind of change that is needed. They assume that disobedience, disorder, and even violence must be risked as the only alternative to continuing slavery.

The role of organized violence is now being carefully considered. During a riot, for instance, a conscious guerrilla can participate in pulling police away from the path of people engaged in attacking stores. He can create disorder in new areas the police think are secure. He can carry the torch, if not all the people, to white neighborhoods and downtown business districts. If necessary, he can successfully shoot to kill.

The guerrilla can employ violence effectively during times of apparent "peace," too. He can attack, in the suburbs or slums, with paint or bullets, symbols of racial oppression. He can get away with it. If he can force the oppressive power to be passive and defensive at the point where it is administered—by the case-worker, landlord, storeowner, or policeman—he can build people's confidence in their ability to demand change. Persistent, accurately-aimed attacks, which need not be on human life to be effective, might disrupt the administration of the ghetto to a crisis point where a new system would have to be considered.

Democracy: A Revolutionary Issue

These tactics of disorder will be defined by the authorities as criminal anarchy. But it may be that disruption will create possibilities of meaningful change. This depends on whether the leaders of ghetto struggles can be more successful in building strong organization than they have been so far. Violence can contribute to shattering the status quo, but only politics and organization can transform it. The ghetto still needs the power to decide its destiny on such matters as urban renewal and housing, social services, policing, and taxation. Tenants still need concrete rights against landlords in public and private housing, or a new system of tenant-controlled living conditions. Welfare clients still need a livable income. Consumers still need to control the quality of merchandise and service in the stores where they shop. Citizens still need effective control over those who police their community. Political structures belonging to the community are needed to bargain for, and maintain control over, funds from government or private sources. In order to build a more decent community while resisting racist power, more than violence is required. People need to create self-government. We are at a point where democracy—the idea and practice of people controlling their lives—is a revolutionary issue in the United States.

VIEWPOINT 5

"A movement which seeks to eradicate shortsighted, mechanistic, anti-humanist conceptions of persons and personal relationships is, in my book, a positive constructive force."

The Women's Liberation Movement Is a Positive Force

Mary C. Segers (b. 1939)

Following a period of relative dormancy after World War II, the feminist movement revived during the 1960s. Betty Friedan's best-selling 1963 book *The Feminine Mystique*, which examined the gap between the belief that women find their greatest fulfillment as wives and mothers (the "feminine mystique") and the discontent many housewives felt with their domestic role, found a receptive audience among American women. In 1966 Friedan and others formed the National Organization for Women (NOW), a political lobbying group that sought the passage of new laws against sex discrimination as well as the enforcement of existing laws. Meanwhile, groups of women active in student protests, the civil rights movement, and other radical movements of the 1960s began meeting to discuss sexism both within these movements and in American society. These discussion groups evolved to form a loosely organized and underground "women's liberation movement" whose goals went beyond NOW's focus on electoral politics and lobbying to include radical critiques of the family, marriage, and sexuality.

The following viewpoint is taken from a 1970 article by Mary C. Segers, a doctoral student at Columbia University in New York

From Mary C. Segers, "The New Civil Rights: Fem Lib!" *Catholic World*, August 1970. Reprinted by permission of the publisher and author.

and a member of the school's Women's Liberation Chapter (Segers later became a political science professor at Rutgers University and the editor of several books on religion and politics). In the article, she provides an overview and appraisal of the developing women's liberation movement, placing it in the context of the evolving position of women in America. Segers argues that although the mass media have highlighted what she terms "the bizarre and the eccentric" facets of the movement, the women in the various "Fem Lib" groups do voice valid concerns regarding their status in American society and the constricting nature of traditional gender stereotypes. The women's liberation movement is valuable, she concludes, because it challenges people to rethink their identities as men and women and gives women greater freedom to explore alternative approaches to work and parenthood.

The bizarre and the eccentric always make "good copy." Perhaps that accounts for the recent deluge of articles on the Women's Liberation Movement in the popular magazines and newsweeklies. After all, women learning karate, burning bras and shrilly denouncing love, sex, marriage, and motherhood are phenomena which fulfill all the requirements of good copy: shocking, gutsy, controversial and therefore "newsworthy." However, on the assumption that beneath the news there is always a story, I propose to find the truth in the eccentric and to describe what are, in my opinion, the genuinely laudable aims of the Women's Liberation Movement.

A Brief History

Feminism, of course, is not new to this country. The Nineteenth Amendment, which granted women the right to vote, was the fruit of a long and sustained effort, born of the abolitionist struggle in the nineteenth century, to enhance the status of women. The suffragettes disappeared from the headlines in the Twenties, but the liberating processes they advocated continued—though not always in the manner they intended. Women began to attend college and to work during the Twenties; they also began to smoke, drink, wear cosmetics and shorten hemlines. If the War brought a large influx of women into the work force during the Forties, the resulting change in their economic status marked women as a new and growing consumer market, fair game for the ingenuity of entrepreneurs and media men. Consumerism and Suburbia meant affluence, household conveniences and more leisure time for women in the Fifties; it also brought to many a vague feeling of discontent and a sense of emptiness and even boredom with their lives as wives and mothers. Young women in the Sixties attempted to find avenues of thought and action (participation in the Civil Rights Movement, for example) other than the traditional route of marriage and motherhood. Instead, they found that, even in "liberation" movements, the role of woman was still that of cook, typist, receptionist and playmate. (As Stokely Carmichael remarked, "The position of women in our movement should be prone.") Finally, if the advent of the pill in the Sixties inaugurated a new era of sexual freedom, approximating that enjoyed by men under the old, now-fading double standard, it also brought an increasing awareness that promiscuity was *not* the avenue to personal fulfillment.

What Women Still Want

Not without reason did a recent TV commercial offer as its main theme, "You've come a long way, baby!" In the first seventy years of this century, a subtle process of social change has brought women a host of new freedoms and opportunities. Why, then, a women's liberation movement now when so much has already been gained? What *are* these new feminists complaining about?

In effect, these women are saying that the liberation process of the last seventy years has not gone far enough, and that what is now required is a fundamental re-evaluation of what it means to be a woman—*and* what it means to be a man. Traditional stereotypes of masculinity and femininity have outlived their usefulness. Women and men are persons, not sex objects and breadwinners. No individual of either sex should feel constrained by social conventions and role conceptions to do only certain things and not others. If a man has a flair for cooking or a "way with children," he should feel free to use these talents without feeling less a man for having done so. If a woman is a trained electrical engineer, she should feel free to pursue her work without being hindered by external discrimination or internal feelings of un-femininity for wanting to do "a man's job." If he and she marry and have children, the division of labor they establish in their home should be based on personal interests and abilities, not on traditional stereotypes of him as father-and-breadwinner and her as housewife-and-mother. What is needed, say these new feminists, are some new role conceptions.

The key to all of this is the word "liberation." The new feminists seek the liberation of women specifically, but they are quick to point out that the achievement of this goal will mean the liberation of men as well. What does this mean? Here I speak simply as one member of the Movement. To me, liberation means a loosening-up of attitudes, a determination to be open-minded, a refusal to indulge in labels and categories. It means the freedom to explore new approaches to work, marriage, fatherhood and motherhood. I am in Fem Lib because I want to destroy stereotypes. If you ask me what I choose to replace the old stereotypes with, I cannot give you an answer because I honestly don't know. But that is the whole point. I prefer open-endedness to the deceptive security of conforming to settled, socially-defined roles. I see a value in exploring new styles of living and acting as men and women. I see positive value in working out my identity as a person and as a woman in an atmosphere free of restricting social conventions and stereotypes. This does not mean that I will not come to the conclusion that woman's peculiar identity is largely bound up with sexuality and with her function of bearing and nurturing new life. It does mean that I will arrive at this conclusion myself and that I will not unthinkingly accept it on the credit of some authority, parental or social. More concretely it means that the next time a man asks me, "What is a pretty girl like you doing studying philosophy?" my answer will be based on the fact that the justification of my activity rests more on his shoulders than on mine.

The Women's Lib Movement

As a Movement, Women's Lib is not nearly so organized as its name suggests. It consists of a variety of organizations, ranging from the reformist, establishment-oriented National Organization for Women (NOW), founded by Betty Friedan of "Feminine Mystique" fame, to more extremist groups such as the New York Radical Feminists whose spokeswoman, Ti-Grace Atkinson, questions the validity of sex and love (never mind marriage and motherhood) as central pillars in a woman's life. Estimates of membership in the multiplicity of small groups that make up the Movement range from 10,000 to 500,000; the fact is that no one really knows how many women are active participants, let alone sympathetic fellow-travelers.

Those attracted to Movement meetings are young, mostly middle class, college-educated women, many of whom have seen previous action in civil rights and peace campaigns. (The current occupational status of women is, I suspect, a factor which may explain why the Movement attracts some women more than others. That is, those in traditionally acceptable "feminine" fields such as fashion, nursing, and school teaching are less likely to become involved than those whose interests, orientation and training have led them to aspire to careers in the traditionally "masculine" professions of law, science, medicine, engineering, and university teaching. Women in this latter category have more obstacles to fight in pursuing their career and are therefore potentially, if not actually, more

In September 1968 approximately two hundred women staged a demonstration against the Miss America pageant in Atlantic City. According to writer and activist Robin Morgan, the protest signaled the moment when radical feminists "announced our existence to the world."

sympathetic with the aims of the Movement.) Widows and divorcees, single and married women gather in private homes in small "self-education" groups to discuss their common experiences and to examine critically their attitudes regarding femininity. Most are career-oriented through training and inclination; their view of marriage and housework is less than romantic. Indeed, a newcomer to any one of Fem Lib's many teach-ins, conferences and workshops must be prepared to encounter negativism, hostility, bitterness and a seething undercurrent of anger at "male chauvinists" who are by definition "oppressors." She or he must also be patient enough to sit through long diatribes of jargon and invective, interlaced with the latest brew of four-letter words.

The hostility and resentment, to be sure, may be misplaced, a point not lost on those who take issue with Fem Lib. Critics argue that the shrill complaints of these women are simply indications of their own inability to accept life's normal difficulties and adjustments. It is not society that is confused, so the argument runs, it is they themselves. The "fault," if there be one, lies in their own personalities.

The Rationality of Feminism

Anyone familiar with the attitudes of [psychologist] Bruno Bettelheim towards the New Left knows this argument is not new. Bettelheim applies it to student militants, claiming that "sickness" is their problem, not society's. However, in my opinion, Bettelheim's view is shortsighted. The argument is deficient for two reasons. First, it ignores objective wrongs of existing society (discrimination against women *does* in fact exist). Secondly, proponents of such an argument ignore the valuable insights we can learn from people who have suffered. One must always be careful, it is true, to distinguish legitimate insights from mere "sour grapes" complaints. One must always take into consideration the possible bias stemming from the personal background and experience of any person who dares to launch a full-scale attack on any social institution. But, as J.S. Mill remarked in *On Liberty*, there is always a kernel of truth in the eccentric and "far out" view. Our task is to isolate that kernel of truth. Suffering— whether it be that of the Fem Lib activist whose personal relations with the men in her life have been unsatisfying or that of the black militant whose interaction with whites has been less than rewarding—brings with it a heightened sense of injustice and a desire to eradicate that injustice. Unfortunately, suffering also brings with it a sense of bitterness, a stridency of tone and an overweening self-righteousness. In approaching Fem Lib, it is the task of the perceptive, discriminating person to discern the kernel of truth beneath the negativism. I guarantee that if one perseveres, one will find the rationality beneath the eccentricity.

Some of the rationality of the Movement is reflected, I think, in the goals they have set for themselves. These center on achieving equal opportunity and compensation in business, the professions and the university; there is no reason, for example, why the salary of a woman and man in the same position should not *be* the same. With regard to the media and advertising, Fem Lib is critical of the commercial image of woman as primarily a sex symbol and consumer of material goods; one group—Media Women—affixes stickers ("This ad insults women") to ads which they consider cheap, demeaning, offensive, and exploitative. The Movement also advocates the establishment of adequately-staffed child-care services for women who work outside the home. For those who have to work (*e.g.* welfare mothers), this is a necessity; for those who want to work, Fem Lib will argue that day-care centers are equally necessary, since such women require activities and outlets outside the home to keep them healthy, active, concerned wives and mothers. Finally, Fem Lib works actively towards the elimination of attitudes and conditioning—social, political and ecclesiastical—which assume the inferiority of women.

Reactions of Men

Male reactions to the Movement are varied. One extreme is reflected in statements such as, "All these women need is some good sex," or, "If women want to be cabbies, mailmen, garbage-men, and soldiers—or draft-resisters—let them go ahead." On a slightly more elevated level, some men question whether Fem Lib activists really want to be liberated to jobs men have and hate (because they are boring and meaningless). Do women really know what they are getting into when they seek entrée into a competitive business world with its hard work and pressures to succeed? Do women really want to be liberated to the power and responsibility which weigh on the man, the husband, the father? After all, who gets ulcers at age thirty-five and heart attacks at age forty in this society?

Liberating Men and Women

Fem Lib's answer to this is that no sensible person wants to see women "liberated into the social role of men." Both roles must be destroyed—that of the dependent female as well as that of the domineering male. Those women who live vicariously through their husband and children (and have no identity other than wife and mother) are basically dangerous people: they threaten to smother their children with affection and overprotectiveness, and they constitute an unfair burden for their men. At issue here is the question of freedom and personal autonomy: whether any one person can be the sole *raison d'etre* for another. Is there not something intrinsically wrong in relying completely upon another person to provide the meaning of one's own life?

Fortunately, a new breed of man is growing up whose ego does not demand that he be the "knight on a white horse" for his woman—who wants a woman to live her own life and create her own identity and meaning because he realizes that he cannot and does not want to do it for her. In the same vein, I think Fem Lib's goal is a new type of woman who can love her man freely because she does not depend on him for economic security or personal and social identity.

Rethinking Personal Identity

The value of Women's Liberation is that it challenges us to re-think individual identity. Hitherto, criteria of femininity and masculinity have been social, conventional and cultural; they may also have been rooted in biological functioning. The question is: need we be enslaved by biological and cultural determinism?

I do not think Fem Lib has given sufficient consideration to this very profound question. In striving for equality and an end to unjust discrimination, the Movement has quite naturally tended to focus on similarities between the sexes; men and women, it is argued, are simply persons having similar talents and abilities and capable of similar achievements. However, I think it is necessary

A Decade of Liberation

Marlene Dixon, a sociologist who taught at McGill University in Canada, writes in a 1969 article in Ramparts *that during the 1960s women—much like blacks, American Indians, poor whites, and other underprivileged groups—have gained a new understanding of their disadvantaged status and of the need to struggle against their oppression.*

The 1960's has been a decade of liberation; women have been swept up by that ferment along with blacks, Latins, American Indians and poor whites—the whole soft underbelly of this society. As each oppressed group in turn discovered the nature of its oppression in American society, so women have discovered that they too thirst for free and fully human lives. The result has been the growth of a new women's movement, whose base encompasses poor black and poor white women on relief, working women exploited in the labor force, middle class women incarcerated in the split level dream house, college girls awakening to the fact that sexiness is not the crowning achievement in life, and movement women who have discovered that in a freedom movement they themselves are not free. In less than four years women have created a variety of organizations, from the nationally based middle class National Organization of Women (NOW) to local radical feminist groups in every major city in North America. The new movement includes caucuses within nearly every New Left group and within most professional associations in the social sciences. Ranging in politics from reform to revolution, it has produced critiques of almost every segment of American society and constructed an ideology that rejects every hallowed cultural assumption about the nature and role of women. . . .

Women are no longer afraid that their rebellion will threaten their very identity as women. They are not frightened by their own militancy, but liberated by it. Women's Liberation is an idea whose time has come.

to define differences as well as similarities between the sexes and to address ourselves to the larger question: what makes a man a man, and what is peculiar and unique to woman-as-woman? Further, how do men and women complement each other? How and why do they need each other? Are differences reducible to genital sexuality, procreation and child-bearing—or is there something more that we can say about the nature of man and woman?

Regrettably, very little research has been done in this area. What has been done suggests that, while goals such as equal opportunity, freedom and pay for both sexes are laudable, there are, nonetheless, some basic, biological male-female differences. It has been found, for example, that males are aggressive, females are passive, though females are tougher and able to endure more pain. A researcher at Stanford University finds that males and females have innate physical temperamental differences, with some overlapping rather than strict, all-or-nothing distribution between the sexes. On a theoretical level, [psychologist] Erik Erikson agrees with Freud that "anatomy is destiny" but argues that Freud misconstrued female identity in emphasizing penis-envy, that is, in concentrating on a woman's lack of what a man has. Rather than stress the loss of an external organ, Erikson prefers to emphasize the female's possession of an inner-bodily space with productive, vital, inner potential. Such physical differences, he continues, determine, to some extent, personality configurations: women have a predisposition to include, to accept, to have and to hold, to nurture and protect, to be molders and shapers. Conversely, men have a predisposition for intruding into outer space, for being active, mobile and aggressive, for being movers and shakers. Erikson is quick to emphasize, however, that "each sex can transcend itself to feel and represent the concerns of the other. For even as real women harbor a legitimate as well as a compensatory masculinity, so real men can partake of motherliness—if permitted to do so by powerful mores" (Erik Erikson, "Womanhood and the Inner Space," in *Identity, Youth and Crisis*, pp. 285–286). It seems to me that Fem Lib is trying to change powerful mores so that people can more freely express their own innate inclinations and predispositions. As one Columbia senior said to me, "Why is it that girls can play cowboys and indians while guys can't play with dolls?" Psychoanalysts are not the only ones to argue that "anatomy is destiny." At a Fem Lib teach-in I attended one speaker categorized sexual intercourse (in all instances, not only in the case of rape) as an act of male aggression and as the prototype of all later male domination in the family, business, industry, society, culture, the university, etc. I find myself disagreeing strongly with this characterization and wondering, á la Bettelheim, what prompted the speaker to make that remark. For it seems to me that intercourse is a sign (a sacramental sign in Catholic theology) of the mutuality that should obtain in a man-woman relationship. That relationship is a complementary one, each person assuming a role and function needed by and complementary to that assumed by the other person. My point is: doesn't intercourse provide clues as to what a heterosexual relationship should be in other areas of life? Aren't tones and nuances ones of mutuality and sharing rather than domination of one partner by the other? The male chauvinist (and we must thank the Movement for emphasizing this) is as odious as the castrating female. Likewise, that a woman should *in practice* have *sole* responsibility, twenty-four hours a day, for the care and rearing of children does not at all follow the fact that these children are the result of a mutually procreative act.

Certain practical implications follow from this, such as a division of the tasks involved in child-care and housework. [Childcare writer] Benjamin Spock has recently lamented the short-sightedness of many women who fail to realize that child-rearing and housekeeping are tremendously challenging, creative, and rewarding endeavors. If this is the case, should men be denied the creative and rewarding satisfactions of cooking, sewing, cleaning, interior decorating, and playing with children?

Obviously, I favor a marriage partnership in which work of all kinds is shared. The fact is that if a woman works outside the home, household tasks must be shared by her and her husband; otherwise, she will find herself trying to do two full-time jobs and losing her sanity in the process. If she doesn't have to work, should she? If she has been trained for a career, she may very well have to—or, again, find herself profoundly discontented. For the fact is—and Dr. Spock would do well to consider it—that even with modern gadgets, housework still has a repetitive quality and a lonesomeness which most work outside the home doesn't have. Perhaps he exaggerates and glamorizes in describing such work as creative and challenging.

Feminism and the New Left

There is a New Left faction in the Women's Liberation Movement which views discrimination against women as just one more manifestation of the inherent "sickness" of advanced industrial society. "Sexism" is the latest evil but it belongs with "Imperialism," "Capitalism" and "Racism" as part of the symptomatology of a repressive society. Of all the movements designed to fight all of these "isms," I think Fem Lib is the most important and will, in the long run, have the greatest impact. This is so because the thrust of Fem Lib is towards a fundamental reevaluation of such basic concepts as person, role, function and relationship. Fem Lib is like the Black Revolution in this respect since it strikes at the basic question of personal identity. Its concerns are more radical (*radix*: root) than the political questions of imperialism, corporate capitalism and "the military-industrial complex." It is easy to deny *personal* responsibility regarding Vietnam or the assassination of Martin Luther King, Jr.; it is not so easy to avoid confronting such issues as the meaning of masculinity and femininity. As the Women's Liberation Movement grows, I predict that it will affect more people than were affected by any of the movements of the Sixties.

A Positive Force

When [German novelist] Gunter Grass was asked by a Columbia University co-ed what he thought of Fem Lib, he replied in six short words: "I don't think it is dangerous." Neither do I. Women and men who refuse to accept as normative the rigid, stereotyped thinking of a culture which boasts of *Playboy* and *Cosmopolitan*—such people are not dangerous. A movement which seeks to eradicate shortsighted, mechanistic, anti-humanist conceptions of persons and personal relationships is, in my book, a positive constructive force.

VIEWPOINT 6

"As a fighting woman myself, I can't forgive Liberation its paralyzing excesses."

The Women's Liberation Movement Is Not a Positive Force

Anne Bernays (b. 1930)

During the 1960s, women ranging from middle-class professionals to college students and veterans of the civil rights and antiwar movements were challenging basic assumptions regarding their place in American society. Their concerns ranged from legalizing abortion to enforcing the 1964 Civil Rights Act (which banned sexual discrimination in education and employment) to attacking the institution of marriage and the traditional societal primacy of heterosexuality. By the end of the decade, the "women's liberation movement," which consisted of loosely organized groups of radical feminists, was attracting increasing attention from the press and the general public.

Not all women agreed with the goals of the various feminist groups. A 1970 Gallup poll reported that 70 percent of American women believed that they were treated fairly by men. Many women were particularly opposed to some radical feminists who argued that all men were enemies and that women should therefore resist oppression by rejecting motherhood, marriage, and sexual relations with men. In the following viewpoint, Anne Bernays, a novelist, expresses her concerns about the women's

From Anne Bernays, "What Are You Supposed to Do If You Like Children?" *Atlantic Monthly*, March 1970. Reprinted by permission of the author.

liberation movement as it had evolved by 1970, when this article was first published. A supporter of women's rights, Bernays nevertheless criticizes some radical feminists for their denunciations of family and men and for their refusal to recognize men and women as being inherently different.

In granting permission to reprint this piece, Bernays wished to emphasize that her views have changed. "If you asked me today if I wrote this piece I would say 'No.' The person who did write it is long gone and buried. I don't even recognize her troglodyte (and somewhat patronizing) attitude."

If it weren't for the disturbing quality that lurks behind every word of Women's Liberation literature, you might be tempted to write off the substantive stuff (men are sexual vampires, marriage is stunting and exploitative—that kind of complaint) as merely whacky. But it is difficult to ignore a movement whose pervasive theme is so resentful, envious, and despairing, and which draws to its liberated bosom thousands of females who would rather break down than build up. Sadder still, while Liberation is irresistible to women who want to be men, it is poison to women who want to be women. Wasteful and self-destructive, this movement may simply be demonstrating in a particularly unappealing form what appears to be society's tendency to atomize and negate, to be compulsively unwilling to compromise and construct. Nevertheless, as a fighting woman myself, I can't forgive Liberation its paralyzing excesses.

At the root of Liberation's determination to disintegrate the sexes is the disabling anxiety that *different* means the same thing as *inferior*. Anybody can see that women are as valuable as men but they are no more the same than ears and eyes are. Women are biologically, constitutionally, and emotionally different from men. Why is this palpable fact so hard for so many women to swallow? Are we as confused as all that?

And while the girls, abetted by certain educationists who ought to know better, are tying themselves into psychic knots trying to prove that the obvious differences ain't so, the larger social issues, among them the measurably deteriorating status of women, continue to smolder. Perhaps for the first time in history, American women have the freedom and opportunity to use their considerable collective energy to do something effective about the way we have been discriminated against.

The Situation of Women and Blacks

In a way, we should not be blamed for our confusion. At least blacks know they are black; it's something they can sink their teeth into. But how many women know they are women, or at least know what being a woman signifies? The analogy to be drawn between the recent racial and sexual explosions is by now almost too weary to be re-cited—except to note the fact that the analogy breaks down at a critical point: namely, in their goals, for while the eventual black goal is psychologically respectable, Liberation's is not.

Despite separatist disclaimers, I'm convinced that blacks will only be satisfied when we all look more or less alike. Most people are profoundly suspicious and hostile about profound physical differences (excluding sexual ones); everybody will be much better off when you can't tell whose parents were white and whose black, when such killing physical differences will be blurred once and for all. But the parallel imperative—that women be just like men—is based on faulty psychological assumptions. For androgyny is not productive; on the contrary, it is irrevocably sterile. You can stir around the races until, like a box of melted crayons, we all come out brown, but you can't do that to male and female.

If women, like blacks, feel that it's about time to do something about our second-class status (and women make up the only *non*minority group I can think of which suffers from the serious effects of minority group self-abasement), more power to us. Until recently we were just the same as prisoners (no money of our own, no political leverage, few career choices, little physical freedom; if home was our castle, we were still under a sort of house arrest). Now that we're out, what are we doing about it? It seems to me we're still too angry, too defiant, too confused to organize ourselves effectively.

Changing Concepts

How did we get this way? For one thing, key concepts have undergone transformations as radical as a sex-change operation. Consider, for instance, the concept of "fulfillment." Until a few decades ago this was a benign word that meant having babies and being a self-sufficient, happy hausfrau. Gradually, while almost no one was looking, it turned itself inside out so that by 1946 or so, it had come to mean just the opposite. It meant get out. It meant you had better find yourself a job that would take advantage of your baffled, bottled-up, urgent, unexpressed need to express yourself to your ultimate mental and emotional capacity. It would be interesting to find out just how many men feel their jobs meet these romantic requirements. To be altogether fair, by the postwar period there wasn't too much left for a woman to do around the house that would fill eight to ten hours, unless she was a compulsive. What was an educated girl going to do *but* go out and fulfill herself in a so-called "man's world," competitively with men, alongside men? So far, all well and good.

No one with any brains would deny that women represent the largest wasted labor force in America, nor that, except for several crucial years, we need and should be given the opportunity to put our gifts—intellectual, artistic, political, whatever—to work on a regular, equal-pay basis. But when Liberation insists that women can be absolute "equals" with men in these spheres, they're ignoring what it's all about. For if women are willing to acknowledge the remotest emotional obligation to husband and children, especially to children during their fragile first five or six years of life, then they can't summon the time, physical energy, and psychic equipment to do two jobs simultaneously. You can't split a woman's life down the middle and expect each half, like a severed worm, to go happily crawling off, to survive and function in perfect health.

Long ago, in the early sixties, Betty Friedan performed a legitimate service for thousands of intelligent ladies by letting them in on her little secret: life has more to offer you women than a sinkful of dirty dishes. Shouting all the way, Mrs. Friedan encouraged women to get up there and claim their seats in the front of the bus.

Mrs. Friedan's rhetoric, however, was as nothing compared with the rhetoric of the Movement. "Sexual suppression is an essential instrument in the production of economic enslavement," says Wilhelm Reich, inventor of the Orgone Box, a telephone-booth-type item you were supposed to sit in for several hours a day while you soaked up sexual wattage. Like so many Liberation writers, Dr. Reich comes up with half-truths which are then worshiped as full-blown realities. The uneasy fact is that sexual suppression and repression do indeed exist as extensive and mutilating problems, but to blame it all on a systematic, conspiratorial attempt by "society" (read "men") is both simplistic and fatally misleading.

There must be something else to blame for the devitalizing anger and the deliberate attempt to defeminize women and for the loss of true sexuality in so many people, both male and female. I suspect that it is that same role-confusion again, compounded by mothers who, unsure of their own sexual identities, don't know what to tell their daughters about men and marriage, and so tell them nothing useful. The result is a perpetual downward cycling of frustration, anger, and envy, based on ambivalent feelings about life itself.

If you can assume that marriage and the family will remain the nucleus of society (and I'm aware this is precisely what Liberation does *not* assume, has no wish to assume), then it is painfully clear that until something or somebody comes along to put the brakes on this runaway confusion, generation after generation of bright girls will wake up sometime after college with a shock, as the pattern repeats itself unchecked, a shock that will have as much to do with *how* and *why* they should function as adult females as with their identity.

If matters were not bad enough, there seems to be a real, gentle conspiracy among the administrators of elite women's colleges to assure their students that they are not merely as good as men but that they *are* men—female men. "You will leave this institution," the girls are told, but not in so many words, "impressively educated. You will go out into a world where you and your male counterparts will have identical careers, job choices, and opportunities. If you happen to get married and have children along the way, you will be able to deal with any *minor problems* that arise on this score." This gentle conspiracy, which glosses over the real facts of life, becomes another accepted myth. If by some miracle, a girl escapes its inevitable backlash, someone else is going to get it in the neck, more probably her husband or her children, those archetypally innocent victims. An unjustified confidence in the ability to drop all such "archaic," "trivial," and "male chauvinist" sex-based distinctions is simply a neatly camouflaged trap.

The victim of this confidence game believes with all her heart that her only satisfactions are going to be those earned by leading an independent life, remaining loyal to abstractions, and doing her own thing. She cannot allow herself to believe that these misty ideals may actually be substitutes for the give-and-take of intensely personal relationships and extended personal commitments—where love is not something you go around talking about but something you do.

Our victim is an easy mark for Liberation. Although she doesn't know it, she is readying herself for a deprived life. It's extremely revealing, I think, that Liberated women don't follow the lead of their black sisters and cry, "Woman is Beautiful." The Liberated girl refuses to think of herself in feminine terms. Like a prisoner of war (the war with men), she will restrict her answer to a stark "I am a person." Since (so their logic lurches along), under the present setup, women possess only the dignity of a sexual object, similar to any other commodity in a market-oriented society, she cannot be beautiful, but only repulsive—and repulsing. No pride is visible here, only fight. The psychic imperatives have blinded her to the pleasures of her own uniqueness.

Male and Female Differences

"Scientists are still busy 'proving' the biological inferiority of women," says sociologist Marlene Dixon in a recent issue of *Ramparts*. This investigation into the clinical differences between male and female, branded by the Movement as sinister, malevolent, male chauvinist, reactionary, and all that, is scientifically quite honorable, even conventional. It is being carried on by both men and women researchers, whose principal aim is to define what most people can see in front of their noses.

Some of the recent findings, while not terribly startling, are interesting for their implications. Jerome Kagan, a professor of developmental psychology at Harvard, an enthusiastic, affable man in his early forties, has been working this controversial vein for several years. Kagan and his colleagues have found clinical evidence that, in general, females are more proficient in verbal skills than males. John Watson, at Berkeley, recently discovered that even in children a few months old, there is a measurable sex-based difference in response to stimulation: specifically, baby girls respond more often to auditory excitation, boys to visual. As Kagan somewhat offhandedly sums up a portion of the findings, "It is not completely bizarre to suggest that the sex differences in . . . vocalization during the first year reflect a subtle difference in cerebral dominance." In other words, the insides of their heads are not the same. Moreover, Kagan has come up with neurological evidence that may explain why "there are many . . . women poets and novelists . . . far fewer woman composers." If the brains of little girls behave differently from the brains of little boys, it seems valid to expect dissimilar personalities, aptitudes, ambitions.

This leads us directly into the delicate area of personality. Even the most repressive male would hardly dare maintain that women have exclusive rights to, say, gentleness, or men, courage. For example, women have very positive, adhesive feelings toward their own small children, and men wouldn't at all mind being physical heroes. (This does not mean, of course, that in a pinch the arrangements can't be turned around.)

Yet, as a lady psychoanalyst recently reminded me, nobody knows how she is going to feel about her children until they arrive. Nonetheless, Liberation maintains that when society undergoes its badly needed overhaul, children can be whisked off to communal nurseries where superbly equipped women will look after them while their mothers go out and fulfill themselves. There's a lot to be said for this kind of substitute home, described recently by [psychologist] Bruno Bettelheim, and for the civilizing effects of a really good nursery with one warm, motherly,

211

consistent woman running the show. It's also perfectly true that an educated adult can't survive solely on a diet of Child for long, uninterrupted periods of time without getting rickets of the mind. But the time your children are with you is short, they grow up fast, and soon all that's left of them is a voice, long-distance, on Sunday afternoon.

Selective Reasoning

Some women might prefer not to have their children removed after breakfast. They may *enjoy* having their kids around, giving them lunch, talking with them, trying to discover the shape of *their* personalities, presiding over domestic war and peace, taking them to buy shoes, even kissing them. Here, in sentimental form, is what is missing in the Liberation's manifesto, which, like scores of radical solutions for injustices, bases its corrective assumptions on selective, fragmentary reasoning. Marlene Dixon says, "All women suffer from economic exploitation, from psychological deprivation, and from exploitive sexuality."

She didn't ask me. She doesn't want to know about women like me, and I can't exactly blame her, for we're her enemy. Just as all males are her enemy. I would like to be there when Miss Dixon debates another professional sociologist, a woman aptly named Patricia Sexton. In Mrs. Sexton's admirable book *The Feminized Male*, she described for us her "ideal woman": "She would be strong, tough, able to take it, ready for rough-and-tumble. . . . As for sex, she would be frank and accepting, if not rather bawdy, and would use the street vernacular where it fits. She would love people—all colors and castes, women as well as men." Mrs. Sexton and I are of one mind, except I regret her use of the conditional tense. Aren't there any flesh-and-blood women to be proud of anymore?

CHAPTER 5

The Activists of the Sixties: Historical Reflections

Chapter Preface

Decades after the end of the 1960s, the period continues to be debated in books and historical studies. Much of the controversy relating to the decade and its legacy focuses on what came to be called the "Movement"—the various, interlinked political and cultural revolutions and activist organizations that began or peaked in the 1960s, including the antiwar, civil rights, student, women's and gay liberation, and environmental movements. The arguments surrounding these various movements often resurface in the differing historical assessments of the decade—in part because the participants in the events of the 1960s and the later chroniclers of that decade are often the same people. "The activists of the [1960s] era keep reliving their youth by writing books about it," notes author and professor Morris Dickstein, "while their conservative opponents . . . never tire of invoking it as the root of all evil."

For many veterans of the movements of the 1960s, the decade was a time of significant achievement. According to noted activist Tom Hayden, who later became a California state senator:

> In the '60s we shook off apathy, ended Southern segregation, expanded voting rights, stopped the Vietnam War, defied an imperial Presidency, empowered the powerless, and became aware of the worse environmental crisis in our history.

Hayden and others concede that sixties activists were not without faults ("We were better at questioning authority than replacing it," admits Hayden), but they maintain that their efforts made American society better, freer, and more open.

Other commentators, however, argue that the legacy of the 1960s has been mostly negative. Many contend that during the 1960s America lost its moral and social moorings amid rampant drug use, sexual openness and promiscuity, and widespread resistance to the authority of cultural, government, and educational institutions. According to Newt Gingrich, the conservative Republican congressman (and part-time history teacher) who was elected Speaker of the House in 1994, the 1960s were a time when disaffected countercultural elitists "taught self-indulgent, aristocratic values without realizing that if an entire society engaged in the indulgences of an elite few, you could tear the society to shreds."

In discussing the 1960s, writes Barbara L. Tischler in her introduction for the book *Sights on the Sixties*, historians must get beyond the extremely divergent views of the decade expressed by Hayden and Gingrich. She argues that many Americans have two simplistic images of the decade: a "good sixties" of the civil rights movement, an optimistic War on Poverty, and the 1967 Summer of Love; and a "bad sixties" of riots, political violence, and a decline of social and cultural standards. Both pictures are not entirely false, Tischler maintains, but they also both simplify the true nature of the decade. "Scholars and students," she contends, "need to transcend the good sixties–bad sixties typology" when examining the decade and its controversial developments.

The historians included in this chapter attempt to do this in appraising the achievements, limitations, and tactics of radical political and cultural activists of the 1960s. The authors agree that many of the visionary goals of the "Movement" were not realized, but disagree on why this happened. Their assessments provide differing conclusions regarding the actions of sixties radicals and the public's response to them.

VIEWPOINT 1

"Sixties movements expressed the voices of those whom society had systematically treated as 'other'—black Americans, Latinos, the poor, Native Americans, women, gays. . . . In place of domination, the Movement sought community."

Activists of the Sixties Were Idealistic and Visionary

Edward P. Morgan (b. 1945)

The nature and legacy of the various protest movements of the 1960s continue to be debated. In the following excerpt from his book *The 60s Experience: Hard Lessons About Modern America*, author Edward P. Morgan traces the development of protest movements of the 1960s from the beginning of the civil rights sit-in movement in 1960 to the killing of four students at Kent State University by National Guard units in 1970. He argues that the Movement—a collective name for the antiwar, civil rights, and other antiestablishment campaigns of the sixties—succeeded in producing radical criticisms of and prescriptions for America that remain valid today. The activists in the sixties movements, he argues, were united by shared democratic ideals of equality, personal empowerment, and community. He attributes their failure in realizing their dreams of social transformation to the fact that America's economy and government proved fundamentally incompatible with their democratic goals. Morgan is a political science professor who has taught at Lehigh University in Pennsylvania and elsewhere. As a college student during the 1960s he was involved in campus politics, civil rights activism, and the antiwar movement.

On February 3, 1960, one month after the junior senator from Massachusetts, John Fitzgerald Kennedy, announced his candidacy for President, the *New York Times* reported in a brief, back-page article from Greensboro, North Carolina, "A group of well-dressed Negro college students staged a sitdown strike in a downtown Woolworth store today and vowed to continue it in relays until Negroes were served at the lunch counter."

Ten years later, the *Times* devoted four front-page columns to a lead article headed, "4 Kent State Students Killed by Troops." Most startling of all was the photograph that appeared nationwide of a young woman screaming for help while kneeling over the body of a slain student.

These two events framed the decade of the 1960s. The Greensboro sit-in evolved out of the civil rights activities of the 1950s and was the spark that ignited a wave of student sit-ins across seventy cities of the South. The Kent State killings occurred during one of several hundred campus protests against the American invasion of Cambodia. After the shock of Kent State, and the subsequent deaths of two black students at Jackson State in Mississippi, over 450 college and university campuses shut down—fifty-one of them for the remainder of the academic year—in what proved to be the largest strike action in United States history. An estimated four million students were involved in the protests of May 1970.

Each event represented an important historical and psychological milestone in this era of protest. The Greensboro sit-ins marked the entry of students into full-scale participation in the civil rights movement. As sociologist Aldon Morris notes [in *The Origins of the Civil Rights Movement*],

> Nineteen sixty was the year when thousands of Southern black students at black colleges joined forces with "old movement warriors" and tremendously increased the power of the developing civil rights movement. . . . From the privileged position of hindsight, it is clear that the student sit-ins of 1960 were the introduction to a decade of political turbulence.

Similarly, although antiwar activity continued until the last

American troops were brought home from Vietnam in 1973, the Kent State and Jackson State killings marked a psychological turning point in the student revolt. Many students realized for the first time that they could die because of their activism, that their government was capable of gunning them down in cold blood. The contrast between Greensboro and Kent State suggests the scale of change over the course of the decade—Greensboro symbolizing the hope and energy of the early Sixties, Kent State the nightmare of repression and social disintegration.

In between these events, the Sixties were stained by assassinations of public figures like John F. Kennedy, Medgar Evers, Malcolm X, Martin Luther King, Jr., and Robert Kennedy. They were years of mass protest, for civil rights and black power, for liberated education, for poor people, women's liberation, gay rights, Chicanos, American Indians, and against the Vietnam war. A host of activist groups of all persuasions materialized, from the Student Nonviolent Coordinating Committee (SNCC), Students for a Democratic Society (SDS), and the Women Strike for Peace, to the New Mobilization Committee to End the War in Vietnam (New Mobe), the Weather Underground, the Black Panther party, and the Radicalesbians.

The Sixties' claim for historical distinction rests on the combination of enormous cultural ferment and political upheaval within a single decade. In effect, the Sixties combined qualities of the 1920s and 1930s. Movements of the Sixties converged while grappling with the most pressing and intractable dilemmas of the post-war world—racism and poverty, pervasive dehumanization in the developed world, and Third World liberation. At their revolutionary peak in 1968, these movements sought to launch, in Daniel Cohn-Bendit's words, "an experiment that completely breaks with that society, an experiment . . . which allows a glimpse of a possibility."

The Sixties were also years of enormous musical energy, from the folk revival in Greenwich Village in 1960 to the British invasion in 1963–1964 and the emergence of rock music in 1965 to the rock festival Age of Aquarius. Marijuana and hallucinogens like LSD were widely used by the young, and sexual experimentation was openly embraced by the youthful counterculture. Scores of underground newspapers appeared across the country, providing a community forum and network for various elements of the Movement. Rules, laws, and social norms changed with staggering speed. Traditional boundaries of acceptable expression were shattered in an enormous burst of innovation and experimentation in literature, theater, and the visual arts. As Michael Arlen described it [in *Living Room War*], the Sixties represented the chaos of a world "coming more and more out from under wraps.". . .

Perspectives on the Sixties

These tumultuous years have inspired reactions ranging from nostalgic recollection to fierce denunciation. . . .

We may distinguish three basic perspectives on the 1960s that reflect distinct social and political outlooks. Two of these—viewpoints we may call "liberal" and "conservative"—lie within the American political mainstream. Citing factors like early socialization, changes in the institutional environment of American life, or simply the pendulum of history, American liberals tend to see the decade as a time when millions of Americans refused to tolerate the gap between institutional practice and the fundamental American ideals of equal rights, free speech, and a foreign policy grounded on universal human rights. Inspired by early civil rights activism and Kennedy rhetoric, young people demanded that their country live up to the values they had been taught.

To a considerable degree, the nation responded with liberal institutional reforms. Unprecedented civil rights legislation permanently changed the face of the Old South; the federal government launched a massive assault on poverty and inadequate education, housing, and health care; universities modified their curricular requirements and social regulations; the draft was replaced by a volunteer army; and the War in Vietnam—a tragic mistake in the view of many liberals—finally ground to a halt. In effect, despite mistakes and short-circuited social programs, the system worked. The Sixties were essentially a noble era of reform.

With remarkable success in the mainstream media, contemporary conservative critics have engaged in a sustained assault on the Sixties, determined to roll back its surge of liberal social and foreign policy: aggressive civil rights enforcement, federal involvement in social services for the poor, affirmative action policies, profit-reducing federal regulations, abortion rights, and most notably, public reluctance to support military intervention overseas, the so-called Vietnam syndrome.

Conservatives argue that the liberal policies of the Sixties and the youth revolt were connected, and that both were carried to excess. The youth revolt was essentially apolitical and self-indulgent, spawned by post–World War II affluence and permissive childrearing. Liberal reformers in government and academia legitimized and thereby helped to unleash the self-indulgent impulses of the young. Liberal political values like free speech, equal rights, and individualism were distorted to justify excessive antisocial behavior. During the early to mid-1980s, a handful of former radicals denounced their earlier political stance while embracing the rising tide of Reaganism.

Both interpretations have merit. Liberals can point to significant accomplishments in civil rights and social welfare legislation. There is also ample evidence that many protesters espoused liberal values, denouncing the hypocrisy of government officials. Conservatives can point to flaws in Great Society programs and instances of excessively self-indulgent or violent behavior on the part of the counterculture and New Left.

However, to limit one's concern to the *relative* effectiveness of the era's liberal reforms, or to concentrate on the manifest behavior of young activists while overlooking the crucial events of that time, is to miss entirely the point of the 1960s revolt. Since both are fully grounded in mainstream institutions, neither perspective can adequately explain movements that launched a fundamental critique of those very institutions.

A Third View

A third view, and one with many variants, has arisen from within the 1960s movements themselves, and has emerged in a host of books that assess distinct movements or recount personal voyages through the Sixties. This view is grounded in the *experience* of the decade's movements and the hard lessons learned about modern America. For many, especially those who were young during that time, the experiences of the Sixties were a formative political education that taught not only painful lessons about American institutions but lessons about themselves.

What can be learned from a systematic review of the Sixties experience? First, young people need to understand, rather than ignore or imitate, the movements of the 1960s—where they came from, how they evolved, and why they evolved as they did. Second, by examining the connections among the movements of that time, we gain a more comprehensive understanding of the meaning of the 1960s in history. And third, the experiences of Sixties movements can provide future movements of human liberation with important lessons about the American political system and its potential for change.

What became known simply as the Movement began with two proactive struggles for change—the civil rights movement and the student New Left. Both were rooted in the postwar world of the 1950s. Each contained an expressive or prefigurative strain—an effort to build and enjoy new democratic social relationships—within an instrumental or political strain aimed at transforming American society. The electric combination of expressive and instrumental strains is one main reason for the enormous energy unleashed during the decade.

The two groups most synonymous with youthful Sixties activism, SNCC and SDS, were acutely affected by the tensions between these two strains. Both expressed an instinctive mistrust of authoritarian rule and hierarchy, a need for loving connection with others, and an emphasis on individual creativity and integrity. These values not only foreshadowed what a "post-revolutionary" America should look like, but they prescribed how the movement to change America should go about this instrumental task. Therein lay the fundamental dilemmas that confronted all movements of the 1960s: how to effect change on a national scale through movements founded on personal relationships and grassroots organizing, a utopian vision, and personal spontaneity; what to do when confronted by a repressive state; how to extend a qualitative, post-scarcity critique of society to those still wanting to be included in that society.

As events unfolded in the 1960s, the relationship between expressive and instrumental politics changed. Initially, activists believed the two were compatible, that they could succeed in transforming society. The result was a contagious, hopeful energy and committed idealism. Over time, buffeted by evasion and resistance, the horror of the Vietnam War, and crushing repression, the hope for fundamental political transformation was shattered; the gap between prefigurative and instrumental politics widened. One outcome was disillusionment, rage, and either disassociation from or aggressive militance toward society. Another was a radicalized critique of modern America, a shift from liberal to radical democracy. The Sixties experience taught activists that their expressive democratic vision was fundamentally incompatible with the root assumptions of American institutions. Let us examine these points in greater detail.

The Sixties Democratic Vision

The two seminal movements of the 1960s, civil rights and the student New Left, expressed a vision of democracy rooted in but distinct from prevailing political values in modern America. At their core, both movements were grounded on four primary values:

(1) *equality,* or the full inclusion of society's dispossessed;

(2) *personal empowerment,* or the liberation of each person from psychological constraints as well as social oppression—a shift from the masculinist "power over" to the feminist "power to";

(3) a *moral politics* grounded on belief in individual growth, compassion for one's fellow human beings—indeed for all life—and intolerance of injustice; and

(4) the central importance of *community* as a locus for meaningful engagement in life and politics.

In sum, the Movement encompassed both a distributive and a qualitative critique of the United States. It railed against the exclusion of black Americans and other groups at the same time that it criticized deep-seated flaws in the very society that excluded these groups.

In its drive to bring American blacks into the mainstream, the civil rights movement insisted that the United States live up to its liberal democratic values of equal rights and universal citizenship. However, it sought equality in a manner that embodied the distinctive Sixties vision of democracy—through direct action that liberated black (and white) Americans from patterns of self-denial and accommodation, through an inspiring moral vision that insisted on justice instead of delay and evasion, and through participatory engagement in one's community.

From Rosa Parks' refusal to give up her seat on a Montgomery bus to the young students who sat in at lunch counters in the face of white violence, to black sharecroppers' defiant determination to register to vote, direct action broke the bonds of accommodation to oppression and forged a commitment to work for justice. . . .

The civil rights movement derived much of its persuasive power from a moral vision of politics based on love rather than an instrumental politics of self-interest, a vision articulated most forcefully by Martin Luther King, Jr. Often overlooked in the post-1960s mass media adulation of King was his, and the civil rights movement's, stubborn insistence on "freedom now" rather than business as usual.

Finally, the civil rights movement sought to transform the experiences of everyday life through engagement in the institutions of community, whether these were the church-based communities of Montgomery's bus boycott, the churches and schools of Birmingham, or the "beloved community" sought by the field workers of SNCC. Community building was an inherent part of working for democracy. As one Freedom Summer [a 1964 civil rights campaign to organize black Mississippians and register them to vote] volunteer recalled, "You've got to build community above all else. If you give people a taste of it, there's nothing you can't do. It's that rich and, I should add, that rare an experience in our society. I never had it until I went South and I . . . *haven't been able to live without it since.*"

The civil rights movement was the formative catalyst for sustained activism throughout the rest of the decade. For many white student activists, the call to heal one of America's deepest wounds was the primary inspiration for their own political activism. In the early to mid-1960s both black and white students flocked to the civil rights cause. The other influential student organization of the decade, SDS, was closely tied to SNCC in its formative years and was responsible for the community organizing effort Economic Research and Action Project (ERAP) in a variety of inner city communities. Indeed, the early years of SDS were patterned after SNCC'S emphasis on participation and organizing for empowerment. Like SNCC, SDS was pulled in different directions by its expressive and instrumental objectives.

The Achievements of Sixties Protesters

Abbie Hoffman combined radical politics, counterculture ideas, and media savvy to become one of the most prominent activists of the 1960s. In a 1986 article in Social Policy *he listed what he considered the major achievements of the movements of the decade.*

I want to emphasize what we pulled off in the 1960s, what I think we achieved.

First of all, we ended Jim Crow. We brought down legal segregation. . . .

We had a movement for freer lifestyles. Wearing your hair long might have seemed frivolous to some of the more straight people on the Left in the 1960s, but I tell you that was a full-time commitment because you were ostracized from your community. You were picked up by the cops. You could get your head shaved. You were kicked out of classes. It had meaning. Now kids can wear their hair long, short, red, blue, pink, shave it off, or whatever. You can wear a bra or not wear a bra, even if you're a guy, it's like okay. So these freer lifestyles were won because of what happened in the 1960s.

Then, of course, there was the war in Vietnam. . . .

If you look at the history of Western civilization, foreign wars in particular have been extremely popular. You can't find another foreign war of aggression fought by such a powerful country where the people rose up and said, "Bring the troops home." But it did actually happen here. . . .

Sure we were young. We were arrogant. We were ridiculous. There were excesses. We were brash. We were foolish. We had factional fights. But we were right.

In addition to racial and social differences, three qualities distinguished SDS and the New Left from SNCC and the civil rights struggle: the articulation of a New Left manifesto in the [1962] *Port Huron Statement*, concentration on the political implications of college and university life, and its transformation to a mass movement in the wake of the Vietnam War. While unremarkable in its policy recommendations, the *Port Huron Statement* nonetheless captured the distinctive flavor of youthful dissent: generational disaffection with an impersonal and acquisitive society, an emphasis on values and human relationships, and the unifying vision of participatory democracy. Reflecting the initial rumblings of campus discontent, SDS decried student apathy, in loco parentis university regulations, and an academic experience that prepared students to adapt to the corporate economy. The latter two themes would be played out on college campuses throughout the rest of the decade. It remained for the war in Vietnam to sharpen the student critique at the same time that it drew thousands of new recruits into the New Left, exacerbating its internal tensions.

Colored by experiences within the civil rights movement and New Left, and battered by the war in Vietnam, all major 1960s movements—from civil rights and New Left to the black power and antiwar movements to the counterculture and the women's and environmental movements—converged in embracing variants of these values.

The antiwar movement rejected a foreign policy that elevated instrumental rationality above moral compassion, and corporate and strategic interests above the right of national self-determination. The counterculture embraced the intuitive wisdom of the people over the technocratic rule of experts, the liberation of the physical and spiritual person from psychological repression, and the quest for loving union with a community of others. The women's movement championed the liberation of women from masculine domination and patriarchy in all cultures. It came to advocate the transformation of society according to a feminist ethic of caring and a community-based feminist praxis.

The ecology movement broadened the definition of domination to include human exploitation of nature, and it extended the notion of community to the entire ecosphere.

From a perspective outside the mainstream, Sixties movements expressed the voices of those whom society had systematically treated as "other"—black Americans, Latinos, the poor, Native Americans, women, gays, Vietnamese peasants, the intuitive and spiritual primitive, and nonhuman nature. In opposing domination, the rape metaphor applied not only to women, but to nonwhites, Vietnamese, and nature. In place of domination, the Movement sought community and celebrated eros, or the union of equals.

In addition to the decade's turbulence, this convergent vision is what distinguishes the 1960s and lays the groundwork for its democratic legacy. The energy from all these movements revitalized the critical left at the same time that prevailing powers were shifting rightward. . . .

The Early 1960s

Several forces came to a head with the election of John Kennedy as president in 1960. The resurgent civil rights movement gained new steam, feeling it had found a sympathetic ear in the White House. Young Americans were inspired by the personable young president's call to serve their country's best interests. A new wave of managerial technocrats was drawn to the analytical pragmatism of the new administration, while died-in-the-wool liberals found government niches from which they could advance the cause of human justice. In effect, Kennedy's pragmatic liberalism (followed by the early years of Lyndon Johnson's Great Society) activated the heady promises of liberal government and scientific progress: social problem solving and a compassionate welfare state, assertion of U.S. preeminence in defense of the "free world," and a belief in economic growth as the key to opportunity for society's dispossessed.

Much of Kennedy's impact derived from his distinctive personality—his mastery of rhetoric and his ability to inspire the public with his vision; the constant image of an administration in motion, tackling crises (some of his own creation) and solving problems that obstructed social progress; his quick intelligence and ability to appear in command of an enormous flow of information; his personal charm and ready wit, especially effective in encounters with the press; and the important fact that he seemed to be responsive to a world in flux.

Kennedy had a particularly poignant effect on the disaffected young who, in Paul Goodman's terms, had been deprived of the romance of patriotism during the 1950s. As Goodman remarked in the mid-1960s, "John Kennedy hit on the Posture of Sacrifice, which was what young people wanted to hear, something to give meaning to the affluent society.". . .

Significantly, Kennedy's rhetoric awakened hope for an expansion of liberal democracy; more Americans would be able to enjoy the benefits of full participation in public life and more people around the world would be able to live and breathe free from poverty and oppression. . . .

Initially, the confidence that things *could* change came from leaders like John Kennedy and Martin Luther King, Jr. In different ways, these two men were gifted with a remarkable ability to convey confidence to their audience; their leadership was a catalyst for many to discard habitual accommodations to the deprivations or petty preoccupations of everyday life. Thus the fight for justice seemed more plausible and rewarding than the more typical flight from injustice. Young people drawn to activism could for a time believe (or want to believe) that their expressive politics would ultimately prevail, that democracy grounded on community and moral purpose was possible. Expressive and instrumental politics were joined.

The result was the high-energy, optimistic early Sixties, the time Carl Oglesby called the Heroic Period of the Movement, its Bronze Age. It seemed, in short, as if America were reclaiming its idealistic heritage, its moral purpose, its promise. Martin Luther

King's memorable "I Have a Dream" speech captured the infectious feeling of the time. The vitality and optimism that came to pervade American society is precisely what seems so remote and so improbable when viewed from afar. For many, these qualities define the Sixties they recall fondly. Tom Hayden recalls, "I still don't know where this messianic sense, this belief in being right, this confidence that we could speak for a generation came from. But the time was ripe, vibrating with potential." As Morris Dickstein has observed of the primary form of cultural expression during these years,

> Folk music was the perfect expression of the green years of the early sixties, the years of integration, interracial solidarity, "I have a dream," and "We shall overcome": the years of the Port Huron statement and the early New Left; the years of the lunch-counter sit-ins and ban-the-Bomb demonstrations. Folk music was a living bridge between the protest culture of the New Left and the genuinely populist elements of the Old Left of the 1930s and after.

Few in the shining moment of 1960 could anticipate the degree to which the awakening of the Sixties would come to pervade all areas of American society in the decade to come. A significant source of energy came from the expressive side of emerging activism. As [historian] Wini Breines observes [in *Community and Organization in the New Left, 1962–1968*], young people were caught up in the creative spirit of defining new forms of social relationship: "The release of suppressed expression was liberating. Most had never experienced anything like it. It went against all the formal and controlled notions of liberal politics, releasing genuinely political, democratic instincts while underscoring the manipulated and anti-political nature of the American political system. . . . Participatory visions and experiments were the fuel that fired the movement's grass roots." Over time, the Movement produced endless alternative or counterinstitutions: co-ops and communes, grassroots and community organizing efforts like ERAP, the Mississippi Freedom Democratic party, free universities and experimental colleges, community control experiments, store-front schools, underground newspapers, feminist consciousness-raising groups and collectives, and ecology action alliances.

Again and again, activists testified to the powerful emotions unlocked by their engagement in community. Jack Weinberg recalled of the Berkeley Free Speech movement, "The FSM . . . has been the most complete experience of my life, the most all-encompassing. . . . It gave me a sense of comradeship we had not known existed." Freedom Summer volunteer Neil McCarthy described his time in Mississippi as "the most frightening and rewarding thing I've done in my life . . . the richest part [of the experience] was the bond you felt with everyone in the project. We were really a family."

In their initial forays into activism, the young began a journey that, as Kenneth Keniston observed, would later evolve into a quest for new pathways of personal development, new values for living, new ways of knowing, new kinds of learning, new formulations of the world, new types of social organization, new tactics of political action, new patterns of international relations, and new controls on violence.

This journey brought them increasingly into conflict with the social and political mainstream, for the Kennedy-Johnson legacy also lay the foundation for the democratic revolt of the disillusioned. As Allen J. Matusow argues [in *The Unraveling of America*], "By his heroic poses, his urgent rhetoric, his appeal to idealism and the nation's great traditions, Kennedy inadvertently helped arouse among millions a dormant desire to perfect America. . . . Only later, during Lyndon Johnson's term as president, would the limits of liberal good will become apparent and the flaws of liberal reform be exposed." Kennedy's was a legacy of rising expectations and shattered illusions, of magnificent promises yet modest results. For many dispossessed people, it was an experience much like opening a long-locked door only to have a chain-lock snap the door back in their face. Sixties movements began *within* the system they were trying to change and ended up struggling *against* that system.

The Process of Radicalization

The process of radicalization began with three crucial ingredients—belief in a community-based, egalitarian democracy; a sharp personal awareness of social ills; and a feeling of confidence that something could be done. As new activists joined the civil rights movement in the South (or the Peace Corps overseas), they came face to face with the compelling need to uproot and eliminate appalling conditions of oppression and powerlessness. Others were moved by the suffering they witnessed at greater distance. For both, what had once been vague and abstract, even invisible, became more immediate and concrete as oppressive conditions came to the surface. In parallel ways, those in other movements were moved by the contrast between their own concrete awareness of suffering, and the inadequacy, even callousness, of society's normal operations. The result was a powerful, personal sense that things had to change.

The combination of moral values, awareness of injustice, and confidence in change produced action, what George Katsiaficas has referred to as the "*eros* effect, the massive awakening of the instinctual human need for justice and for freedom." In the 1960s this meant joining activist organizations or more established service agencies like the Peace Corps, or, most profoundly, engaging in direct action or "putting your body on the line." Black sharecroppers risked death to register to vote, young men refused draft induction, women dared to leave abusive mates.

In a variety of forms, personal action set in motion the remaining stages of the radicalization process, although obviously not everyone traveled the same path or the same distance in that process. Initially, direct action produced a heady sense of empowerment, described by participants as a combination of fear and ecstasy resulting from taking risks to change one's environment. It also reinforced the personal commitment to work for justice. Out of this profound personal engagement came the distinctive personal politics of the Sixties. In contrast to the more compartmentalized, abstract mainstream process, political action was bound up with personal authenticity.

The moral catalyst for change therefore came from outside the institutions of government. During the early years of the civil rights movement, the interplay between activists and liberal officials in the federal government was the primary dramatic setting for the contradictions of liberal democracy, a process later played out in the antiwar movement. For those who had been optimistic, disillusionment began to set in. Endangered SNCC field workers came to see the federal government as a disinterested observer rather than a participant in remedying the injustices of Southern racism. College students came to see the traditional curriculum reflecting the vested interests of future employers. Antiwar activists rejected the authority of an administration that continually promised "light at the end of the tunnel." Hippies fled from the nightmarish violence of society while also rejecting the increasingly violent tactics of the New Left. Women activists were appalled to discover that their New Left boyfriends mirrored oppressive strains of the larger society. Ecologists despaired at society's perpetual "progress" toward ecological disaster. . . .

While the process of radicalization took place at different times within each movement, it also colored the tone of the decade as a whole. In 1964–1965, events coming on the heels of the president's assassination signaled a basic shift in the national dynamics of change. In 1964, Congress passed the Civil Rights Act, followed by the Voting Rights Act and an avalanche of social legislation including the War on Poverty. Yet civil rights activists involved in the Mississippi Freedom Summer campaign were sharply alienated by the failure of the Democratic party to seat the Mississippi Freedom Democratic party at the 1964 convention. The first major urban riots of the decade exploded in

Harlem and Watts, and in 1965, the first cries of "black power" were heard. Freedom Summer veterans also returned to college campuses in the North and began to mobilize the student movement, beginning with the Berkeley Free Speech movement.

Most crucially, the United States unofficially declared war on Vietnam through the Gulf of Tonkin Resolution, and began massive bombing and deployment of the first wave of ground troops. Nothing alienated, and in many cases radicalized, a broader segment of the young more than the war in Vietnam. The government's promise of winning the hearts and minds of the Vietnamese was shattered by the hideous experience of the war and of the young men who were shipped home in coffins or with broken bodies or damaged spirits.

These events helped usher in the "high Sixties," a time of mass movement characterized by two ultimately incompatible traits: a growing radical awareness of society's deeply rooted resistance to change, coupled with activists' still confident commitment to bring about change. As faith in leaders and the political process faded, the sense of efficacy came from participation in a momentous collective enterprise. As Ann Oakley recalls [in *What Is Feminism?*],

> The extraordinary intimacy experienced by people who have fallen in love is akin to that felt by participation in great political movements: one's sensory world expands, becomes more intense, the boundaries between people become diffused, ordinary human selfishness is replaced by an unusual altruism, and everyday routines and language become inappropriate to the description and working out of a relationship that cancels time by becoming "an eternalization of the present."

The euphoria was powerful. Yet the seeds of an apocalyptic vision and an exaggerated belief in one's own power lurked beneath the surface. . . .

As the promise of the early Sixties disintegrated, activists experienced what Todd Gitlin has called "radical disappointment." They came to see their liberal allies as morally hypocritical, and the system as deeply entrenched and in need of more fundamental or radical change. They discovered that liberal rhetoric obscured a determination to maintain prevailing institutional arrangements. The liberal establishment spoke the language of democracy, but meant a democracy in which the powerful continued to hold most of the power. When push came to shove, those who held power rebuffed the claims of those who sought change. In short, activists came to be radicalized when they realized that liberalism inspired a form of personal activism and democracy that it ultimately could not tolerate, much less satisfy.

The tension between expressive and instrumental politics became too strong. As SDS national secretary Clark Kissinger asked, "How can one live his values in the movement and yet change an industrial society of 180,000,000 people?" Activists increasingly felt the urge to disassociate from a society that seemingly expected them to "sell out" as a price for their participation. Many exercised a "great refusal," rejecting participation in society on society's terms. At different times, radical disassociation emerged in the black separatist movement, the creation of counterinstitutions like experimental colleges and free schools, the noncooperation or expatriation of draft resisters, the amazing and sometimes bizarre array of lifestyles in the counterculture, the creation of radical and lesbian feminist communities, and the total rejection of commercial technologies exhibited in elements of the counterculture and ecology movements. The only recourse, many felt, was to remove the stain of cooperation with a society that demanded amoral complicity in immoral acts.

Radical disappointment also fed activists' anger, not only at the system's injustice but at sympathetic liberals' willingness to compromise with the perpetrators of injustice. The result was renewed activism with a harder edge, a growing militance that in turn sharpened the conflict with society. Camus' words, "There are times . . . when the only feeling I have is one of mad revolt," describe a growing feeling in the decade's later years. As Todd Gitlin recalled, "The war was driving us nuts." Something had to give. . . .

Coming Apart

In 1968, it all came apart. The bloody Tet Offensive exploded administration myths about the "light at the end of the tunnel" in Vietnam. Senators Eugene McCarthy and Robert Kennedy challenged the President for the Democratic nomination, and Lyndon Johnson withdrew from the presidential race. Martin Luther King, Jr., and Robert Kennedy, the two mainstream political figures who held out the greatest hope for change, were shockingly, yet almost predictably, assassinated. Students took over five buildings at Columbia University and defiantly held them until a brutal police assault ended the occupation. Americans became aware of the global extent of revolt as a student-worker strike immobilized Paris, and Soviet tanks rolled into Prague to crush the Czech uprising. Finally, the Democratic National Convention in Chicago itself grimly recalled Prague as National Guardsmen patrolled the barbwired city and Chicago police assaulted protesters and reporters outside the convention hall. As Hans Koning recalled [in *Nineteen Sixty-Eight: A Personal Report*], "The essence of 1968 was a clarity of perception. It was as if a curtain had been raised, a veil lifted. The clichés, platitudes, and myths of our pub-

lic life . . . were suddenly seen as such." The late Sixties were ush-
ered in by the election of Richard Nixon and Spiro Agnew. The
Movement began to spin out of control.

While the mid-Sixties had taught activists that the system was
capable of enormous evil, it had also seemed responsive to mass
movements that clearly demanded change, especially as the numbers of those demanding change swelled. The late Sixties taught
activists that the system was only symbolically responsive. Also,
as Richard Flacks argued in 1966, the Vietnam War revealed a
fundamental dilemma for the New Left:

> It has helped to build the Left. But people on the Left can't re-
> sponsibly worry about much else as long as it goes on. And the
> more they accept the responsibility for trying to end the war,
> the more militant they become—and the more they sense their
> own impotence, isolation, and alienation from the larger
> society. . . . The war helps to build the radical movement, but
> the necessary obsession to work to end it is, in many ways, in-
> compatible with *achieving* such a movement.

By this time, the system was fighting back, seemingly determined
to crush the Movement. Government repression was pervasive.
Under Director J. Edgar Hoover, the FBI not only kept Movement
activists under surveillance, they used provocateurs to instigate
violence at innumerable demonstrations, and infiltrators who
fanned the flames of factionalism within the black power movement and underground press. They pressured corporations like
Columbia Records not to advertise in the underground papers,
and planted damaging disinformation about Movement activists
in the mainstream press. Local police, most notoriously in
Chicago and Oakland, harassed and arrested black and white
radicals, shut down underground newspapers, and even killed
several Black Panthers in dubious shoot-outs. The conspiracy trial
of the Chicago Seven [antiwar and political radical leaders accused of inciting riots in Chicago in 1968] provided an insane
kind of comic relief within the Movement, yet sent the clear message that there *was* a conspiracy by the Nixon administration to
eradicate the Movement. Movement paranoia increased apace. It
all became terribly real at Kent State in 1970.

As society's resistance stiffened, the tendency to disassociate
led to a splintering of Movement alliances. Black militants
clashed with feminists, as did one SDS faction with another, hippies with politicos, men with women, straights with gays—each
with its own agenda. Ultimately the disassociation could not be
sustained. . . .

More generally, the Movement's twin strains, the prefigurative
creation of a new democratic community and the instrumental
drive to transform institutions, fractured. As hope died late in the

decade, the personal politics of the 1960s tended to become *either* personal *or* political, either expressive or instrumental. The movements of the Sixties evolved toward two opposite extremes. One extreme expressed a militant perseverance to change society even if it meant abandoning the personal morality that originally inspired Sixties movements. The organized New Left, the heirs of SNCC and SDS, emphasized an instrumental revolutionary politics in which the ends justified the often violent means. The politics of experience was replaced by borrowed dogma from the Marxist-Leninist tradition. Amidst squabbles over "Revolutionary Korrectness," in Abe Peck's phrase, the New Left embraced "tyrannies in the name of democracy." It thereby left itself open to the accusation that it mirrored the moral degradation of the system it opposed so violently. And the New Left provided an obvious scapegoat for the effort to turn the United States to the right.

The opposite extreme, represented by counterculture dropouts, championed an abandonment of political concerns and a preoccupation with inner or private reality. Recoiling from the heavy turbulence of political struggle, many young people (especially the younger phalanx of the Sixties generation) abandoned the Movement's declining political hopefulness and demonstrated little awareness of the economic roots of the social mores they rejected. This was the key to the counterculture's vulnerability, the reason it deteriorated into excessive disassociation only to be largely absorbed by the mainstream culture. However shortsighted, excessive, or naive the counterculture may have been, it represented a deeply felt need to escape the alienating mainstream culture, to turn inward and explore personal qualities repressed in conventional society, and to live in more intimate connectedness with others, all of which were elements at the core of Sixties prefigurative politics.

Most of the young did not move to either extreme. Seasoned activists clung to whatever sense of community they could find, even if that community was largely defined by what it was not. Many continued to turn out for massive antiwar protests while grappling with issues closer to home. The period of radical disassociation also provided the psychological space that enabled many to see society more clearly, thereby revitalizing a Left critique. It nourished a vast multitude of experiments and meetings of the mind, all exploring visions of democracy, community, and personal empowerment. Together with feminism and ecology, which were the two new pro-active movements of the late 1960s and early 1970s, these participatory experiments are part of the unfinished democratic legacy of the Sixties.

Meanwhile, as America went back to business, the Movement

licked its wounds and began to take a look at what it had and had not accomplished, where it had gone wrong, ways in which the system perpetuated itself, and the reasons for this perpetuation. As Hans Koning put it,

> It is tiring to look reality in the eye, nearly as hard as looking at the sun, looking at death. No one can keep that up. Challenging it may be, but no one wants seven days a week of challenge.

> The powers-that-be, whose empire had been shaken and threatened by our sixties insight, took advantage of our weariness and invited this nation to relax and feel good.

Since the Sixties, society has gone in two directions, one effectively rejecting the democratic and communitarian vision of the Sixties, the other continuing to embrace that vision in various forms.

Hard Lessons

For many activists—those who come together to reflect on Sixties movements and events, those who continue to embrace the prefigurative democratic vision of the Sixties in their lifestyles and their work, and those who are actively committed to any of the myriad movements that reflect those values—the Sixties experience is part of a continuing path of political commitment and personal growth. In large part, this movement for democracy is grounded on lessons learned through the experiences of the 1960s.

Many activists' experiences forged their consciousness of the underside of American life that has not been and cannot be obscured by politicians' rhetoric about standing tall, government propaganda about overseas ventures, or mass media hype about winning the Cold War. If the Sixties experience demonstrated anything, it was the dramatic difference between the "advertisement" and the "product." The intensity and emotion of Sixties experiences have, over time, led to a radical assessment of American culture and institutions.

At the core of Sixties lessons was the awareness that, whatever virtues they might possess, American institutions are fundamentally incompatible with the democratic vision that inspired and drew so many to activism. Instead of eradicating racial oppression, a system under fire cautiously removed its most blatant forms of expression, ultimately rendering invisible those who bore the double burden of racism and class inequality. Instead of eliminating poverty, this system, amidst great flourish and for a limited period of time, produced program after program that softened the cruelest edge of suffering for those fortunate enough to benefit. Instead of empowering people, the system relied increasingly on experts who in the best of times provided the needy with incremental material and psychological gains. Instead of a politics grounded on moral compassion, activists encountered resistance to their moral claims justified by the "higher good" of system maintenance. Instead of a culture that valued the full flowering of individuality, they found a society that purports to leave people alone yet barrages them daily with inducements to fit into the mass culture. Instead of the flourishing of community, they encountered faceless bureaucracy, distant arenas of political decision-making, and a marketplace that accelerated the extinction of traditional communities and the natural landscape. And, of course, instead of an America making the world safe for democracy, they discovered a bipartisan, elite-driven foreign policy virtually crushing the lifeblood out of a small Asian nation, all to prove its commitment to sustaining the American empire. These lessons were pounded home by the traumatic shocks of the decade: assassinations, sellouts by party politicians, arrests, violent assaults by police or National Guard, and the searing reality of Vietnam.

These experiences converged to teach two deeper lessons. First, the oppression and dehumanization targeted by Sixties movements were not so much the result of bad men as they were sustained by the incentives and rewards that characterize America's most hallowed institutions—free elections, two-party competition, representative democracy, a free press, universal education, a capitalist economy, and the American tradition of political liberalism. Second, these institutions are inherently incapable of eradicating the ills that so galled activists—poverty, racial and sexual inequality, narrowly technocratic education, an aggressive foreign policy, and the destruction of community and the environment.

"Many protesters in the sixties shouted and claimed the right to speak for all. They often revealed contempt for working people."

Activists of the Sixties Were Elitist and Alienating

David Farber (b. 1956)

David Farber teaches history at Barnard College in New York and is the author of *Chicago '68* and *The Age of Great Dreams: America in the 1960s.* He was editor of *The Sixties: From Memory to History,* a collection of essays by various historians; excerpts from his own contribution to the anthology are presented here. Farber examines the public reaction to the protest movements of the 1960s, including the violence between police and protesters in Chicago in 1968. He argues that political and cultural radicals who questioned and sought to change American society failed in their goals in part because their countercultural ideas and political tactics had little relevance for working-class Americans—many of whom, he asserts, viewed protesters as arrogant and elitist. The words and actions of the activists, he argues, estranged large numbers of people and ultimately helped the cause of political conservatism. Farber asserts that politicians such as Richard Nixon, elected president in 1968 and 1972, and Ronald Reagan, elected governor of California in 1966 and president in 1980, were able to use public disaffection with activists to further their careers and agendas. He focuses especially on the career of Nixon, arguing that his dramatic political comeback after losing the 1960 presidential election to John F. Kennedy occurred largely because he appealed to voters who were alienated from protesters and tired of the decade's tumultuous events.

At the close of the sixties, a machinist tried to explain his sense of frustration. He tried to explain how he divided up the world. He was struggling to say something never expressed in the mass media, never taught at the universities. What he felt was so obvious and in some ways so gross a truth that it escaped most of America's professional observers and commentators. What he felt was that what some people called the establishment and anti-establishment forces were really just two sides to the same coin:

> The way I see it, you've got these people who run the big companies. Then you've got others who run the newspapers and the magazines and the television stations, and they're all full of themselves. . . . They're full of long lectures. . . . They can take anything and make it into what they want. I guess they're just smart talkers. . . . What I don't like about the students, the loudmouthed ones, is that they think they know so much they can speak for everyone, because they're right and the rest of us aren't clever enough and can't talk like they can. . . . There are people in this country who make all the noise and have their hands on most of the money. . . . I have a friend, he and I work together, and he says he wishes they'd get rid of each other, the rich guys and the college radicals.

Many working-class Americans hated the student protesters of the sixties, not because they disagreed with the students' opinions on this issue or that (more working people opposed the war in Vietnam than did people of the upper and middle classes), but because they could not stomach the idea of the nation not only being run by corporate elites but also listening so seriously to the clamorous claims of the corporate elites' privileged children. Richard Nixon tried to take people's resentment against all the "smart talkers" and "loudmouths"—young and old—and turn it into a potent political weapon.

To some extent, he came by his strategy honestly. Nixon had these same feelings of resentment. They were bred into him during his boyhood in the provinces. They were seared home in his post–law school search for a job in New York City, where one elite law firm after another turned him away, his brilliance and ferocious drive not enough, in their sophisticated eyes, to make up for his humble past.

Nixon knew these feelings—of being excluded, of being mocked by those who felt themselves charged with reproducing

American culture in their own powerful image. And from the start of his meteoric political career, Nixon knew the political utility of unleashing and directing the angry feelings generated by sociocultural exclusion. Nixon blasted off into the political stratosphere when—in Spring 1948—as an unrefined congressman from provincial southern California, unsure of dress or Washington protocol, almost bereft of cultural capital, he took on a paradigmatic "smart talker," Alger Hiss—Harvard man, State Department snob.

At their very first meeting, Nixon regarded Harvard Man Hiss as suspiciously "too mouthy." Nixon ended Hiss's high-flying government career, a career that at the time promised to be far more glorious than Nixon's own, by calling the man a communist traitor and making the charge stick. Here was a classic example, said Nixon, of a man who used his fancy words to sell out the country that too many quiet, simple folk had just died defending during World War II. . . .

Nixon and Populism

In part, Nixon was then playing on the raw nerve of American populism. He knew the scorn a great many Americans felt for the well born and the well educated—paradigmatically, the East Coast Ivy league elite. For Nixon, this scorn for the proverbial Harvard Man was not simply a political tool—it coursed through his veins. Early in his presidency he secretly ordered his chief of staff, when looking for young people to bring on board the ship of state, "as far as the universities are concerned, [to] just rule out the east even though there are some good ones here and go to the midwest to try to find some decent people. I consider this new direction as being of the highest priority. I want absolutely no deviation from it." Nixon's populist resentment resonated, and he gained support as he expressed his revulsion for a world of privilege and a network of power that many Americans saw as unearned.

Americans' populist resentment of class privilege was, however, neither a historical constant nor unnuanced. In 1960 Americans had scorned Richard M. Nixon, the hard-trudging "iron-butt" from Whittier, California, for Harvard Man, never- worked-a-day-in-his-life John F. Kennedy. When Barry Goldwater had campaigned on the old virtues in 1964 and snickered about sawing off the eastern seaboard and letting it float out to sea, he had garnered only 38 percent of the vote. A good many Americans' feelings about East Coast privilege, cosmopolitanism, and academic credentials were complicated. What they liked and disliked about the world of the privileged, as well as exactly who they considered privileged and why, was changing. It was open to manipulation.

Shortly after Nixon was sworn in as president, a Justice Department official, whose charge it was to go into polarized communities and mediate between civil rights protesters and their white adversaries, tried to put his finger on what made so many Americans so angry about the swirling protests, demands, and challenges of the sixties: "The values we held so dear are being shot to hell. . . . Everything is being attacked—what you believed in and what you learned in school, in church, from your parents. So the middle class is sort of losing heart. They had their eyes on where they were going and suddenly it's all shifting sand."

Polls and surveys gave credence to the idea that a good many Americans were angry about protesters and their clamorous attacks on what many Americans thought of as the "American way." By the fall of 1969, an astounding 84 percent of white Americans assented to the claim that college demonstrators were treated too leniently. The ayes went up to 85 percent when the statement read, "black militants are treated too leniently." At the close of the 1960s, white Americans overwhelmingly disapproved of the main noisemakers in the United States.

But what exactly did a large majority of white America see as so threatening about student protesters, antiwar demonstrators, and black militants? What "values" were being "shot to hell" by these dissidents? These were questions without sure answers but questions politicians needed to answer in the late 1960s and early 1970s.

Protesters and American Values

Back in 1964, Republican nominee for the presidency, Barry Goldwater, in a case of premature articulation, had run on the "values" question. "We must, and we shall," he orated, "return to proven ways—not because they are old, but because they are true." What exactly those values were, though, even Goldwater seemed unwilling—or perhaps, more interestingly, unable—to state clearly. What he did make clear was that the Democrats had sought to replace bold actions in defense of those values with nothing more than slippery rhetoric: "During four futile years the Administration which we shall replace has distorted and lost the faith. It has talked and talked and talked the words of freedom but it has failed and failed and failed in the works of freedom." Goldwater, without as stark a canvas as would be available to Nixon in the late 1960s and early 1970s, struggled to paint Republicans as the party of "the creative and the productive" and Democrats as a cabal of garrulous politicians who thought America could be built on "bureaucratic make-work," "bread and circuses," "spectacles," and "scandals." Goldwater, in an almost prescient way, wanted to define himself and the Republicans as the party of the work ethic, of industrial capitalism, and the family farm. He attacked the Democrats, to use contemporary terms, as a bunch of postmodern, postindustrial, paper shufflers. In the early 1960s, not enough Americans were willing to accept this rhetorical sleight of hand. By the late 1960s, the divide he sought to picture between those who produced and those who schmoozed would gain greater visceral meaning with the prime-time events all America watched.

The Sixties Are Over

In a 1995 article in Culture Wars, *Michael Bauman, a professor of religion and culture at Hillsdale College in Michigan, attacks the ideas of the dissidents of the 1960s, especially his own.*

I confess to believing at one time or another nearly all the pervasive and persistent fantasies of the '60s. In the words of Joni Mitchell's anthem for the Woodstock nation, I thought all I had to do was "get back to the land to set my soul free." I thought that flowers had power, that love could be free, and that the system was to blame. By 1968, I had the whole world figured out. I knew the cause of every evil—America—and I knew the solution to every problem—freedom and tolerance. . . .

Like almost all dissidents of my generation, I was a protester without a plan and a visionary without a vision. I had not yet learned that you see only what you are able to see, and I was able to see only the egalitarian, relativistic, self-gratifying superstitions of the secular, wayward, Left. Please do not think that this was simply a case of prelapsarian innocence. It was not. It was ignorance and it was evil, although I would have denied it at the time. . . .

The '60s are over, and it's a good thing. The '60s were a bad idea, if for no other reason than because the '60s had no ideas, only selfish desires hiding behind the shallow slogans and free-lance nihilism emblazoned on psychedelic bumper stickers, slogans like "I dissent, therefore I am." The only things about which we were intellectually modest in the '60s were the claims of objective truth. We seemed unable to wrap our minds around even the most obvious ideas. We seemed unable to realize, for example, that you cannot raise your consciousness until you have one. The '60s were perhaps the most unconscious decade in centuries. It was a time of suffocating intellectual mediocrity, from which our nation has not yet recovered.

There they were, on television and in the papers: hippie visionaries, black power fire-eaters, and New Left revolutionaries. They made fun of Americans' hard work and the ethics that put a man on the line day in and day out. They made fun of the good life, the new-car-in-the-garage life, that the hard work paid for. They rejected "respectability" and "decency," terms that they argued had come to mean little more than buying the right products from the right stores so that you looked like everybody else and smelled like everybody else and mowed your lawn like everybody else. The protesters seemed to give the same "stink eye" to both production and consumption, to the old virtues and the new values.

Yippie activist and mass media manipulator extraordinaire Abbie Hoffman, for example, envisioned a society where the machines would do all the factory work and Americans would devote themselves to community good when not reveling in adolescent fantasies. The New Left and the protesters simply never spoke about work as a locus of political consciousness or radical energies. The black power advocates demanded that white America fork over reparations and good jobs and free housing. No one seemed to pay attention to the hard work, to the daily grind, to the effort it had taken so many Americans to make something from nothing. Nor did they seem to understand the economic breakthrough so many Americans felt themselves living through: suddenly, regular, hard-working Americans could and did command a host of luxurious goods and services. As many Americans saw it, the protesters railed against this and they chanted about that but never did they seem willing to do what was necessary to bring a better life to their families and to themselves. *That is how many heard the protesters.*

As one of Nixon's supporters, a bank worker and part-time security guard, raged: "Every time I used to hear on television those spoiled-brat students singing 'we shall overcome,' I'd think of my dad. *There's* someone who has overcome, let me tell you. . . . His father . . . was killed working in a coal mine. Then his mother died giving birth to a child and there was no money for a doctor. . . . But he got a job in Western Union when he was thirteen, and he's been working for them ever since." What the student protesters seemed not to know and too many black activists failed to acknowledge was that many white working people well remembered a time when they had done without, when they had suffered hard times and unemployment. In 1968 Alabama governor and presidential aspirant George Wallace told cheering crowds that he had grown up in a house without indoor plumbing, he had held the short end of the stick, but he had not gone yelling and demanding this and that, he had not rioted, he had soldiered on.

Protesters paid little to no mind to the history of white working people in the United States—conceding little to their struggle to make ends meet and to create meaningful lives in fast-changing times. They seemed to give no respect to the hard work it had taken and still took most Americans to earn the modestly pleasant life-styles they had chosen for themselves. What protesters seemed to offer in the place of the rewards of hard work, in the minds of many Americans, was talk—the free speech movement, the filthy speech movement, participatory democracy, chanting, singing, dancing, protesting. And, as many nonyoung, nonblack Americans believed, all of the talk was aimed at the television cameras. The cameras' red lights stayed on, often enough, because the young protesters knew the new language of entertainment value—"the whole world is watching," they chanted to the cameras. The protesters meant that the whole world was watching the political battle, but many heard the chant differently—"the whole world is watching . . . Them and not Us."

Social critic Christopher Lasch, in *The True and Only Heaven*, excoriates "the habit of criticism" that gushed forth, he argues, from "the dominant culture" in the 1960s and 1970s. From a lower-middle-class point of view, he writes, "the habit of criticism" appeared to invite people to be endlessly demanding of life, to expect more than anyone had a right to expect." As Lasch notes, many white working people saw this "habit of criticism" as a direct repudiation of the dignity of the limited lives that they had fought to earn and they quietly accepted. He quotes a white Catholic housekeeper's contempt for her privileged employers:

> The house is full of talk. . . . He's read something that's bothered him and she's read something that's bothered her. They're both ready to phone their friends. The kids hear all that and they start complaining about what's bothering them—about school, usually. They're all so *critical*. I tell my kids to obey the teacher and listen to the priest; and their father gives them a whack if they cross him. But it's different when I come to fancy Cambridge. I want to scream sometimes when I hear those brats talking as if they knew everything.

Many Americans felt threatened by a world in which hard work and hard knocks seemed to earn less and less respect and less and less money. They felt threatened by a world in which their labor, they felt, was deemed less praiseworthy than somebody else's angry demands. Barry Goldwater, in the 1964 campaign, tried to bestir these feelings, as protests by black Americans in particular touched many white Americans' fears about losing their places in the economic and social hierarchy, as well as their limited arenas of autonomy.

The Wallace Campaign

George Wallace in the 1968 campaign pushed hard at those fears. He understood, more clearly than Goldwater, that a great many white Americans felt caught in a paradox. They felt economically beleaguered in the midst of plenty. Paychecks were shredded by high taxes, homes were mortgaged, cars were paid off a month at a time, mass-produced splendors were bought on credit. Even what they had—and it is crucial to note that they had much more than their parents had had—they did not securely have. They were in thrall to credit companies, banks, corporations, and the Internal Revenue Service. That they had, to a large extent, put themselves in such a position was not something Wallace or his audience dwelt on. Wallace did not point a finger at people's own avarice or the acquisitiveness big business pushed at Americans from all directions. Instead, Wallace told white working men and women, in the basic speech he gave around the country in 1968, that what little there was left to the average American was being challenged by the students, the black activists, the intellectuals, and the liberal federal government. In his rambling, visceral way, he listed for his enthusiastic audiences what he claimed all the "pointy-heads" and "protesters" meant to "take away": "We're talking about domestic institutions, we're talking about schools, we're talking about hospitals, we're talking about the seniority of a workingman in his labor union, we're talking about the ownership of property. . . . We don't need guidelines to tell us and we don't need half a billion dollars being spent on bureaucrats in Washington of your hard earned tax money to check every school system, every hospital, every seniority list of a labor union . . . let them know that a man's home is still his castle."

Wallace used racism as a unifying subtext in his speeches. But his real power came from his ability to tell his audiences that their racism was justified because racism was one of the few weapons they had standing between them and further loss of control over their lives and the lives of their children. More than 20 percent of Americans said in the fall of 1968, before they reconsidered the utility of voting for a third-party candidate, that they supported Wallace. Wallace, they believed, understood their anger against all the cosmopolitan forces and organized shouters. By 1968 Richard Nixon knew that he had a competitor who meant to rub raw the same angry feelings that he meant to massage.

The Clash in Chicago

George Wallace, in 1968, tried to mutate a racist populist politics of the Old South into a national politics of resentment. Richard Nixon, picking up on the cultural politics of Barry Goldwater and then California governor Ronald Reagan, tried to quietly unite the producing classes with the capitalist producers against the "critical" and protesting segments of society. Mayor Richard J. Daley, arguably the most powerful local politician in the United States during the 1960s, more powerfully and accurately reflected the political sensibility of at least white northern working people. Daley truly was a kind of organic intellectual of the silent majority.

Daley was born into an Irish Catholic working-class family. His father had been, at the local level, a union activist and had suffered job loss and discrimination as a result. Much of Daley's political success hinged on union support and the good working relations such support created. Although Daley had sweeping support in Chicago, his base remained the southside neighborhood, Bridgeport. He was born at 3602 Lowe Street and never left; he raised his own family half a block away at 3536 Lowe. While he was host of the 1968 Democratic National Convention and the protests that went with it, Daley's political values and understandings of sixties-style protest were put on national display.

Daley still achingly and very much paradoxically believed in an older productionist model of economy and politics, even as his constituents had begun to embrace and be embraced by a consumerist and therapeutic ethos that privileged buying power and a mutable life-style. As a politician, even a local one, Daley was a dinosaur and he knew it, even as he fought it. He had no respect for sound bites, spin control, photo opportunities. He knew the world was changing and changing away from his world in which personal loyalty overrode any ideology, in which a patronage job meant more for a family than any federal program, and in which a precinct captain's political advice stood ahead of a thirty-second-lie broadcast during prime time. Daley feared the loss of a political world in which what programs you brought to whom was replaced by one in which attitudes you sold in living color determined from whom you got support.

Like many of the people Nixon spoke to with such insight, Daley saw in the protesters simply an extreme version of all those who used language and symbols and the sheer manipulation of desire to override an older world of hard work and concrete acts and the complicated reality of making ends meet. As Daley and his police force made clear during the 1968 Democratic convention, to them the radical protesters appeared as a part of a bigger enemy—a class enemy.

The mass media loomed large in the mayor's list of enemies, just as it did in Richard Nixon's. Daley saw the mass media and the protesters as two sides to the same problem. Daley, in answering a hostile question from a reporter about why he did not give protesters permission to march through his city, impishly turned the question around and expressed the contempt he and others felt: "We are talking to the hippies, the Yippies, and the flippies and everything else. . . . We are talking to the newspapers and some of them are hippies and Yippies. And to the TV and radio, and a lot of them, I guess, are the leaders in these movements." Daley was kidding on the square; the protesters and the mass media were all outsiders in his community. More seriously, Daley tried to express his vision to his fellow Democrats when they assembled in Chicago right before the 1968 convention. He suggested: when the reporters ask you questions that you don't want to answer, just don't. Power, he argued, did not have to stem from the lens of a camera.

A Chicago policeman, questioned a few days later why he and others beat and bloodied news reporters, gave the epigrammatic answer, they "act like they own the street." But, the policeman believed, they did not. They just visited the streets, observed them, reported about them. They did not really do anything on them— they just used them as a backdrop for stories they made up in their heads and then tried to put into everybody else's. For the mayor, the convention was the same thing. Reporters and the networks and the protesters all came to do the same thing—to make of a working meeting a symbol for the nation. The talkers and shouters were most interested in colorful images, blowups, and hard feelings. As Daley saw it, they did not care about, let alone understand, the hard work of lining up votes and making deals. The mass media, like the protesters, talked as if their words meant more than people's deeds, indeed, more than the dead American boys about whom they chanted, whom they numbered and flashed on the screen in ten-second images. Mayor Daley was a political dinosaur. And after 1968, in part because of the aesthetically displeasing violence at the 1968 Democratic convention, nobody even made believe that a presidential nominating convention was anything but an extended commercial aimed at marketing certain messages.

When Mayor Daley was confronted by the press about his orders to stop the antiwar protests in Chicago in 1968, over and over, he asked hostile reporters, "What programs do they have, what do they want?" And all along he knew that what they wanted was not what he could even begin to deliver. Daley knew how to make a brokered political deal. The protesters he saw on Michigan Avenue and in Lincoln Park were a part of something postpolitical, something new that spoke to images and feelings and the existential wonder of feeling yourself raging on the streets of "America," where the cameras could flash your soul into everybody's living rooms.

The protesters, Mayor Daley felt, were not his kind of people. Most Americans knew this too. "The world hears those demonstrators making their noise. The world doesn't hear me and it doesn't hear a single person I know. Fancy, fast talking students, gabby they are, gab, gab," said the wife of a fireman and part-time carpenter whose son died in Vietnam.

In the logorrhea of the new world in which words were made to stand for more than deeds and images for more than realities, the fireman's wife knew that her son had died, in a way, because he was not a good talker. He had not used student deferments or psychiatrist reports or clever letters to his draft board or any of the other manipulations of the selective service regulations so many well-educated people called on to keep out. The members of her family were not good talkers, just as the machinist quoted earlier was not. In the new information age, these were people accustomed to, but often no longer making, things. In an age where soft drinks that cost more to market than manufacture earned billions, the old lines of division made little sense. And Americans of all socioeconomic castes felt the change and wondered how to maintain their dignity and their economic viability.

For many Americans whose lives were already torn between a belief that said dignity came in your ability to shape a small piece of reality and a life-style that said pleasure came bundled in purchasable quantities, the kind of political protest practiced by white radicals and even by civil rights leaders like Martin Luther King, Jr., seemed to offer them little chance of improved conditions. Whereas the heartfelt beliefs of a Daley and the manipulations of a Nixon proffered a world in which the real lives they had produced mattered, the world invoked by the protesters seemed like nothing more than an ineffective burned offering simulated by the image merchants that sold them their everyday dreams. . . .

This is not to suggest that all Americans bought the false faith in the dignity of the working man sold by a Nixon or later by a Reagan. A welder put it well: "You can't fool a workingman too long. Nixon isn't fooling me. He's an old Wall Street lawyer, right. . . . My Dad never lets me forget what a struggle the workingman had in this country, to get the unions working." Most union men and women continued to pull the lever for Democrats throughout the Nixon years. But overwhelmingly most Americans did not accept the demonstrators or the demonstrators' supporters or sympathizers—the national Democratic party—as spokespeople for them (and, of course, the demonstrators were not really trying to speak for them). They saw in the protesters just another sector of the elite, less reasonable and less concerned about economic viability, bidding for power and walking a path to power that offered those who could not give orders in the new code of consumption nothing more than they already had. Indeed, in the new activists' loud demands for affirmative action programs and a nonsexist, nonracist society, a good many white men, at least, found only new threats and new diminutions to their already circumscribed world.

In a world divided between those who spoke and those who were silent, many protesters in the sixties shouted and claimed the right to speak for all. They often revealed contempt for working people and showed much ignorance about those people who still wondered if it was not what you said that counted but what you did. During the sixties, many people held on to a kind of anachronistic faith in the importance of production—of being working people—and they half-mourned a world that had never come to be. Unlike Richard Nixon, too many protesters failed to consider the meaning of so many Americans' silence. Instead, the protesters' verbosity allowed them to be set up by savvy politicians as scapegoats for any and all problems that encroached on Americans' tenuous hold on a satisfactory life.

Finishing Off the Sixties

Richard Nixon preyed on the sixties protesters who talked about a revolution that offered most Americans nothing but heartache. In 1972, while he was running against Senator George McGovern of South Dakota, Nixon's campaign strategists reveled in cultural politics. A secret campaign strategy memo paints a vivid picture: "Portray McGovern as the pet radical of Eastern Liberalism, the darling of the *New York Times*, the hero of the Berkeley Hill Jet Set, Mr Radical Chic. . . . By November he should be postured as the Establishment's fair-haired boy, and RN postured as the Candidate of the Common Man, the working man." Nixon and his campaign team understood what Mayor Daley of Chicago had tried to explain a few years earlier and what working people around the country were quietly feeling; the *New York Times*, the University of California professoriat, student radicals, and the establishment had more in common with each other than any one of them had with most working people. All the talkers . . . Nixon could argue convincingly, were remaking America in their own image and leaving little dignity— economic dignity eventually, psychic dignity by the late sixties— for the common folk who were willing to labor in productive ways for the good things that America offered its working people.

Richard Nixon understood how to tap such feelings. He knew how to lure enough working people who felt left out of the cultural code that seemed to be America in the 1960s to put together a winning campaign. He would help to chart a new culture. Like a very different kind of Moses, he would not be allowed to lead his people into this new land. Stopped by Watergate, he would watch from his California exile.

He would watch, however, as others followed his lead. Hollywood listened to the fury that marked liberal McGovern's crushing defeat. New films with truck driver heroes appeared. CB radios that let anyone sing into the airways became a market sensation—"Breaker, Breaker, that's a bear in the air, Good Buddy," the nation would learn to say. Fundamentalist preachers and New Right social conservatives would learn to use new technologies and marketing tools to reach huge audiences that Madison Avenue and the universities and the New Left and the Democratic party had long ignored. The silent majority would gain a voice in the 1970s. Then Ronald Reagan would come and put all of these ducks in a row. The silent majority, Nixon's America, would finish off the sixties. With anger and uncertainty and little charity, led by rich men whose real interests were very different from their own, this no longer so silent majority would be about the business of charting America's course into the twenty-first century.

For Discussion

Chapter One

1. In his 1961 speech, did John F. Kennedy frame his call for America to send a man to the moon in such a way as to make criticism of the moon program—such as that expressed by Carl Dreher—seem defeatist or unpatriotic? Explain your answer.

2. What elements are there in John F. Kennedy's speech that might help account for America's subsequent involvement in the Vietnam War? Explain.

3. Barry Goldwater attacks Lyndon B. Johnson for "relying on the overturned doctrine of turning our problems, our lives, and our liberties over to a supposed elite in an all-powerful central government." In your opinion, is this a fair summary of Johnson's views as expressed in the opposing viewpoint? Why or why not?

4. Are the "creative federalism" described by Max Ways and the "liberal corporatism" named by Richard Flacks different labels for the same phenomenon? Are the elements of the Great Society that Ways finds most alluring the same ones that Paul Goodman and Flacks find most objectionable? Explain what these elements are and why they are the source of disagreement.

5. What common themes can be found in the arguments of conservative Barry Goldwater and those of Paul Goodman and Richard Flacks, who are both identified with political and cultural radicalism? What are the major differences?

Chapter Two

1. On what principles does Lyndon B. Johnson rely to defend U.S. involvement in Vietnam? What principles does Martin Luther King Jr. cite in his statement of opposition to the war? Which principles are employed by both Johnson and King? In your opinion, whose interpretation of these principles is more valid? Explain.

2. What connections do Martin Luther King Jr. and J. William Fulbright make between the war in Vietnam and social unrest in American cities? In your opinion, are the links they describe convincing? Why or why not?

3. What are the differences between "honorable" and "unpatriotic" dissent, according to Dwight D. Eisenhower? Do you agree with his distinction? Would you use different criteria to distinguish the two? Explain your answer.

Chapter Three

1. What do the opening words of the Port Huron Statement reveal about its writers? Do they see themselves as representing all young Americans?

2. Irving Kristol criticizes campus radicals for being apolitical and for failing to propose or demand "a single piece of legislation from their government." Could his comments apply to the Port Huron Statement? Why or why not?

3. Compare and contrast the opinions on American society expressed by "Sonny" with those expressed in the Port Huron Statement. Are the opinions expressed largely the same, or are there fundamental differences between them?

4. Jack Newfield presents an "outside" critique of the hippies, while the Communications Company presents more of an "inside" view. Compare and contrast the arguments and the rhetorical styles of the two pieces. What are the similarities and differences? Whose use of language is more effective? Why?

5. Margaret Mead interviewed people who were at Woodstock, while Philip P. Ardery Jr. extrapolated from his own personal experience at the festival. What are the strengths and weaknesses in each approach in assessing an event such as Woodstock? Which author do you think provides the more convincing evaluation?

Chapter Four

1. In what ways does Julius Lester repudiate Martin Luther King Jr.'s vision as expressed in King's "I Have a Dream" speech. What alternative vision does Lester provide? In your opinion, who presents the more realistic view of race relations in America? Why?

2. What link does Richard Nixon attempt to establish between urban riots and the civil disobedience practiced and advocated by civil rights leaders? Among those who advocated civil disobedience was Martin Luther King Jr. Could elements of his "I Have a Dream" speech be construed as causing disrespect for law and order? Explain.

3. Does Tom Hayden implicitly or explicitly condone violence in his article about riots and revolution in New Jersey? What does he say is necessary for "meaningful change" in the nation's ghettos? Is his argument persuasive? Why or why not?

4. Some historians argue that the revival of feminism in the 1960s can be traced to the civil rights movement, both for inspiring people to demand equality and for ignoring the issue of gender equality. Is there evidence to substantiate this view in the viewpoints by Martin Luther King Jr. and Julius Lester? In the viewpoints by Anne Bernays and Mary C. Segers? Explain your answers.

Chapter Five

1. What criticisms does Edward P. Morgan offer of both "liberal" and "conservative" perspectives on the 1960s? Do you agree with his argument that both perspectives fail to provide a full picture of the decade? Why or why not?

2. Both Edward P. Morgan and David Farber argue that many Americans were alienated by young radical activists in the 1960s, but they

differ on the reasons why people were disaffected. What reasons does each author give? Whose reasons do you find more compelling? Why? Could each author's argument contain elements of truth? Explain.

General Questions

1. Compare and contrast Martin Luther King's 1963 "I Have a Dream" speech (found in chapter 4) with his sermon attacking the Vietnam War (found in chapter 2). What are the main differences in style and content? What changes do they reveal in King's thinking and his sense of hope for America? What do they suggest about the changes that took place in America between 1963 and 1967?

2. Todd Gitlin, writing in the *American Prospect*, identifies two general "strands" of sixties activism—one striving for maximizing personal freedom without constraints, the other emphasizing solidarity with the poor and disadvantaged. Gitlin maintains that these two strands often contradicted each other. Can this generalization be applied to the viewpoints in this volume? Classify the viewpoints according to which strand they belong to. Do any viewpoints defy categorization? Explain.

Chronology

February 1, 1960	Four black college students stage a sit-in protest against racial discrimination at a Woolworth's lunch counter in Greensboro, North Carolina.
April 1960	The Student Nonviolent Coordinating Committee (SNCC) is founded to coordinate the growing civil rights sit-in movement.
May 1, 1960	U-2 spy plane pilot Francis Gary Powers is shot down over the Soviet Union; the incident worsens U.S.-Soviet relations.
May 9, 1960	The federal government approves the first birth-control pill as safe for general use.
September 26, 1960	Candidates Richard M. Nixon and John F. Kennedy engage in the nation's first televised presidential campaign debate.
November 8, 1960	Kennedy defeats Nixon in the closest presidential election since 1888.
January 3, 1961	The United States breaks off diplomatic relations with Cuba.
March 1, 1961	President Kennedy establishes the Peace Corps.
March 21, 1961	The United States sends military advisers and aid to Laos.
April 17, 1961	The Bay of Pigs fiasco: American-trained and -supplied Cuban exiles fail in their efforts to depose Fidel Castro.
May 5, 1961	Alan Shepard becomes the first American in space.
May 25, 1961	President Kennedy pledges to put an American on the moon by the end of the decade.
August 13, 1961	East Germany closes the Berlin border and begins construction of the Berlin Wall.
December 11, 1961	Kennedy sends four hundred American combat troops to South Vietnam.
1962	In *Engel v. Vitale* the Supreme Court rules that even a nondenominational prayer in a public school is unconstitutional; in *Baker v. Carr* it is ruled that legislative districts must be relatively equal in population.

Michael Harrington publishes *The Other America,* detailing the problem of poverty in the United States; *Silent Spring* by Rachel Carson raises public consciousness of environmental degradation.

February 20, 1962 John Glenn becomes the first American to orbit the earth.

June 11–15, 1962 The Port Huron Statement is issued by Students for a Democratic Society (SDS).

October 22– The discovery of Soviet missiles in Cuba brings the
November 2, 1962 world to the brink of nuclear war; the Cuban missile crisis is defused when the Soviet Union withdraws its missiles in the face of a U.S. naval blockade.

December 31, 1962 The number of U.S. military personnel in South Vietnam reaches eleven thousand.

February 19, 1963 Betty Friedan's *The Feminine Mystique* is published.

April/May 1963 Civil rights demonstrators led by Martin Luther King Jr. are attacked with fire hoses and police dogs in Birmingham, Alabama.

June 10, 1963 Kennedy signs into law the Equal Pay Act, making it illegal to set different pay scales for men and women who perform the same job.

August 5, 1963 A nuclear test-ban treaty is signed by the United States, the Soviet Union, and Great Britain.

August 28, 1963 The March on Washington draws over 250,000 civil rights activists to the nation's capital.

September 7, 1963 Four black girls are killed in a church bombing in Birmingham, Alabama.

November 1, 1963 President Ngo Dinh Diem of South Vietnam is overthrown in a military coup with the acquiescence of the American government; he is later assassinated.

November 22, 1963 President John Kennedy is assassinated in Dallas, Texas; Vice President Lyndon Johnson assumes office; captured alleged assassin Lee Harvey Oswald is murdered two days later.

January 8, 1964 President Lyndon B. Johnson declares an "unconditional war on poverty" in his State of the Union address.

January 23, 1964 The Twenty-fourth Amendment to the Constitution, which outlaws the poll tax in federal elections, is ratified.

February 1964	The Beatles arrive in the United States for their first American tour.
May 22, 1964	In a commencement address at the University of Michigan, President Johnson calls on the United States to create a "Great Society."
June 21, 1964	Civil rights workers James Chaney, Michael Schwerner, and Andrew Goodman disappear from Philadelphia, Mississippi; six weeks later their bodies are discovered in an earthen dam by FBI agents.
July 2, 1964	President Johnson signs the Civil Rights Act of 1964, prohibiting discrimination in employment and places of public accommodation.
August 10, 1964	The Gulf of Tonkin Resolution is passed by Congress, authorizing military action against North Vietnam in response to purported attacks on U.S. ships off the Vietnamese coast.
August 20, 1964	President Johnson signs the Economic Opportunity Act, which calls for the "maximum feasible participation of the poor" in antipoverty programs.
September–December 1964	The Free Speech Movement: students at the University of California at Berkeley protest after university administrators try to limit political activities on the campus; 796 arrests are made on December 3.
September 27, 1964	The Warren Commission concludes that Lee Harvey Oswald, acting alone, killed President Kennedy.
November 3, 1964	Johnson overwhelmingly defeats Senator Barry Goldwater to win a full presidential term.
February 7, 1965	President Johnson orders bombing raids on North Vietnam.
February 21, 1965	Black leader Malcolm X is assassinated.
March 21–25, 1965	Martin Luther King Jr. leads a voting-rights march from Selma to Montgomery, Alabama.
April 17, 1965	The first major demonstration against the Vietnam War takes place in Washington, D.C.
April 28, 1965	President Johnson sends U.S. Marines to the Dominican Republic to prevent a communist takeover.
July 25, 1965	Acclaimed folk singer Bob Dylan breaks cultural barriers by performing with a rock band at the Newport Folk Festival.
July 30, 1965	President Johnson signs the Medicare bill into law.
August 6, 1965	President Johnson signs the Voting Rights Act of 1965.

August 11–16, 1965	Race riots in the black ghetto of Watts in Los Angeles leave thirty-five dead and hundreds injured.
October 1965	Cesar Chavez of the United Farm Workers Union organizes a national boycott of grapes in support of striking farmworkers.
October 3, 1965	The Immigration Reform Act eliminates many immigration restrictions.
November 27, 1965	Novelist Ken Kesey, author of *One Flew over the Cuckoo's Nest,* and a band of his followers known as the "Merry Pranksters" distribute LSD at the first "acid test" open to the public.
January 1966	Automatic student deferments from the draft are abolished.
June 1966	"Black Power" becomes the popular slogan of young black civil rights activists during a civil rights march in Mississippi.
June 13, 1966	In *Miranda v. Arizona* the Supreme Court declares that authorities must inform a criminal suspect of his or her constitutional rights at the time of arrest.
July 1966	Urban riots strike Chicago, Brooklyn, and Cleveland.
October 1966	The National Organization for Women (NOW) is founded.
	The Black Panther Party is founded in Oakland, California.
November 8, 1966	Ronald Reagan wins his first race for public office when he is elected governor of California.
January 14, 1967	A San Francisco Be-In draws national attention to the hippie scene.
June 1967	The Beatles release their most influential album, *Sergeant Pepper's Lonely Hearts Club Band.*
June 16–18, 1967	The Monterey Pop Festival popularizes countercultural rock music and marks the beginning of the "Summer of Love."
July 1967	The American troop commitment to the war in Vietnam reaches four hundred thousand.
July 23, 1967	Race riots in Detroit, Michigan, and Newark, New Jersey, leave 693 dead.
October 21, 1967	National Stop the Draft Week climaxes with a March on the Pentagon by fifty thousand antiwar protesters.
November 9, 1967	The first issue of *Rolling Stone* is published.

1968	The American Indian Movement (AIM) is founded in Minneapolis.
January 1968	The first all-female antiwar demonstration, organized by the Jeannette Rankin Brigade and the Women's Strike for Peace, is held in Washington, D.C.
January 30, 1968	The Tet Offensive by North Vietnamese and Viet Cong forces stuns the American military leadership and shakes the American public's confidence in America's mission in Vietnam.
February 8, 1968	*Soul on Ice* by Eldridge Cleaver is published.
March 1, 1968	The Kerner Commission on Civil Disorders publishes its report on the causes of the riots of 1967; it declares that the country is becoming "two societies—one white, one black—separate and unequal."
March 12, 1968	Senator Eugene McCarthy, an antiwar candidate, surprises many by finishing a strong second in the New Hampshire primary with 42 percent of the vote.
March 16, 1968	Senator Robert Kennedy joins the race for the Democratic presidential nomination.
	In the My Lai massacre in Vietnam, U.S. troops indiscriminately kill innocent Vietnamese villagers.
March 31, 1968	President Johnson announces he will not seek reelection as president.
April 4, 1968	Martin Luther King Jr. is assassinated by James Earl Ray in Memphis, Tennessee.
April 23–30, 1968	Student radicals at Columbia University take over campus buildings.
May 1968	Peace talks to end the war in Vietnam begin in Paris.
June 5, 1968	Senator Robert Kennedy is assassinated hours after winning the California primary.
August 25–28, 1968	Hubert H. Humphrey is nominated for president at the Democratic National Convention in Chicago; antiwar demonstrators in a nearby park are beaten by local police.
September 7, 1968	Feminists protest the Miss America Pageant at Atlantic City, New Jersey.
November 5, 1968	Republican candidate Richard Nixon defeats Humphrey for the presidency; American Party candidate George Wallace finishes a distant third.
January 1969	U.S. troop strength in Vietnam reaches a peak of 543,000.

March 1969	The United States begins a secret bombing campaign in Cambodia.
June 18–23, 1969	SDS holds its last national convention and breaks into factions.
June 27, 1969	A riot outside the Stonewall Bar in Greenwich Village in New York City signals the start of a militant gay liberation movement.
July 21, 1969	Neil Armstrong becomes the first human to set foot on the moon.
August 15–17, 1969	The Woodstock Music and Arts Festival in White Lake, New York, draws several hundred thousand people.
September 24, 1969	The "Chicago 8" conspiracy trial begins; eight defendants, including Abbie Hoffman, Tom Hayden, and Bobby Seale, are accused of inciting violence during the 1968 Democratic Convention.
October 8–11, 1969	The Weathermen, a splinter faction of SDS, hold four violent "Days of Rage" in Chicago.
November 1969	The American public learns of the 1968 My Lai massacre.
December 1, 1969	The first draft lottery of the decade is held.

Annotated Bibliography

Judith Clavir Albert and Stewart Edward Albert, eds. *The Sixties Papers: Documents of a Rebellious Decade.* New York: Praeger, 1984. A large source anthology concentrating on radical political writings.

Terry H. Anderson. *The Movement and the Sixties.* New York: Oxford University Press, 1995. A comprehensive history of radical politics in the United States from the Greensboro, North Carolina, sit-in of 1960 through the Wounded Knee confrontation of 1973.

David M. Barrett. *Uncertain Warriors: Lyndon Johnson and His Vietnam Advisers.* Lawrence: University Press of Kansas, 1993. A history of U.S. policy concerning the Vietnam War between 1965 and President Lyndon Johnson's decision not to run for reelection in 1968.

Larry Berman. *Lyndon Johnson's War: The Road to Stalemate in Vietnam.* New York: Norton, 1989. A concise account of American policy towards Vietnam between 1965 and 1968.

Michael R. Beschloss. *The Crisis Years: Kennedy and Khrushchev, 1960–1963.* New York: HarperCollins, 1991. A comprehensive history of the relationship between John F. Kennedy and Nikita Khrushchev at the height of the Cold War between the United States and the Soviet Union.

Mary C. Brennan. *Turning Right in the Sixties: The Conservative Capture of the GOP.* Chapel Hill: University of North Carolina Press, 1995. An account of the efforts of conservatives to take control of the Republican Party from moderates during the 1960s and the legacy of their success.

Clayborne Carson. *In Struggle: SNCC and the Black Awakening of the 1960s.* Cambridge, MA: Harvard University Press, 1981. A history of the Student Nonviolent Coordinating Committee (SNCC) from its origins in 1960 to its demise in the early 1970s that records its shift from interracial idealism to racial separatism.

Dan T. Carter. *The Politics of Rage: George Wallace, the Origins of the New South, and the Transformation of American Politics.* New York: Simon & Schuster, 1995. A biography of George Wallace and a study of the impact of his ideas and political strategy on racial politics during the 1960s and after.

William H. Chafe. *Never Stop Running: Allard Lowenstein and the Struggle to Save American Liberalism.* New York: BasicBooks, 1993. A compelling biography of the leader of the "Dump Johnson" movement in 1968 and his efforts to end the war in Vietnam without destroying the liberal base of the Democratic Party.

David Chalmers. *And the Crooked Places Made Straight: The Struggle for Social Change in the 1960s.* Baltimore: Johns Hopkins University Press, 1991. A compact history of the struggle to bring about significant social change during the 1960s written by a historian who was a participant in some of those struggles.

Noam Chomsky. *At War with Asia.* New York: Pantheon, 1970. An attack on the "historical misadventure" that was the American war in Vietnam written by a noted linguist-turned-critic of American foreign policy.

Eldridge Cleaver. *Soul on Ice.* New York: McGraw-Hill, 1968. Essays and letters written from prison during the 1960s by a radical African American and leader of the Black Panther Party.

Mitchell Cohen and Dennis Hale. *The New Student Left: An Anthology.* Boston: Beacon Press, 1966. A collection of essays and manifestos by student radicals interpreting, exhorting, and criticizing their own movement.

Peter Collier and David Horowitz. *Destructive Generation: Second Thoughts About the Sixties.* New York: Summit Books, 1989. A retrospective on the 1960s written by two former radical activists who are now highly critical of sixties radicals.

Charles De Benedetti. *An American Ordeal: The Anti-War Movement of the Vietnam Era.* Syracuse, NY: Syracuse University Press, 1990. A sympathetic account of the origins, goals, and conduct of the American peace movement during the Vietnam War.

David DeLeon, ed. *Leaders from the 1960s: A Biographical Sourcebook.* Westport, CT: Greenwood Press, 1994. A useful compendium of biographical sketches of leading activists, writers, and cultural figures of the 1960s and their activities subsequent to that decade.

John D'Emilio and Estelle B. Freedman. *Intimate Matters: A History of Sexuality in America.* New York: Harper & Row, 1988. A general history of sexuality in America that places the sexual liberation of the 1960s in historical context.

Alice Echols. *Daring to Be Bad: Radical Feminism in America, 1967–1975.* Minneapolis: University of Minnesota Press, 1989. A history of the feminist movement that places it in the context of other social movements of the era.

Sara Evans. *Personal Politics: The Roots of Women's Liberation in the Civil Rights Movement and the New Left.* New York: Knopf, 1979. A history of the early years of modern feminism that argues that the movement grew directly out of women's disaffection with the male-dominated civil rights movement.

David Farber. *The Age of Great Dreams: America in the 1960s.* New York: Hill & Wang, 1994. An overview of the decade that analyzes everything from the Great Society and the civil rights movement to rock music and the drug culture.

David Farber, ed. *The Sixties: From Memory to History.* Chapel Hill: University of North Carolina Press, 1994. A collection of essays by historians examining various aspects of the decade.

Lewis Feuer. *The Conflict of Generations: The Character and Significance of Student Movements.* New York: Basic Books, 1969. A comparative history of twentieth-century student movements in Europe and the United States that is highly critical of the student New Left of the 1960s.

David J. Garrow. *Bearing the Cross: Martin Luther King Jr. and the Southern Christian Leadership Conference.* New York: William Morrow, 1986. A major biography of the moral and political leader of the modern civil rights movement.

James N. Giglio. *The Presidency of John F. Kennedy.* Lawrence: University Press of Kansas, 1991. A balanced study of the Kennedy administration.

Todd Gitlin. *The Sixties: Years of Hope, Days of Rage.* New York: Bantam, 1987. Part history and part memoir of the decade written by a former Students for a Democratic Society (SDS) activist.

Todd Gitlin. *The Whole World Is Watching: Mass Media and the New Left, 1965–1970.* Berkeley and Los Angeles: University of California Press, 1980. An analysis of media coverage of the New Left and its impact on New Left leaders who were transformed into media celebrities.

Robert Alan Goldberg. *Barry Goldwater.* New Haven, CT: Yale University Press, 1995. A biography of the Arizona senator and 1964 presidential candidate.

Peter Goldman. *The Death and Life of Malcolm X.* New York: Harper & Row, 1973. Less a biography of Malcolm X than an assessment of the impact of his life and his death on American society and the black civil rights movement.

Doris Kearns Goodwin. *Lyndon Johnson and the American Dream.* New York: Harper & Row, 1969. An intimate portrait of the last years and months of the Johnson presidency written by one who was accorded great access to the president and those near to him.

Richard Goodwin. *Remembering America: A Voice from the '60s.* Boston: Little, Brown, 1988. A memoir by a speechwriter for and adviser to John Kennedy, Eugene McCarthy, and Robert Kennedy.

Lewis Gould. *1968: The Election That Changed America.* Chicago: Ivan Dee, 1993. A well-written history of this turbulent year.

Michael Harrington. *The Other America.* New York: Macmillan, 1962. A study of poverty in America through the early 1960s that influenced both the Kennedy and Johnson administrations.

Tom Hayden. *Reunion.* New York: Random House, 1988. The autobiography of one of the key leaders of the Students for a Democratic Society (SDS).

Kenneth J. Heineman. *Campus Wars: The Peace Movement at American State Universities in the Vietnam Era.* New York: New York University Press, 1993. A history of mounting student radicalism in response to the war in Vietnam on four large campuses: Michigan State University, Kent State University, Pennsylvania State University, and the State University of New York at Buffalo.

Max Heirich. *The Spiral of Conflict: Berkeley, 1964.* New York: Columbia University Press, 1970. The definitive history of the Free Speech Movement at the University of California at Berkeley that spawned a good deal of the student radicalism of the 1960s.

George C. Herring. *America's Longest War: The United States and Vietnam, 1950–1975.* New York: Knopf, 1979. An acclaimed single-volume account of the American role in the war in Vietnam.

Jerome Himmelstein. *To the Right: The Transformation of American Conservatism.* Berkeley and Los Angeles: University of California Press, 1990. An intellectual history of conservatism in America and how it changed during the 1960s.

Abbie Hoffman. *The Best of Abbie Hoffman.* New York: Four Walls Eight Windows, 1989. Writings of the famous sixties activist, including selections from *Revolution for the Hell of It, Woodstock Nation,* and *Steal This Book.*

Gerald Howard, ed. *The Sixties: Art, Politics, and Media of Our Most Explosive Decade.* New York: Paragon House, 1991. A collection of writings of the decade on culture, politics, and their intersection.

Paul Jacobs and Saul Landau, eds. *The New Radicals: A Report with Documents.* New York: Random House, 1966. A collection of classic statements of 1960s radicalism that connects advocates of peace, sexual freedom, black civil rights, and feminism.

Roger Kahn. *The Battle for Morningside Heights: Why Students Rebel.* New York: William Morrow, 1970. A narrative of the student riots at Columbia University in 1968 written by one sympathetic to the students and critical of the educational establishment.

Charles Kaiser. *1968 in America.* New York: Weidenfeld and Nicholson, 1988. An engaging account of a tumultuous year in the history of the United States.

Kenneth Keniston. *Young Radicals: Notes on Committed Youth.* New York: Harcourt, Brace, and World, 1968. A brief for student radicals written by a noted American scholar of the young.

James Simon Kunen. *The Strawberry Statement: Notes of a College Revolutionary.* New York: Avon, 1968. A memoir and call to action by a participant in the 1968 Columbia University student uprising.

Michael J. Kurtz. *The Crime of the Century.* Knoxville: University of Tennessee Press, 1982. A thoughtful examination of the Kennedy assassination that criticizes the Warren Commission and presumes the existence of a conspiracy without naming the specific conspirators.

Timothy F. Leary. *Flashbacks: A Personal and Cultural History of an Era.* New York: St. Martin's Press, 1990. The autobiography of the celebrated drug guru of the 1960s.

David Levy. *The Debate over Vietnam*. Baltimore: Johns Hopkins University Press, 1991. An extended essay on the arguments for and against American policy on the war in Vietnam.

Guenter Lewy. *America in Vietnam*. New York: Oxford University Press, 1978. A history of American involvement in the Vietnam War that criticizes the antiwar protest movement.

Norman Mailer. *Armies of the Night: History as Novel*. New York: New American Library, 1968. An account by a leading American novelist of the October 1967 antiwar march on the Pentagon.

Christopher Matthews. *Kennedy and Nixon*. New York: Simon & Schuster, 1996. A dual biography of the two key political figures of the 1960s that seeks to minimize the political differences between them.

Allen J. Matusow. *The Unraveling of America: A History of Liberalism in the 1960s*. New York: Harper & Row, 1984. An absorbing history of the rise and fall of domestic liberalism in the 1960s with an emphasis on Keynesian economics, the civil rights movement, the major Great Society programs, and the student rebellion.

Walter A. McDougall. *. . .the Heavens and the Earth: A Political History of the Space Age*. New York: Basic Books, 1985. A political analysis of decisions that initiated and perpetuated the space race between the United States and the Soviet Union.

Joe McGinnis. *The Selling of the President, 1968*. New York: Trident Press, 1969. An inside look at the new media politics of the 1960s and the marketing of Richard Nixon to the American voters.

Douglas T. Miller. *On Our Own: Americans in the Sixties*. Lexington, MA: D.C. Heath, 1996. A solid overview of the major events and personalities of the decade.

James Miller. *"Democracy Is in the Streets": From Port Huron to the Siege of Chicago*. New York: Simon & Schuster, 1987. A history of the Students for a Democratic Society (SDS) and its descent from idealism to violence during the 1960s.

Timothy Miller. *The Hippies and American Values*. Knoxville: University of Tennessee Press, 1991. A survey of counterculture thought and an assessment of the ethics of drugs, sex, rock music, and communal living as they were practiced during the 1960s.

Daniel Patrick Moynihan. *Maximum Feasible Misunderstanding: Community Action in the War on Poverty*. New York: Free Press, 1969. An extended essay that argues that reformers' efforts to ensure "maximum feasible participation" of the poor ultimately ensured the failure of the War on Poverty.

Charles Murray. *Losing Ground*. New York: Basic Books, 1984. A conservative critique of Great Society programs and their effects on poverty and other social problems.

Jack Newfield. *A Prophetic Minority*. New York: New American Library, 1966. A history of the New Left with special emphasis on the Students for a Democratic Society (SDS), which the author holds in high regard.

William O'Neill. *Coming Apart: An Informal History of America in the 1960s*. New York: Quadrangle Books, 1971. A witty history of the decade that deals with everything from the state of the presidency to the counterculture.

Kenneth O'Reilly. *Racial Matters: The FBI's Secret Files on Black America, 1960–1972*. New York: Free Press, 1989. The most comprehensive account yet written of the relationship between the Federal Bureau of Investigation and black activists during the 1960s.

Herbert Parmet. *JFK: The Presidency of John F. Kennedy*. New York: Dial Press, 1983. An account of the Kennedy administration by a veteran historian of the Democratic Party in the twentieth century.

Hugh Pearson. *The Shadow of the Panther: Huey Newton and the Price of Black Power in America*. New York: Addison-Wesley, 1994. A study that is at once a history of the Black Panther Party; a biography of one of its founders, Huey Newton; and a critique of the black-power ideology of the 1960s.

Abe Peck. *Uncovering the Sixties: The Life and Times of the Underground Press*. New York: Pantheon, 1983. An overview of the radical underground newspapers of the 1960s.

Norman Podhoretz. *Breaking Ranks*. New York: Harper & Row, 1979. The memoirs of a journalist and thinker who became more conservative in reaction to the events of the 1960s.

Gerald L. Posner. *Case Closed*. New York: Random House, 1993. A history of the Kennedy assassination and its aftermath that defends the findings of the Warren Commission.

Howell Raines. *My Soul Is Rested: Movement Days in the Deep South Remembered*. New York: G.P. Putnam's Sons, 1977. An oral history of the civil rights movement from the perspective of those who participated in it.

Charles A. Reich. *The Greening of America*. New York: Bantam, 1971. A defense of the counterculture by a Yale Law School professor.

W. J. Rorabaugh. *Berkeley at War: The 1960s*. New York: Oxford University Press, 1989. A history of a university that was the scene of numerous campus eruptions during the 1960s.

Anthony Scaduto. *Bob Dylan: An Intimate Biography*. New York: New American Library, 1973. The first full biography of this leading figure of American popular culture of the 1960s.

Bobby Seale. *Seize the Time*. New York: Random House, 1970. The manifesto of a leading Black Panther and one of the "Chicago Seven" who was put on trial (and subsequently acquitted) for his alleged role in the riots at the 1968 Democratic convention.

Melvin Small and William D. Hoover, eds. *Give Peace a Chance*. Syracuse, NY: Syracuse University Press, 1992. A collection of scholarly essays concerning the antiwar movement with emphasis on strategy and tactics, the impact of the movement on women, and the course of protest in the schools.

Robert Stephen Spitz. *Barefoot in Babylon: The Creation of the Woodstock Music Festival, 1969*. New York: Viking, 1979. An engaging account of Woodstock and its lasting impact on American popular culture.

Jay Stevens. *Storming Heaven: LSD and the American Dream*. New York: Atlantic Monthly Press, 1987. A study of the spread of the use of LSD and the drug's role in creating the sixties counterculture.

Amy Swerdlow. *Women Strike for Peace: Traditional Motherhood and Radical Politics in the 1960s*. Chicago: University of Chicago Press, 1993. A narrative account of the 1960s peace organization Women Strike for Peace written by one of the key leaders of this group.

Irwin and Debi Unger. *America in the 1960s*. St. James, NY: Brandywine Press, 1988. An overview of the decade that covers the civil rights movement, the growth of feminism, the antiwar movement, and the tragic events of 1968.

William L. Van Deburg. *New Day in Babylon: The Black Power Movement and American Culture, 1965–1975*. Chicago: University of Chicago Press, 1992. A history of the black power movement of the 1960s that argues that it was a broad-based cultural movement that promoted African American identity and had a lasting, positive impact on American society.

Tom Wells. *The War Within: America's Battle over Vietnam*. Berkeley and Los Angeles: University of California Press, 1993. A comprehensive history of the peace movement and a positive assessment of its impact on policy makers.

Harris Wofford. *Of Kings and Kennedys: Making Sense of the Sixties*. New York: Farrar, Straus, and Giroux, 1980. The personal and political memoirs of a young member of the Kennedy administration who was deeply involved in the civil rights movement.

Leonard Wolf, ed. *Voices from the Love Generation*. Boston: Little, Brown, 1968. A collection of extended interviews with residents of the Haight-Ashbury hippie community.

Index

institutions, 233
principles of, 123-24
Democratic National Convention
(Chicago, 1968), 230, 242-46
democratic society
need to build, 79-80
Dickstein, Morris, 226
Dien Bien Phu, Vietnam, 94
Die, Nigger, Die! (Brown), 191
Diggers, 144, 149
Dissent, 75
Dixon, Marlene, 202, 211
domino theory, 107
Dreher, Carl, 33
drugs, 218
in hippie movement, 137, 141
DuBridge, Lee, 35
Dylan, Bob, 144

ecology movement, 224
and process of radicalization, 228
Eisenhower, Dwight D., 35, 68, 107
Erikson, Erik, 202-203
the Establishment
institutions of, are incompatible with
democratic vision, 233
and resistance to change, 229
role of, 71
Evans, M. Stanton, 48
Evers, Medgar, 148
assassination of, 218
Excellence (Gardner), 72

Farber, David, 235
Federal Bureau of Investigation (FBI),
231
Feminine Mystique, The (Friedan), 195
feminism, 196
see also women's movement
Feminized Male, The (Sexton), 212
Flacks, Richard, 67
Foreign Affairs, 101
foreign policy, U.S.
antiwar movement's view of, 224
Fortune magazine, 53, 87
freedom, in the United States
government is threat to, 49-50
Freedom Rides, 173-75
Freedom Schools, 177
Freedom Summer, 222
Free Speech Movement, 122, 127, 226
Friedan, Betty, 195, 209
Fulbright, J. William, 98

Gardner, John W., 61, 72
Gitlin, Todd, 229, 230
Goldwater, Barry, 45, 69, 237

call for values by, 238
on communist threat, 47-49
position on Vietnam, 84
on purpose of government, 47-49
Goodman, Paul, 67
Grass, Gunter, 204
Great Society, 40-41, 43
criticism of, 48
definition of, 44
is aggrandizement of the
Establishment, 72
is unpersuasive as a moral incentive,
74
role of federal government in, 55
theory of, 70
war in Vietnam inconsistent with
goals of, 99-101
Greensboro sit-in, 217
Gulf of Tonkin, 146
Gulf of Tonkin Resolution, 229

Haight-Ashbury, 144, 149
Hamer, Fannie Lou, 180
Hard Times (Kopkind), 155
Harriman, Averell, 129
Hayden, Tom , 75, 118, 188, 226
highway construction, 77
in Appalachia, 69
hippie movement
beginnings of, 137
drug use in, 137, 141
nihilism of, 145
as reaction to U.S. drift to right, 146
rejection of New Left by, 228
sexism of, 147
sexuality in, 139-41
and sharing, 138-39
Hippie Trip, The (Yablonsky), 133, 140
Hiss, Alger, 237
Ho Chi Minh, 95, 96, 107
Hoffman, Abbie, 158, 223, 240
Hoover, J. Edgar, 231
Housing and Urban Development,
Department of, 63
Humphrey, Hubert H., 91
Huxley, Aldous, 137
Huxley, Thomas, 100

Jefferson Airplane, 144
Job Corps, 53
Johnson, Lyndon B., 40, 43, 84, 91
consensus politics of, 65-66
on riots in Newark and Detroit, 189
support of Civil Rights Act by, 176
on U.S. objectives in Vietnam,
86-90
youth's perception of, 146

265

973.923   The 1960s.
DUD

$20.96   3246

DATE